ABSTRACT ART

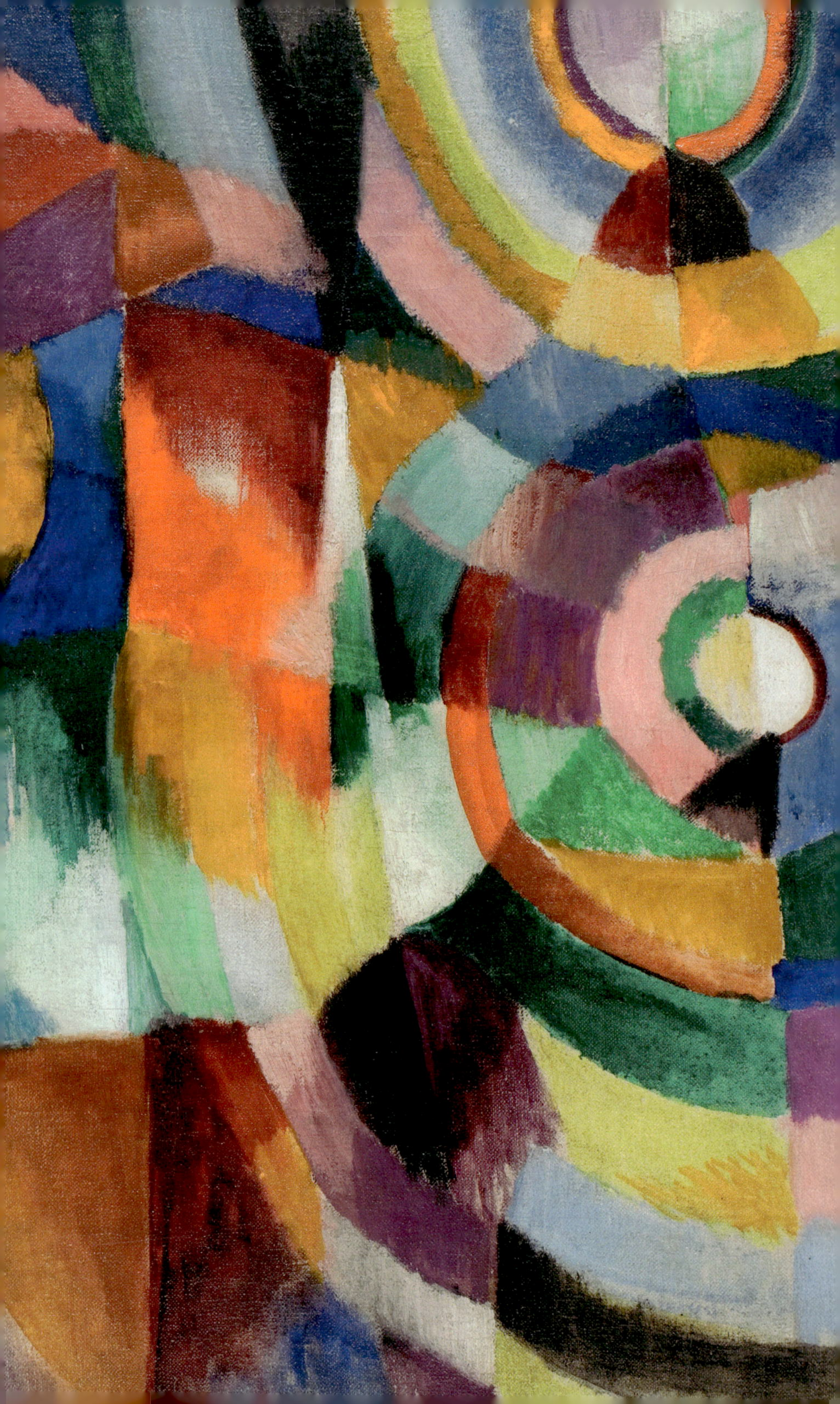

ABSTRACT ART

—

STEPHANIE STRAINE

—

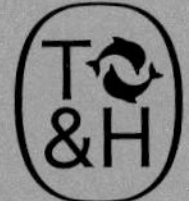

CONTENTS

6   **INTRODUCTION**

8   **MULTIPLE BEGINNINGS**
10   Hilma af Klint
12   Wassily Kandinsky
14   Giacomo Balla
16   František Kupka
18   Piet Mondrian
20   Kazimir Malevich
22   Paul Klee
24   Olga Rozanova
26   Sonia Delaunay-Terk
28   Sophie Taeuber-Arp
30   Liubov Popova
32   El Lissitzky
34   Naum Gabo
36   Katarzyna Kobro

38   **CONSTRUCTING AN ABSTRACT VOCABULARY**
40   Marlow Moss
42   Emma Kunz
44   Paule Vézelay
46   Ben Nicholson
48   Henryk Stażewski
50   László Moholy-Nagy
52   Lucio Fontana
54   Mary Martin
56   Saloua Raouda Choucair

58   Yves Klein
60   Piero Manzoni

62   **ABSTRACT EXPRESSIONISM AND ITS LEGACIES**
64   Mark Rothko
66   Barnett Newman
68   Len Lye
70   Lee Krasner
72   Norman Lewis
74   Jackson Pollock
76   Morris Louis
78   Agnes Martin
80   Zao Wou-Ki
82   Ellsworth Kelly
84   Helen Frankenthaler
86   Cy Twombly
88   Sam Gilliam
90   Frank Bowling

92   **GLOBAL GEOMETRIES**
94   Fahrelnissa Zeid
96   Carmen Herrera
98   Rubem Valentim
100   Monir Shahroudy Farmanfarmaian
102   Carlos Cruz-Diez
104   François Morellet

106 Lygia Pape
108 Bridget Riley
110 Frank Stella
112 Hélio Oiticica
114 Nasreen Mohamedi

116 **MINIMAL, CONCEPTUAL AND PROCESS ART**
118 Anne Truitt
120 Ruth Asawa
122 Sol LeWitt
124 Donald Judd
126 Charlotte Posenenske
128 Robert Ryman
130 Gerhard Richter
132 Rasheed Araeen
134 Eva Hesse
136 Lee Ufan
138 Daniel Buren
140 Judy Chicago
142 Howardena Pindell

144 **ABSTRACTION IN THE DIGITAL AGE**
146 Helen Pashgian
148 Sheila Hicks
150 Dóra Maurer
152 Takesada Matsutani
154 El Anatsui

156 Tomma Abts
158 Johanna Unzueta
160 Rana Begum
162 Zhao Yao
164 Tomm El-Saieh

166 **Major Group Exhibitions of Abstract Art**
168 **Glossary**
172 **Further Reading**
173 **Index**
175 **Picture Acknowledgements**

INTRODUCTION

This book offers a glimpse into a diverse array of abstract art, journeying across the entire span of the twentieth century and into the twenty-first. The artists you will discover in this book took many different paths to reach their version of abstract art – and there are almost limitless alternatives to what is covered here.

So just what is abstract art? To answer that question, we must recognize that no single explanation exists for such a vague concept: there is no movement or style that defines 'abstract'. It simply means art that does not directly represent reality, with no recognizable objects, people, places or stories depicted. It is an ever-changing field that more than one hundred years after its widespread emergence continues to inspire and challenge artists across the world. As an umbrella term, it can describe an impossibly vast range of artistic work, with no consistency of material, theory or technique. It is also necessary to acknowledge that many abstract artists themselves dislike 'abstract' as a description – believing it to be too imprecise to be useful.

Abstraction has its roots in many art movements of
the nineteenth and early twentieth centuries, including
Impressionism, Expressionism and Cubism, all of which
came close to registering pure colour, line and shape, while
still intending to convey representation. This book does not
focus on these many important precursors to abstract art,
or the thousands of years of abstract forms and patterns
within many non-western artistic traditions.

Abstract art does not exist in opposition to reality; in fact,
it enriches our understanding of the world, enabling artists
to communicate through a universal visual language. A new
vocabulary was built from the near-simultaneous arrival
of abstract art in multiple locations just before the First
World War. This emergence had political implications,
certainly in relation to utopian expressions of freedom
and idealism. Some of the most important moments in
twentieth-century abstract art, including the Bauhaus
in Germany and Suprematism in Russia, have strong
links to left-wing political beliefs, so much so that the
story of abstraction is inextricably connected to the
history of social change across the century.

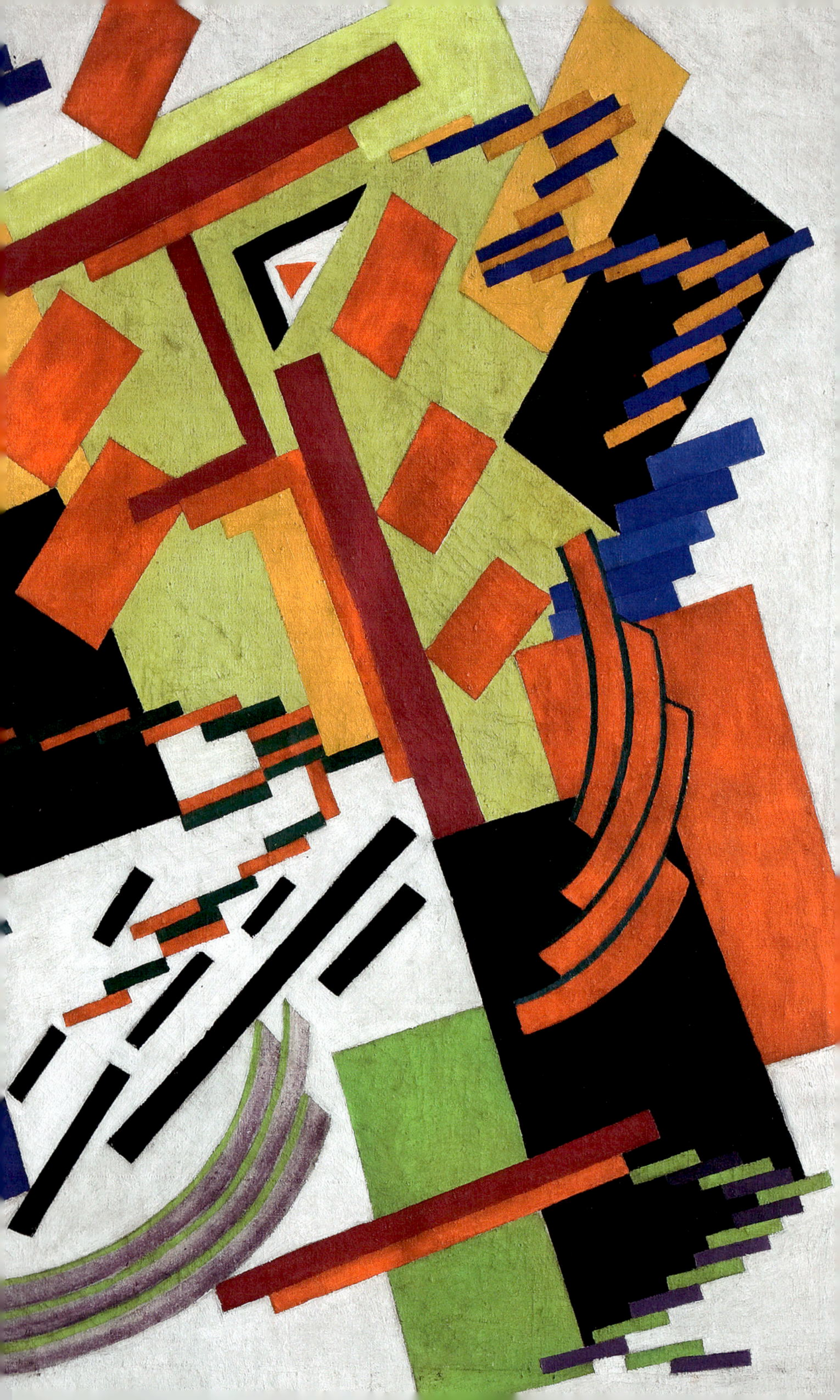

MULTIPLE BEGINNINGS

-

Things have disappeared like smoke . . .
art approaches creation as an end in itself
and domination over the forms of nature

-

Kazimir Malevich

1915

HILMA AF KLINT
1862–1944

Born in Stockholm, Hilma af Klint began attending séances as a teenager, and although she did not find them wholly satisfying, this early interest in psychic and spiritual matters remained throughout her life. In 1880, the same year she began her artistic training at Stockholm's Technical School, af Klint's sister Hermina died at the age of ten. This traumatic event prompted the eighteen-year-old Hilma to seek further religious nourishment.

Af Klint belonged to the first generation of women to gain an education at the Royal Academy of Fine Arts in Stockholm, where she studied for five years, graduating as an accomplished portrait and landscape painter. Her move towards a pioneering form of abstraction occurred almost two decades later as a result of her sustained interest in spiritualism and theosophy – a religious philosophy based on achieving mystical insights into the divine nature of God. Af Klint's abstract paintings were an escape from the limits of the physical world, and an attempt to go beyond what is visible. Her works use a complex code of different symbols to express hidden dimensions and messages. Af Klint emphasized that she was a mediumistic receiver of this new abstract visual language: 'The pictures were painted directly through me, without any preliminary drawings, and with great force. I had no idea what the paintings were supposed to depict; nevertheless I worked swiftly and surely, without changing a single brush stroke.'

In af Klint's will she stipulated that her work could not be shown publicly until twenty years after her death – her spirit guides advised her never to share her creations. Ultimately, this took more than forty years, with her inclusion in a 1986 group exhibition in Los Angeles, 'The Spiritual in Art: Abstract Painting 1890–1985'.

Hilma af Klint
Group IV, No. 2, The Ten Largest, Childhood (Grupp IV, nr 2, De tio största, Barnaåldern), 1907
Tempera on paper, mounted on canvas, 315 x 234 cm (124⅛ x 92¼ in.)
The Hilma af Klint Foundation, Stockholm

***The Ten Largest* captures the phases of life from childhood to old age using startling colours and shapes, in one of the earliest non-representational series of paintings in the western world. In this second abstract image of *Childhood*, af Klint derives some forms from nature, including flower petals, to inform a composition that has no equivalent in reality.**

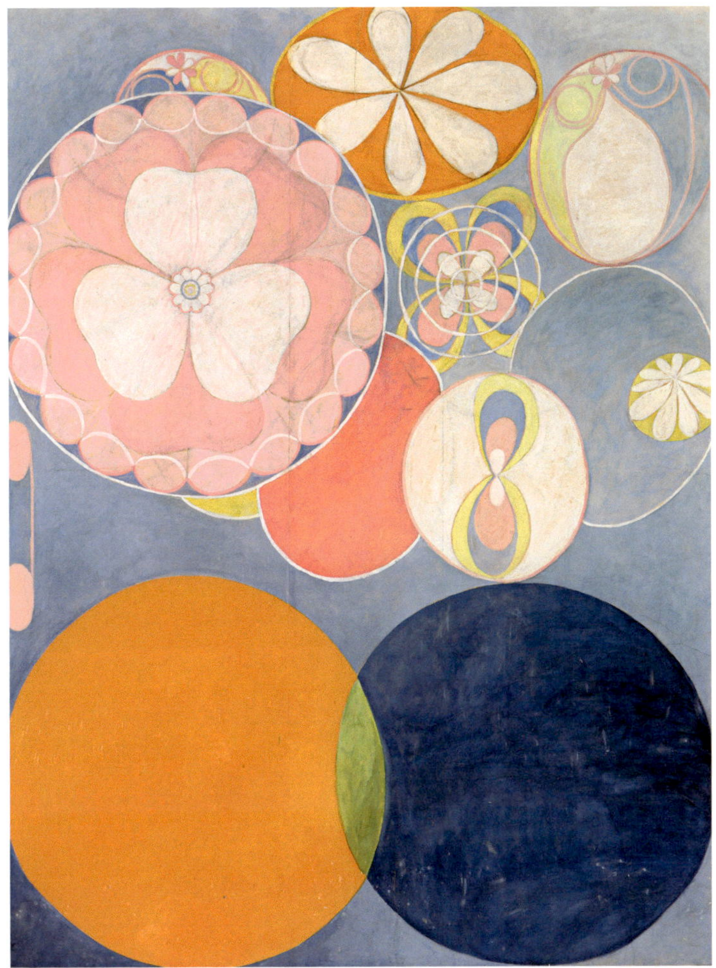

KEY EVENTS

1896: With her group 'The Five', af Klint and four other women conduct séances and make contact with spirits they name 'The High Ones', channelling their messages via automatic drawings.

1906–15: Af Klint completes her major body of work, *The Paintings for the Temple*, comprised of 193 paintings that together illustrate a spiritual evolution.

2018–19: The Solomon R. Guggenheim Museum, New York, stages an exhibition, 'Hilma af Klint: Paintings for the Future', attracting the largest audience in the museum's history.

WASSILY KANDINSKY

1866–1944

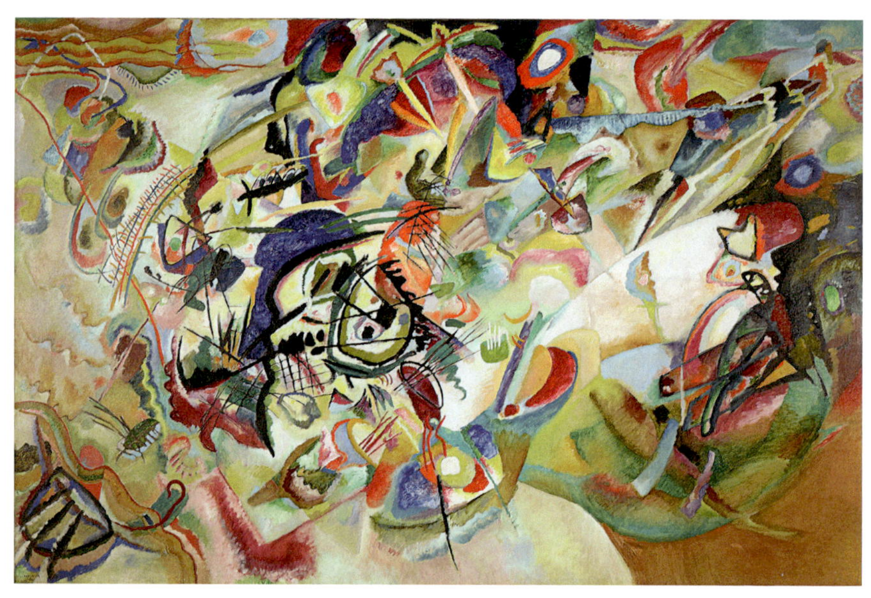

Moscow-born Wassily Kandinsky left behind a successful academic career in economics and law to take up painting at thirty. He relocated to Munich to study at its Academy of Fine Arts. In dialogue with his partner, artist Gabriele Münter, he developed an intensely colour-saturated, dynamic approach to landscape painting, with simplified forms verging on abstraction. Kandinsky and Münter also co-founded the Expressionist art movement Der Blaue Reiter (The Blue Rider) which operated in Munich between 1911 and 1914. These years were an important precursor to Kandinsky's subsequent advance towards abstract painting, although he never fully relinquished spiritual allusions or landscape references. His work during this time also reflected a sense of tumultuous uncertainty and impending violence, as the world moved closer to conflict.

In one of his most influential texts, 'Concerning the Spiritual in Art', Kandinsky claimed that 'colour is a means of exerting a direct influence upon the soul'. Kandinsky's writing offers lyrical parallels between art and music, reflecting his melodic painting technique. He divided his paintings into three categories that also recalled musical terminology: Impressions, Improvisations and Compositions – which he reserved for his most fully realized large-scale works. Only ten Compositions were ever completed. After producing the first, Kandinsky turned for inspiration to the innovative music theories of composer Arnold Schoenberg, with whom he developed a close correspondence.

Returning to Moscow at the outbreak of the First World War, Kandinsky briefly became involved with government work, helping to establish the Museum of Painterly Culture. He soon realized that his spiritual approach to painting was at odds with the impending Soviet doctrine of state atheism and left once again for Germany in 1921. He was a master at the Bauhaus School of Art and Architecture from 1922 until its closure by the Nazis in 1933.

Wassily Kandinsky
Composition VII, 1913
Oil on canvas, 200 x 300cm (78¾ x 118⅛ in.)
The State Tretyakov Gallery, Moscow

This painting has over thirty preparatory sketches associated with its two-month development, although it took Kandinsky just three days to complete the final painting. Its abstract forms might be partly derived from earlier paintings including *All Saints Day I* (1911), as well as Christian apocalyptic themes such as the Last Judgement and Resurrection, although these external references are obscured.

KEY EVENTS

1909–10: Drafts his 'Concerning the Spiritual in Art' manifesto, articulating his progression towards abstraction. The text is published in December 1911, the same month Kandinsky exhibits his important painting *Composition V* in Munich. Multiple translations appear in quick succession.

1926: Publishes his second theoretical text, 'Point and Line to Plane', informed by his new teaching methods and colour theories developed at the Bauhaus.

GIACOMO BALLA

1871–1958

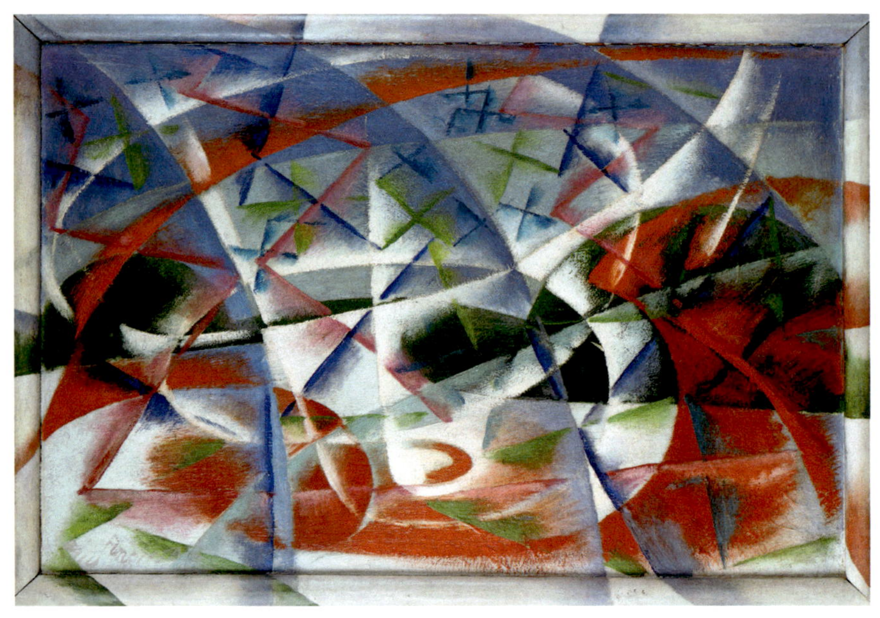

Abstract art in the early twentieth century rarely emerged in isolation from real-world innovations and progress. The Italian art movement Futurism is an important example of engineering and technology profoundly affecting the visual arts. It was founded by the poet Filippo Tommaso Marinetti in Milan; the first manifesto was published in *Le Figaro* newspaper in 1909. Futurism was concerned with overthrowing the burden of history and past artistic traditions, to focus on scientific advancements such as the dizzying speeds achieved by the modern aeroplane and car. Its adherents admired the new industrial city and depicted a world in constant motion, often fracturing images to achieve effects based on light prisms. Their intensely patriotic fervour led the group, especially Marinetti, towards an association with Italian fascism from 1919 onwards.

The Turin-born painter Balla did not exhibit with the Futurists until 1913, although he did sign the group's second Futurist painting manifesto in 1910. Previously working in Rome as a portrait painter and caricaturist, Balla completely overhauled his artistic practice in 1913 as a result of his involvement with Futurism, selling off all his past work and making the declaration 'Balla is Dead!' He would go on to sign all new paintings with the inscription 'Futurballa', emphasizing his commitment to modernity.

In 1913 he also began a new series of paintings, *Abstract Speed*, focusing on the power and speed of the automobile. Balla almost totally abstracted its subject matter – a car travelling through a landscape – from reality, while heightening the sensation of smooth, continuous movement. In each of the three works, Balla continued his painting over the surface of the frame, implying that his new abstract vision of the world could escape into the space of the viewer.

Giacomo Balla
Abstract Speed + Sound
(*Velocità astratta +
rumore*), 1913–14
Oil paint on millboard
in artist's painted frame,
54.5 cm x 76.5 cm
(21½ x 30⅛ in.)
The Solomon R.
Guggenheim Foundation,
Peggy Guggenheim
Collection, Venice

Thought to be the central panel of a triptych of paintings, this work retains some allusions to a landscape, particularly the blue sky in its top half. The small cross motifs that appear across the surface represent the sound of the painting's title, while the swooping curves imply the automobile's sleek industrial design merging with its surrounding landscape.

KEY EVENTS

1916: Balla is commissioned by the Ballets Russes to design the stage set for their production of Igor Stravinsky's *Feu d'Artifice*. His design emphasizes geometric forms, beams of light and the movement of colours.

1915: Together with Fortunato Depero, Balla authors the *Manifesto of the Futurist Reconstruction of the Universe,* which calls for a total transformation of everyday life through art.

1918: Balla publishes his 'Manifesto of Colour' in an exhibition catalogue, which encourages a form of dynamic painting based on explosions of colour.

FRANTIŠEK KUPKA
1871–1957

Born in Opočno in eastern Bohemia (present-day Czech Republic),
Kupka first studied at Prague's Art Academy, before moving to
Vienna in 1892 to train at the city's Academy of Fine Arts. In
Vienna he also developed an interest in eastern philosophy and
theosophy, one inspiration for his embrace of abstraction years
later. His final relocation was to Paris in 1896, where he produced
a wide variety of creative commissions, including poster designs,
book illustrations and satirical drawings for newspapers.

Kupka was profoundly influenced by the first Futurist manifesto,
which appeared in Paris in 1909. Partially as a result, his work
shortly afterwards began to move towards arrangements of abstract
shapes and colours, inspired by various theories of motion, the light
and colour of Gothic stained-glass windows, as well as the interplay
between music and painting. His use of the music term 'fugue' for
many of his paintings suggests this close relationship between sonic
and visual manifestations.

Kupka's two paintings *Amorpha: Warm Chromatics* and *Amorpha:
Fugue in Two Colours* were shown at the Autumn Salon in Paris, 1912.
They were the first wholly abstract works to be exhibited publicly
in Paris, where they prompted a scandalized response from an
audience unaccustomed to their lack of representational content.
These ground-breaking works were created following a progressive
sequence of over fifty drawings charting Kupka's evolution from
observational study to 'non-objective' painting. The artist began by
observing his stepdaughter Andrée playing with a red and blue ball
in the garden, trying to capture its arc of motion through the air, as

František Kupka
*Amorpha: Fugue in
Two Colours*, 1912
Oil on canvas,
211 x 220 cm
(83⅛ x 86⅝ in.)
National Gallery
Prague, Prague

**The painting's limited
palette of black, blue,
red and white puts
a stark emphasis on
the synthesis Kupka
achieves with the looped,
intertwined curves. They
suggest the passage of
time as well as movement
in space, as trajectories
criss-cross each other,
implying multiple throws
of the ball into the air.**

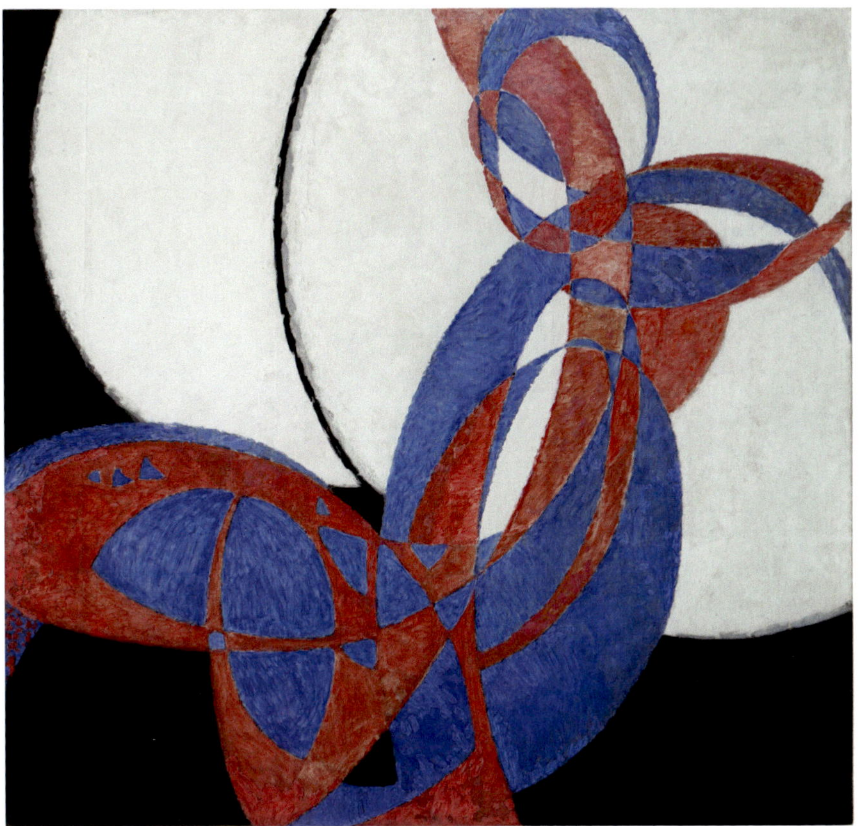

well as her presence. Gradually he eliminated all naturalistic forms,
to concentrate on the linear trajectory of the ball's movement:
a pure abstraction without any residual references to the human
body or its physical environment.

KEY EVENTS

1912: Exhibits in the Cubist room of the Autumn Salon, Paris,
  although he resists being too closely associated with any
  one particular school or group of artists.

1923: Kupka's text *Creation in the Plastic Arts* is published
  in Prague, although completed in Paris a decade earlier.

1931: Kupka is a founding member of the artist group
  Abstraction-Création, alongside Hans (Jean) Arp, Albert
  Gleizes, Jean Hélion, Auguste Herbin, Theo van Doesburg
  and Georges Vantongerloo.

PIET MONDRIAN
1872–1944

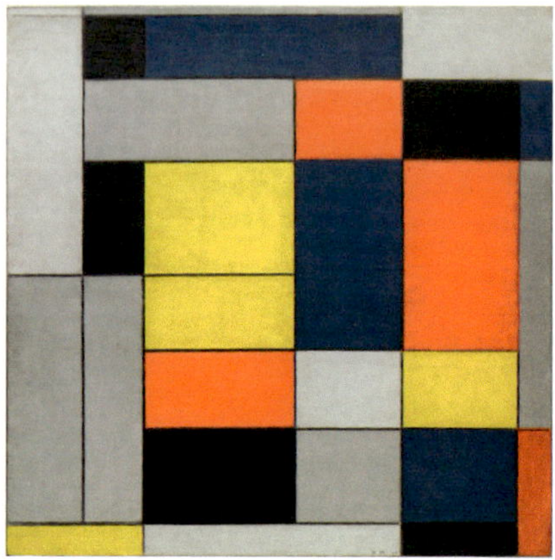

Born Pieter Cornelis Mondriaan, Jr in Amersfoort, the Netherlands,
up until 1908, Piet Mondrian worked in a naturalistic style, painting
landscapes and still lifes influenced by Dutch Impressionism and
Symbolism (in different ways these late nineteenth-century art
movements offered alternatives to the direct depiction of reality).
In 1911 he was inspired to move to Paris after seeing the radical
compositions of Cubist works by Georges Braque and Pablo Picasso
at the first 'Modern Art Circle' exhibition in Amsterdam. During
his first few years in Paris, Mondrian developed his own distinctive
abstracted vision.

The First World War was declared during a visit home to the
Netherlands in 1914. Mondrian was unable to return to Paris
until 1919. During this time, in dialogue with other members of
the De Stijl abstract art group, he restricted his colour palette
further and concentrated on the grid, completely eliminating
ovals and diagonals.

Mondrian published his text 'Dialogue on the New Plastic'
in two issues of the journal *De Stijl* in 1919. It takes the form of
a conversation between a painter and a singer, who expresses
his doubt concerning the painter's shift to a purely abstract art.
'I see nothing in these rectangles,' the singer declares, perhaps
not unreasonably. In the text, the painter (whom we assume to
be Mondrian himself) reasons that: 'In painting you must first try

Piet Mondrian
*No. VI / Composition
No. II*, 1920
Oil on canvas,
99.7 x 100.3 cm
(39⅜ x 39½ in.)
Tate Collection, UK

**In this De Stijl-era
painting, Mondrian
combines black and grey
tones with the three
primary colours (blue, red
and yellow) mixed with
grey, in an interlocking
asymmetrical scheme
containing a variety
of different-sized
rectangles.**

Piet Mondrian
*Composition with Blue:
Schilderij No. 1: Lozenge
with 2 Lines and Blue*, 1926
Oil on canvas,
61.1 x 61.1 cm
(24⅛ x 24⅛ in.)
Philadelphia Museum
of Art, Philadelphia

**Mondrian rotates his
canvas 45 degrees to
transform its perfect
square into a diamond.
The right angle created
by the intersection of
the two black lines
produces a small blue
triangle against the
canvas edge. The vast
majority of the painting's
surface remains an
austere, pure white.**

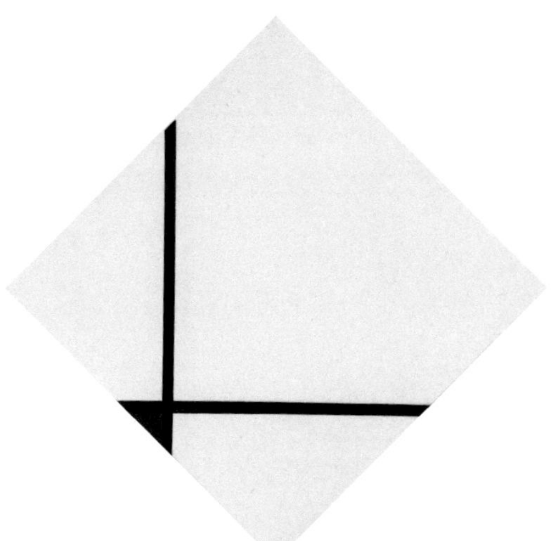

to see *composition, colour, and line* and not the representation *as representation*. Then you will finally come to feel the subject matter a hindrance.'

The artist considered his essay 'Neo-Plasticism: The General Principles of Plastic Equivalence' (published in French in January 1921) to be his definitive statement on his invention of 'neo-plastic' art, in which he makes the following dramatic claim: 'For let us not forget that we are at a turning point of culture, *at the end of everything ancient: the separation between the two is absolute and definitive* . . . Because the obstacle of form has been destroyed, the new art affirms itself as *pure plastic*.'

After many years in Paris, Mondrian sought refuge in London in 1938, just prior to the outbreak of the Second World War. From there he moved to New York in 1940, where he would live for the remaining four years of his life, continuing to publish texts on abstraction and adapting his style in response to the city's architecture and jazz music, as indicated by the title of one of his final works, *Broadway Boogie Woogie* (1942–3).

KEY EVENTS

1917: Mondrian is a founding member of the Dutch art group De Stijl, alongside Theo van Doesburg, Bart van der Leck and Georges Vantongerloo. The group extends their geometric approach to abstraction beyond painting and sculpture, to encompass architecture and graphic design.

1936: Nine of Mondrian's paintings are included in the monumental group exhibition 'Cubism and Modern Art' at the Museum of Modern Art, New York, NY.

KAZIMIR MALEVICH
1878–1935

Born in Kiev, Ukraine, to a Polish family and later based in Moscow, artist and theorist Malevich quickly absorbed many European avant-garde movements of the early twentieth century, travelling to Paris in 1912 to experience Cubism. He also participated in many exhibitions organized by artist collectives, such as the *Donkey's Tail* group show (1912) influenced by Russian folk art.

Malevich launched a new art movement, Suprematism, in Petrograd (now St Petersburg) at 'The Last Exhibition of Futurist Painting 0,10 (Zero Ten)' in December 1915. It presented an original visual language that used only simple shapes and colours, without narrative distractions. Alongside this exhibition he published a pamphlet, *From Cubism to Suprematism: The New Realism in Painting*, in which he first used the term 'non-objective' to describe his abstract art. This can be considered Malevich's manifesto for his new art movement, which was inherently political in many ways, not least its pronounced anti-elitism. In it he writes: 'I have transformed myself *in the zero of form* and dragged myself out of the *rubbish-filled pool of Academic art*.' Later in the text he argues that: 'The artist can be a creator only when the forms in his picture have nothing in common with nature . . . Colour and texture in painting are ends in themselves.'

This doctrine of simplification and purity of form would guide Malevich for the next decade. After the October Revolution (1917), he taught at art schools in Vitebsk, Belarus, Leningrad and Kiev, refining and communicating his theories of Suprematism to the next generation of artists. In 1927 he travelled to Warsaw for his first solo exhibition outside of Russia, where he was welcomed by former students including the Constructivist sculptor Katarzyna Kobro.

Kazimir Malevich
Black Square, 1915
Oil on linen canvas,
79.5 x 79.5 cm
(31⅜ x 31⅜ in.)
The State Tretyakov
Gallery, Moscow

This is one of four versions of Malevich's *Black Square*, and thought to be the earliest, although the artist himself later re-dated the work to 1913, probably erroneously. At 'The Last Exhibition of Futurist Painting 0,10' Malevich hung his *Black Square* up high in one corner of the room: a place traditionally reserved in Russian homes for the Orthodox icon of a saint. It became a symbol for a new age of revolution.

KEY EVENTS

1913: *Black Square* starts life as a theatre curtain in Malevich's
stage design for the Futurist opera *Victory over the Sun* in
St Petersburg.

1919: Malevich participates in the 'Tenth State Exhibition'
in Moscow, debuting his painting *Suprematist Composition:
White on White* (1918).

1927: Publishes his book *The Non-Objective World*.

1930: Malevich is forced to abandon abstraction after a two-
month imprisonment by the government of Joseph Stalin
that now views abstract art as 'decadent'. Malevich paints in
a government-approved Socialist Realist figurative style for
the remaining five years of his life.

PAUL KLEE
1879–1940

Klee was born in Münchenbuchsee near Bern to a music teacher
father and singer mother. During his schooling in Switzerland, Klee
was unsure whether to become an artist or musician, but shortly
after graduating in 1898 he relocated to Munich to pursue the
study of drawing. He married the pianist Lily Stumpf in 1906,
travelled throughout Europe and continued to produce artistic work
in relative isolation, without much critical or commercial success.
A meeting with Wassily Kandinsky in 1911 enabled Klee to connect
with a wider network of artist peers. In 1912 Kandinsky and Franz
Marc invited Klee to participate in the second exhibition of The Blue
Rider group in Munich. While he was never an exclusively abstract
artist, Klee's work contributed significantly to an understanding of
how colour could operate independently of subject matter. His time
at the Bauhaus, beginning in 1921 with his appointment to direct the
bookbinding workshop and teach a course in practical composition,
solidified his reputation as an influential theorist of colour. He later
taught painting and design for weaving when the Bauhaus moved to
Dessau from 1925 to the school's closure in 1932.

Klee's thesis 'On Modern Art' was first given as a lecture at the
Jena Kunstverein in 1924, and only published in 1945, after the
artist's death. In it he proclaimed, 'what tremendous possibilities for
the variation of meaning are offered by the combination of colours'.
This emphasis that colour alone can be consequential, without
the support of storytelling or forms from nature, is summed up
in Klee's assertion to his students that 'to paint well means only
this: to put the right colours in the right spot'. Throughout his
career he produced over 10,000 works, mainly small-scale drawings
and watercolours.

Paul Klee
*Static-Dynamic Gradation
(Statisch-Dynamische
Steigerung)*, 1923
Oil and gouache on paper
bordered with gouache,
watercolour and ink,
mounted on cardboard,
43.5 x 29.2 cm
(17⅛ x 11½ in.)
The Metropolitan
Museum of Art,
New York

**This watercolour is one
of many works that
Klee created to aid his
teaching at the Bauhaus.
In it he explores the
relationship between the
colour variations, and
the rigidity of the grid as
their governing structure.**

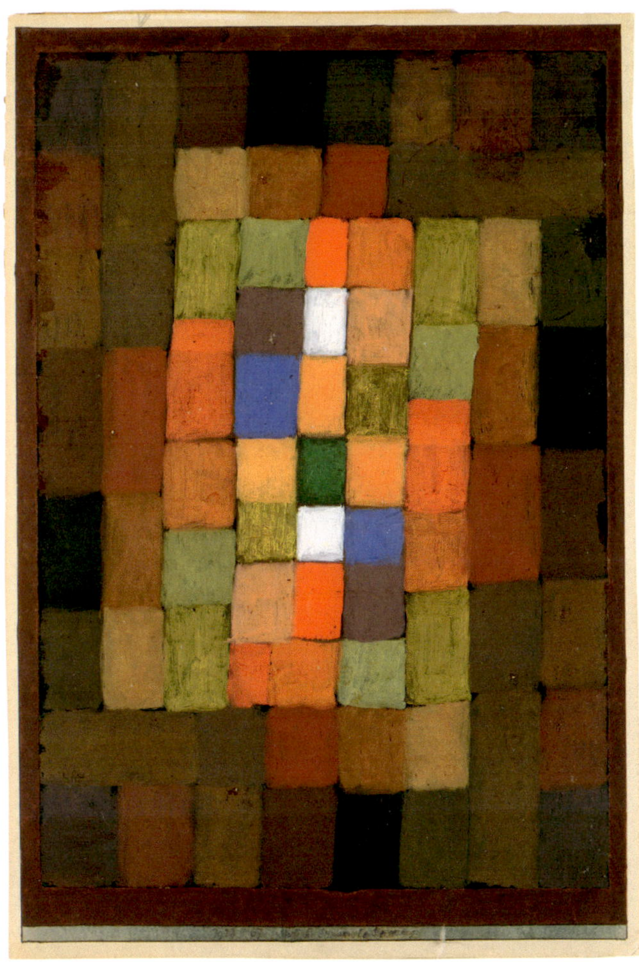

KEY EVENTS

1914: Travels to Tunisia with artists August Macke and Louis
 Moilliet, a trip that proves inspiring for his colour palette and
 exploration of light.

1924: The first American exhibition of Klee's work is organized
 by Katherine S. Dreier of the Société Anonyme, New York, NY.

1925: Klee's *Pedagogical Sketchbook* is published as a part of
 a series of Bauhaus books, based on his extensive lectures at
 the school.

OLGA ROZANOVA
1886–1918

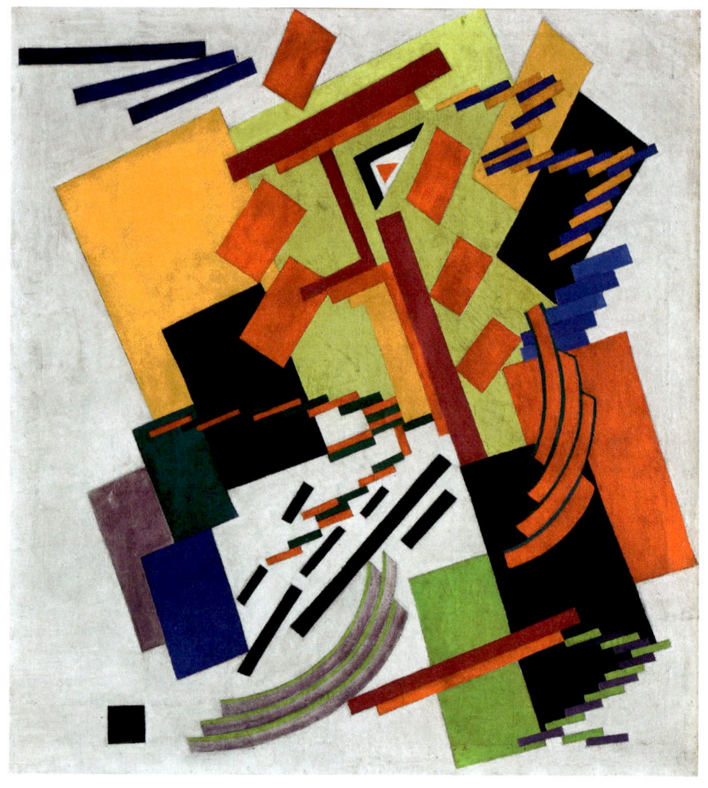

Olga Rozanova
*Non-objective
Composition*, 1916
Oil on canvas,
102 x 93.5 cm
(40¼ x 36⅞ in.)
Ekaterinburg Museum of
Fine Arts, Yekaterinburg

Rozanova's abstract
visual expression does
not rely on precise
geometric shapes. Every
painted rectangle in this
composition of diagonals
is imperfect, skewed
or tilted, creating a
dynamic effect of
movement and rhythm.

Olga Rozanova attended various art schools in both Moscow and
St Petersburg before establishing links with the Union of Youth
– an avant-garde artist society based in St Petersburg from 1909
to 1917. Rozanova was closely associated with the development of
Futurism in Russia, and later aligned herself with the Suprematist
art movement led by Kazimir Malevich.

In 1913 Rozanova published her essay 'The Bases of the New
Creation and the Reasons Why it is Misunderstood' in the Union of
Youth journal. In it, she describes her journey towards abstraction
in expansive terms: 'How does the world reveal itself to us? How
does our soul reflect the world? In order to reflect, it is necessary to
perceive. In order to perceive, it is necessary to touch, to see.' She
heralds a new era: 'The era of the final, absolute liberation of the
Great Art of Painting from the alien traits of Literature, Society,
and everyday life. Our age is to be credited with the cultivation of
this valuable world view.' This suggests that abstract art could in fact
provide a valuable new perspective on the world, rather than be seen
to turn its back on it.

After participating in 'The Last Exhibition of Futurist Painting
0,10' in Petrograd, Rozanova joined the Supremus group,
established by Malevich as the official group (and journal) for
his new artistic movement. Rozanova's artistic style adapted and
evolved as a result of this affiliation, and for the remaining short
years of her life she produced paintings and drawings in a wholly
abstract style with elegant colour harmonies and rhythms. Malevich
considered Rozanova to be his best and most talented disciple, and
undoubtedly his work was also influenced by her presence. At the
age of thirty-two, Rozanova succumbed to diphtheria in Moscow.

KEY EVENTS

1915: Participates in the fifth 'Jack of Diamonds' group
exhibition, alongside artists including Kazimir Malevich and
Liubov Popova.

1915: Contributes fashion and textile designs to the exhibition
'Women Artists for the Victims of War' in Moscow.

1918–19: Major posthumous exhibition of 250 works by Rozanova
in Moscow.

SONIA DELAUNAY-TERK
1885–1979

Ukrainian Sonia Terk's formal studies began at Karlsruhe's art academy in 1904, followed two years later by further training in Paris. This was a momentous time for the development of modern art in the city, following the first public exhibition of the Fauves (Wild Beasts) – Expressionist painters renowned for their bold use of colour. Terk's early works display a Fauvist influence, as well as references to Cubism, Futurism and other avant-garde movements that were collectively building towards abstraction.

Sonia Terk met fellow painter Robert Delaunay in 1907; they were married in late 1910. In about 1911 they collaborated on a style of purely abstract art based on bright colour contrasts and rhythmic geometric shapes that they described as 'Simultanism', referring to the fast-paced energy of modern life and its advances in communication and technology. The key inspiration for this new visual language came from Delaunay-Terk's fabric design: a baby blanket she made for their new son, Charles, which referenced the collaged textiles of Russian peasants as well as Cubist spatial arrangements. This synthesis (of painting and textiles; of folk techniques and modern abstraction) would guide Delaunay-Terk throughout her career, as she criss-crossed between applied and fine arts. She designed everything from books, posters and tapestries to cars, handbags and ballet costumes. Her work was one of the definite expressions of modernity, and she became a symbol of its freedoms.

The Delaunays were famous in Paris for their Thursday evening salons, where an intoxicating mix of artists, musicians and poets (including Hans Arp and Sophie Taeuber-Arp) would gather to debate the latest artistic responses to modern life. Delaunay-Terk later described the relationship between the visual arts and creative writing in these interwoven terms: 'Painting is a form of poetry, colours are words, their relations rhythms, the completed painting a completed poem.'

Sonia Delaunay-Terk
Electric Prisms (*Prismes électriques*), 1913
Oil on canvas,
56 cm x 47 cm
(22⅛ x 18⅝ in.)
Davis Museum at
Wellesley College,
Wellesley

This early series of paintings explored the effects of electric streetlights on the city of Paris, deriving an utterly abstract geometric composition from a visual experience rooted in everyday reality.

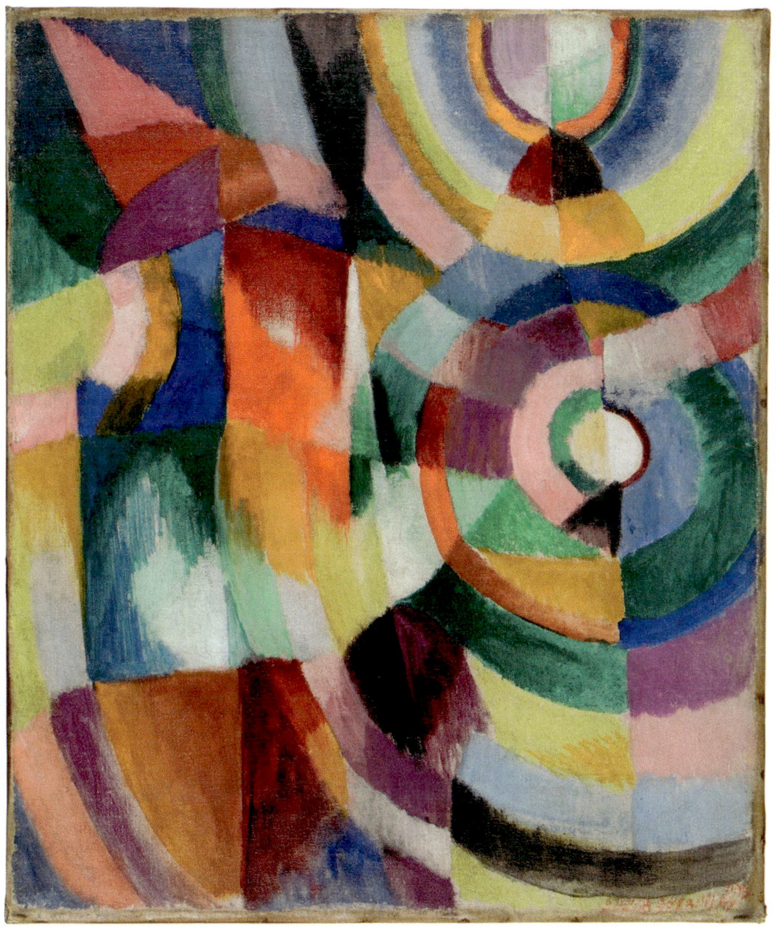

KEY EVENTS

1913: Collaborates with poet Blaise Cendrars to illustrate his
poem *Prose of the Trans-Siberian and of Little Joan of France*, a
multimedia artwork that they describe as the 'first simultaneous
book', which unfolds accordion style to a scroll almost 2 metres
(6⅝ feet) long.

1927: Delivers the lecture 'The Influence of Painting on the Art
of Clothes' at the Sorbonne University, Paris, which underscores
her interdisciplinary approach to fine art, design and fashion.

1964: Delaunay-Terk becomes the first living female artist to be
given a retrospective exhibition at the Louvre Museum, Paris.

SOPHIE TAEUBER-ARP
1889–1943

A pioneering Swiss abstract artist, Sophie Taeuber was one of the earliest to work across a wide range of applied arts (particularly textiles), as well as drawing, collage, painting and sculpture. She first studied at an applied art school in St Gallen, then in autumn 1910 moved to the experimental textile workshop of Wilhelm von Debschitz, part of a Munich art school that became an influential model for the Bauhaus some years later.

Returning to Switzerland after this training, Taeuber met her future husband, the Dada artist Hans (Jean) Arp, in Zurich in 1915, and in the same year she joined the Swiss Association of Craftsmen. Soon Taeuber-Arp and Hans Arp began to make works of art in partnership, creating cut-paper collages and wooden sculptures together, utilizing the geometric forms common to both their practices, but most fully informed by Taeuber-Arp's advanced fabric designs. Taeuber-Arp also made an important contribution to Dada's cross-disciplinary and subversive art scene based on chance improvisation. In the early 1920s she moved away from the strict verticals and horizontals that had become her signature motif, to develop forms that contained a heightened sense of movement. The couple lived between Paris and Zurich for many years, while Taeuber-Arp maintained her Swiss teaching position.

Taeuber-Arp later co-founded the multilingual artist magazine *Plastique* (1937–8) and became a member of the artist groups Cercle et Carré and Abstraction-Création. Her major contribution to both the Dada art movement and abstract art in the 1910s and 1920s was for decades under-recognized both by her fellow artists and by later art historians, perhaps owing to some innate prejudice against abstract art when applied to the design of useful objects.

Sophie Taeuber-Arp
Vertical, horizontal, squared, rectangular, 1917
Gouache on paper,
23 x 15.5 cm
(9⅛ x 6⅛ in.)
Private collection

Working as a textile design teacher in Zurich, Taeuber-Arp made many gouache preparatory designs that were meant to inform the production of textiles. These drawings also stand independently as important works of geometric abstraction.

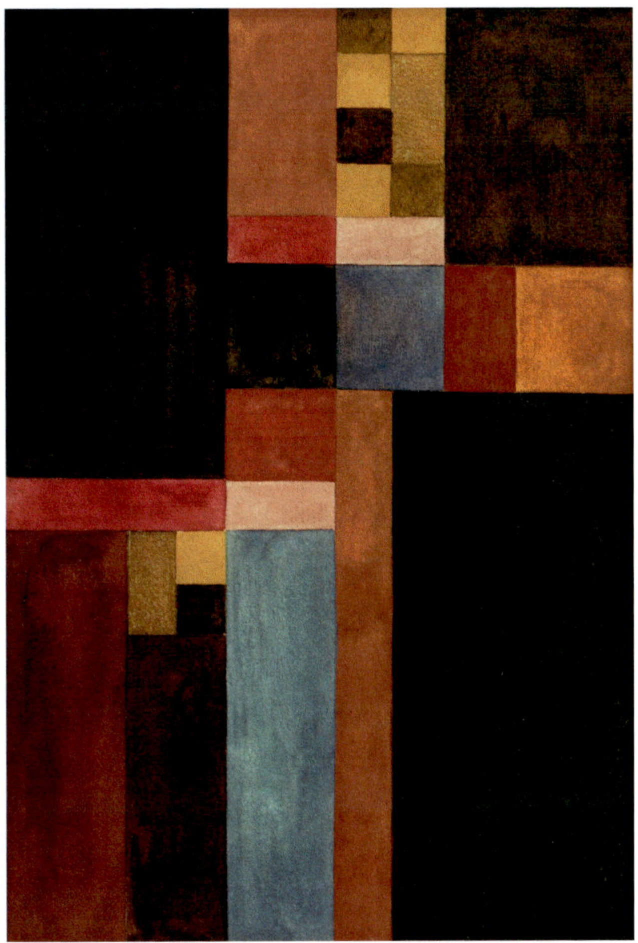

KEY EVENTS

1916: Taeuber-Arp performs daring modern dances at the home
of Dada, Zurich's Cabaret Voltaire, with dance legend Mary
Wigman.

1922: Trip to Florence and Siena with Hans (Jean) Arp; they marry
in October in Ticino.

1925: Taeuber-Arp's tapestries are shown in the 'International
Exhibition of Modern Tapestries' at the Toledo Museum of Arts,
Toledo, OH, in the United States.

1938: Her works are included in the 'International Exhibition
of Surrealism' in Paris.

LIUBOV POPOVA
1889–1924

Born near Moscow, Liubov Popova studied and travelled widely throughout her home country and Europe to learn about contemporary art movements such as Italian Futurism. Visiting Paris in 1912, she trained with Cubist artists Henri Le Fauconnier and Jean Metzinger. For the next three years her own paintings were deeply influenced by Cubism's multiple, fragmented perspectives, deconstructing the reality of objects in space.

In 1915 Popova participated in two major exhibitions that heralded the arrival of a purely abstract art in Russia: 'Tramway V: First Futurist Exhibition of Paintings' and 'The Last Exhibition of Fururist Painting, 0,10', alongside Malevich and Rozanova. The following year Popova joined Supremus. In her artist's statement for the catalogue of the 'Tenth State Exhibition: Non-Objective Creativity and Suprematism' in Moscow, April 1919, Popova ascribed certain values to what she termed 'not painting, but the depiction of reality', including: 'illusionism, literariness, emotions and recognition.' Under 'Painting' she listed qualities such as 'painterly space, line, colour (Suprematism), energetics (Futurism), texture'. In this clear articulation of painting as definitively abstract in character, Popova, like many artists at this time, makes a distinction between the old expressive values centred upon representation and storytelling, and the new, revolutionary art in which all superfluous elements – including emotion – are to be omitted.

Following the Russian Revolution, Popova abandoned oil painting to design fabrics for mass production that reflected the new Constructivist doctrine of making art useful. Her designs used primary colours, repetition and simple geometric shapes, often subjected to pattern dislocations to add energy and movement to

Liubov Popova
Space Force Construction, 1920–21
Oil with wood dust on plywood, 112.3 x 112.5 cm (44¼ x 44⅜ in.)
State Museum of Contemporary Art, George Costakis Collection, Thessaloniki

This work dates from the period in which Popova turned towards more utilitarian forms of abstract production, utilizing a limited colour palette and strict economy of means. She considered these paintings only as 'preparatory experiments towards concrete material constructions'.

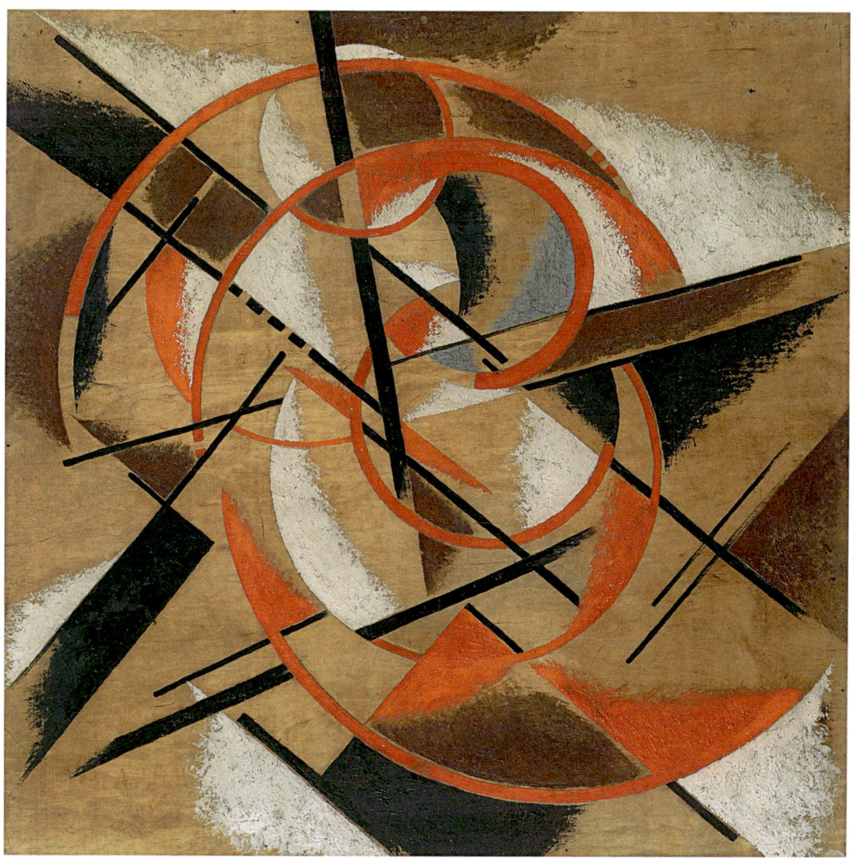

the fabric surface. Popova also designed theatre costumes and sets, books, ceramics and clothing. In 1921 she declared: 'Our new aim is the organization of the material environment, i.e. of contemporary industrial production, and all active artistic creativity must be directed towards this.'

KEY EVENTS

1923: Popova responds to a call-out in the *Pravda* newspaper for artists to contribute designs to the First State Textile Printing Factory, Moscow. She works at the factory with fellow Constructivist artist Varvara Stepanova.

1924: A posthumous exhibition is organized by Popova's fellow artists, in which they display her paintings and textile designs side by side.

EL LISSITZKY
1890–1941

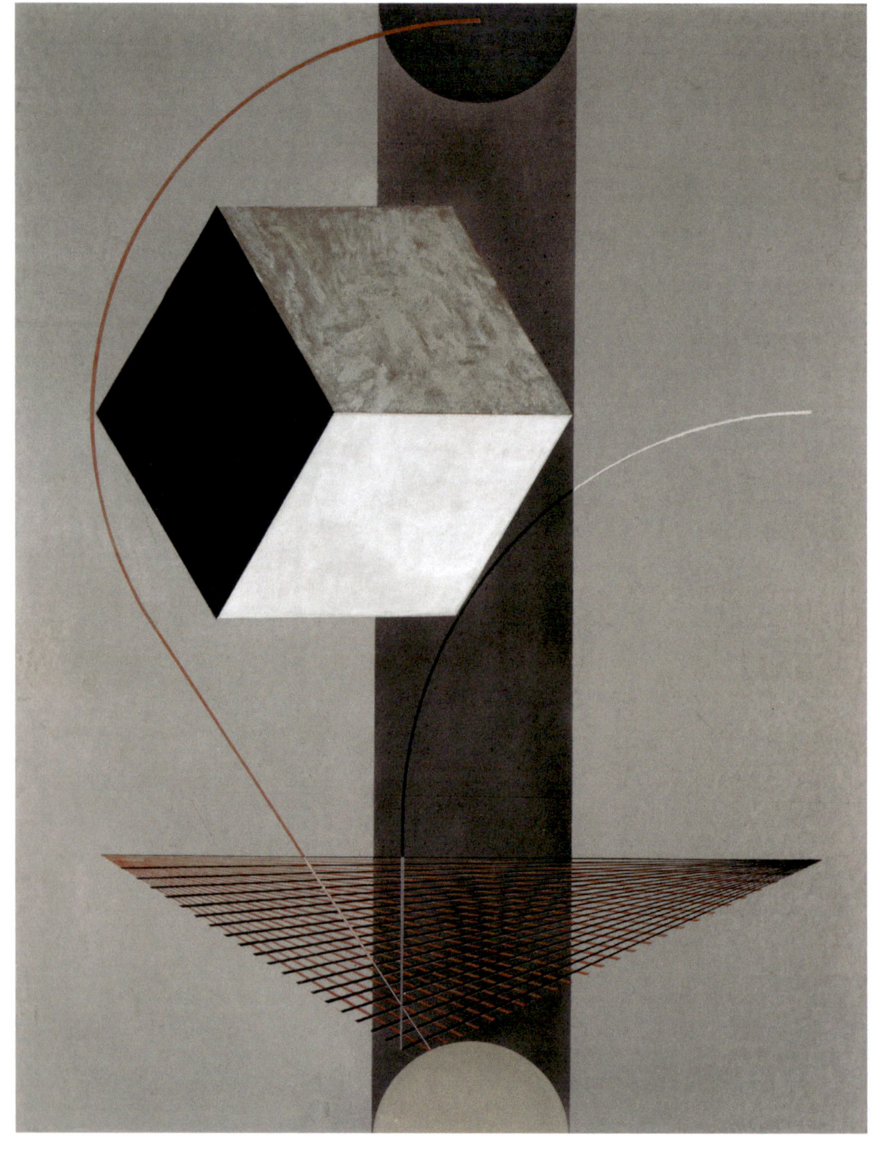

El Lissitzky
Proun 99, c.1923–5
Water-soluble and
metallic paint on wood
129 x 99.1 cm
(50⅞ x 39⅛ in.)
Yale University Art
Gallery, New Haven

***Proun* is a Russian
acronym for 'project for
the affirmation of the
new'. El Lissitzky created
many works under this
title, including a *Proun
Room* that expanded the
abstract geometries of
his paintings into three-
dimensional space. In
the Russian Revolution's
aftermath, the project
was an attempt to
visualize what this new
society might look like.**

Lazar Markovich Lissitzky, known as El Lissitzky, was a Russian interdisciplinary artist and designer who worked across many fields including typography, photomontage and graphic design. His diverse output was unified by the belief that abstract art could be a catalyst for social and political progress. After studying architecture in Germany, Lissitzky returned to Russia at the outbreak of the First World War. He became a disciple of Kazimir Malevich, teaching alongside him at the Vitebsk Art School and becoming part of his UNOVIS (Advocates for the New Art) group, founded in 1919. They worked to integrate Suprematist abstract ideas into all aspects of society, from architecture and street decorations to books and textiles.

El Lissitzky arrived in Berlin at the end of 1921 as the Russian cultural ambassador to Weimar Germany. In Düsseldorf in 1922, he participated in the 'Congress of the International Union of Progressive Artists', an initiative designed to foster links between Soviet Constructivism and related avant-garde movements in western Europe. At the conference, Lissitzky stated that: 'In Russia, we have fought a hard but fruitful struggle to realize the new art on a broad social and political front.' He also argued that:

The new art . . . like science, can be described with precision and is by nature constructive. It unites not only pure art, but all those who stand at the frontier of the new culture. The artist is companion to the scholar, the engineer and the worker.

Always forward looking, at this time of momentous change El Lissitzky advanced the idea that abstract art was a language of logic, and a unifying force.

KEY EVENTS

1919: Creates his most legendary work of design, the Soviet propaganda poster *Beat the Whites with the Red Wedge*, which uses abstract means for political ends.

1941: At the end of his life, El Lissitzky produces his final artwork – another Soviet propaganda poster, promoting the building of tanks in the fight against Nazi Germany.

NAUM GABO

1890–1977

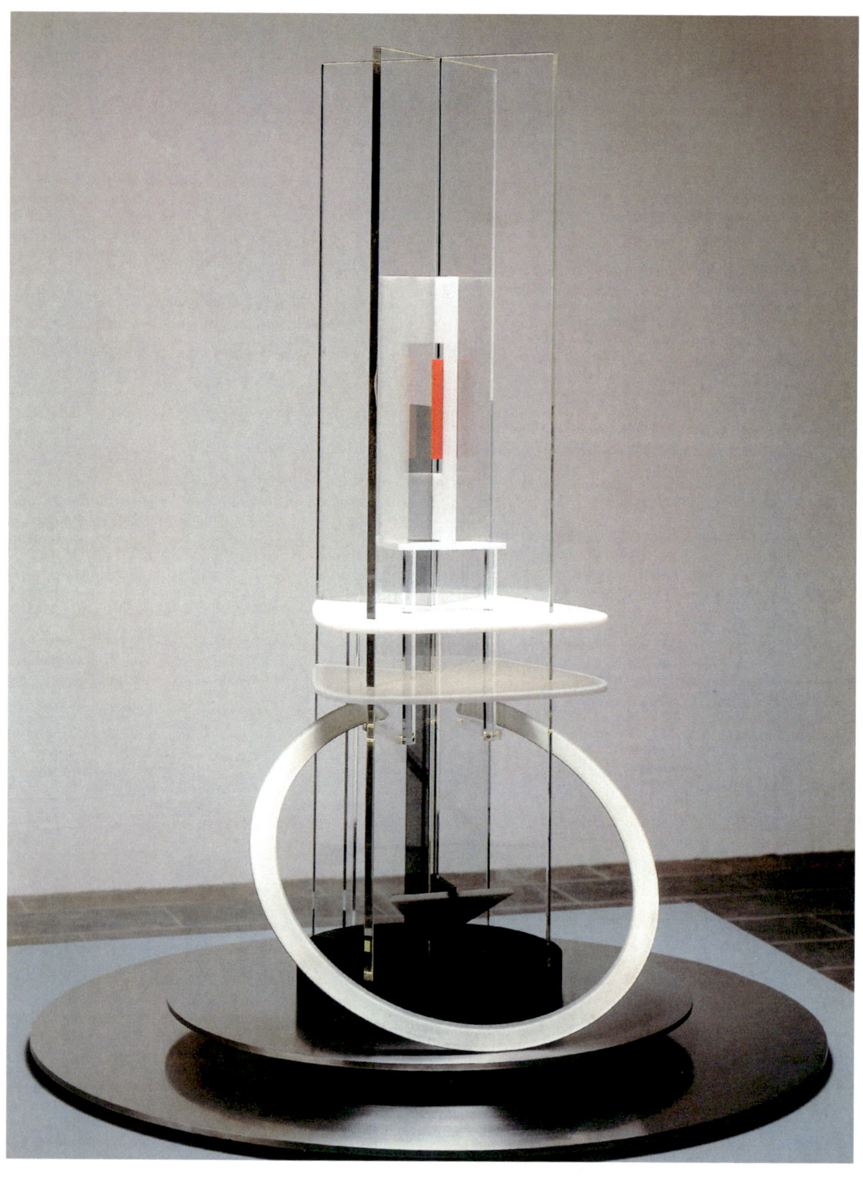

Having first studied medicine, natural sciences and engineering, Russian-born Naum Gabo began to construct small geometric sculptures in Oslo in 1915. He quickly became a leading Constructivist artist after returning to Russia following the 1917 Revolution. Gabo believed in the value of art to society, and in the close alignment of the arts and sciences. Freed from the obligation to imitate nature, Constructivist Art was concerned with both the material and spatial presence of an object. Gabo's interpretation of the movement also emphasized the spiritual – as well as social – dimension of artistic practice. As he urged in an early manifesto: 'Art should attend us everywhere that life flows and acts . . . at the bench, at the table, at work, at rest, at play.'

Gabo spent the years 1917–22 in Moscow, in close dialogue with other leading abstract artists including Kandinsky, Malevich and Vladimir Tatlin. Gabo travelled to Berlin in 1922 under the auspices of organizing the Soviet government-backed 'First Russian Art Exhibition' in the city; ultimately, he would never return to the Soviet Union, spending a decade in Berlin before moving on to Paris. His early use of transparent plastics reveals his ongoing fascination with scientific advancements in new material production. Gabo's pioneering use of cellular acetate in the interwar period later required many of his sculptures and models to be remade in more durable Perspex, due to the plastic compound's unanticipated material deterioration.

Gabo was based in England from 1936 to 1945, where he became friends with the leading British sculptors Barbara Hepworth and Henry Moore. His final move was to the United States in 1946. For several years in the mid-1950s Gabo was a professor in the Graduate School of Architecture at Harvard University, before realizing several large-scale public sculptures in the latter years of his life.

Naum Gabo
Column, c.1923
(reconstructed 1937)
Perspex, wood, metal
and glass, 104.5 x 75 cm
(41¼ x 29⅝ in.)
The Solomon R.
Guggenheim Museum,
New York

The artist considered this crucial work (of which there are several variations) to represent his 'search for an image which would fuse the sculptural element with the architectural element into one unit'. *Column* was originally conceived as a public monument to the Soviet Constitution c.1920, although this was never realized.

KEY EVENTS

1920: Publishes the 'Realistic Manifesto' which is co-signed by his older brother, artist Antoine Pevsner. It sets out key definitions for Constructivism and makes the case for a new abstract sculpture that is industrial in character.

1932–5: Joins the group Abstraction-Création in Paris.

1936: Participates in the important group exhibition 'Abstract and Concrete' in London.

KATARZYNA KOBRO
1898–1951

Born in Moscow to a German-Russian family, Kobro was educated
in the Soviet Union but spent the majority of her adult life in
Poland. In 1918 she joined the Trade Union of Painters in Moscow,
whose members included Malevich, Rozanova and Tatlin. Later that
year she moved to Smoleńsk, where she produced her first sculpture
and married fellow Constructivist artist Władysław Strzemiński
in 1920. Together they worked for the Russian Department of
Education, and also led an artistic workshop (IZO-studio). At the
same time they ran a division of the Suprematist group UNOVIS
(Advocates for the New Art) and so continued their artistic dialogue
with Malevich and El Lissitzky from a distance.

Settling in Poland around 1924, Kobro's approach to working
in three dimensions began with Cubist-inspired spatial renderings
of the human body, as seen in her early series of plaster nudes.
Many of her subsequent abstract geometric arrangements (often
elliptical and cuboid in shape) have a dynamic sense of constant
motion. In 1929 Kobro published a statement on her work, in which
she declared: 'It should be definitively, irreversibly and once-and-
for-all acknowledged that sculpture is neither literature, symbolism
or psychological emotion. Sculpture is simply the shaping of form
in space.'

Many of her early works were suspended constructions
with moving parts. Often the visual ideas tested out by Kobro's
prototypes and her sculptures were intended to be transferred into
architectural or industrial designs, in order to create functional
solutions for living. Kobro was exiled from Poland during the
Second World War owing to her German-Russian background, and
consequently many of her sculptures were destroyed or lost during

Katarzyna Kobro
Abstract Sculpture (1)
(*Rzeźba abstrakcyjna [1]*)
1924
Painted wood, metal and
glass, 72 x 17.5 x 15.5 cm
(28⅜ x 7 x 6⅛ in.)
Museum Sztuki, Łódź

**This is the earliest of
Kobro's sculptures
to survive, and
demonstrates her interest
in rejecting 'any attempt
at ornamentation,
aestheticization or
contemplation in art'.**

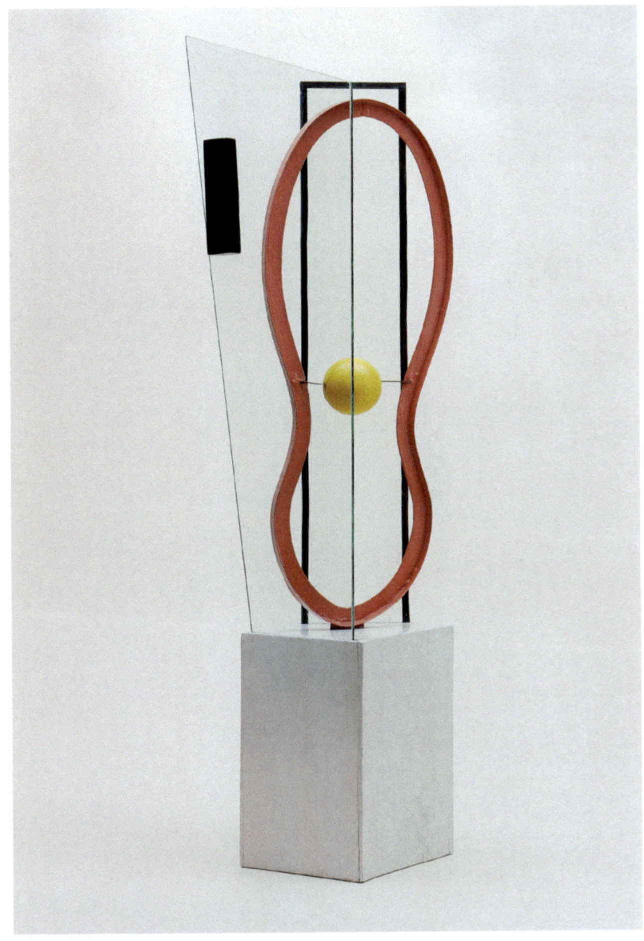

this time of upheaval. Some of her earliest works of the 1920s were
reconstructed from photographs in the 1960s by the art historian
Janusz Zagrodzki, author of the first publication on Kobro's practice.

KEY EVENTS

1924: Kobro becomes a member of the avant-garde Blok Group
  in Warsaw.

1931: Kobro helps to establish the International Collection
  of Modern Art in Łódź.

1998: A major retrospective of Kobro's work is organized by
  the Museum Sztuki, Łódź.

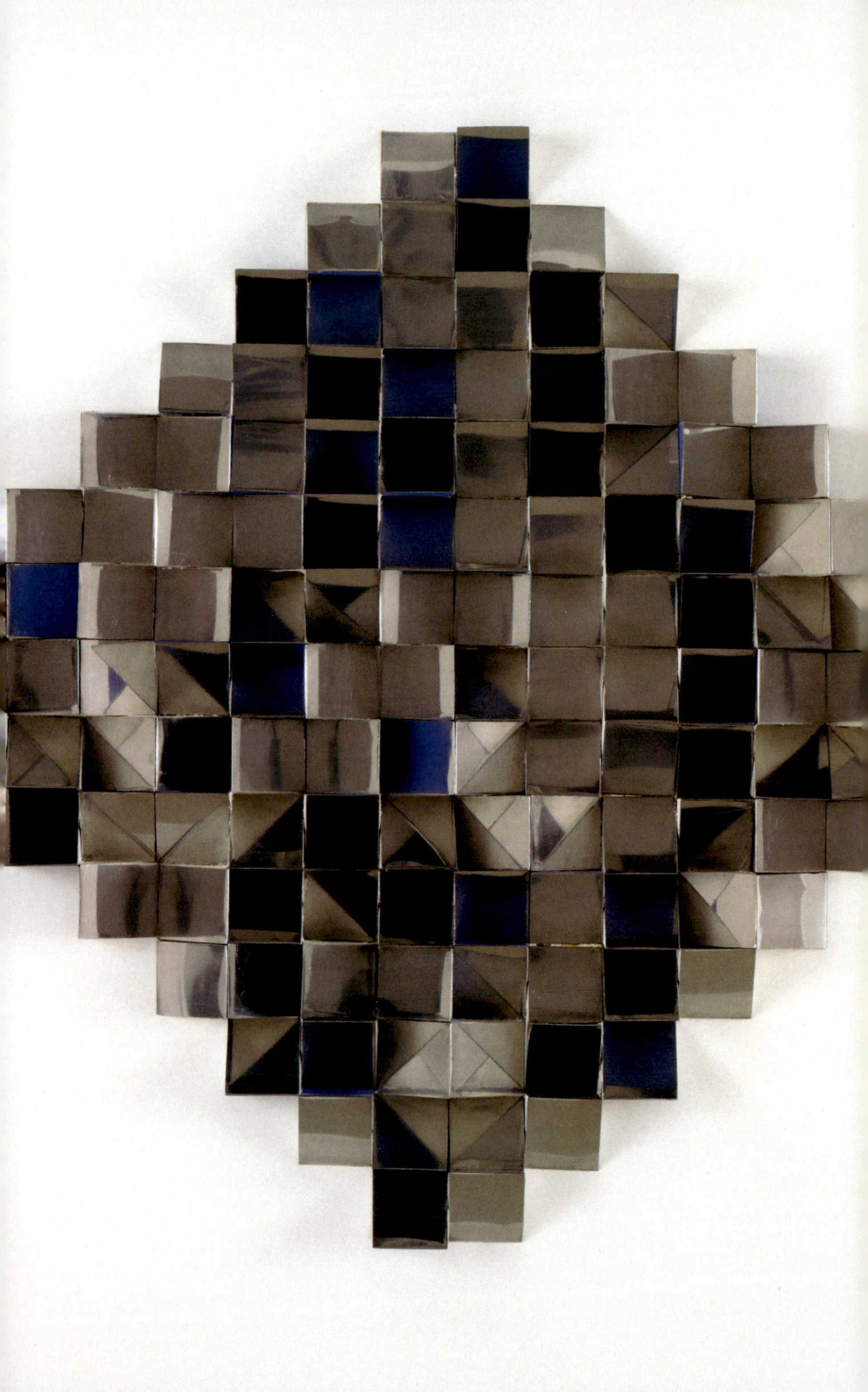

CONSTRUCTING AN ABSTRACT VOCABULARY

-

About 'abstract' art: . . .
After all, every movement of human life is affected
by form and colour, everything we see, touch, think
and feel is linked up with it

-

Ben Nicholson
1941

MARLOW MOSS

1889–1958

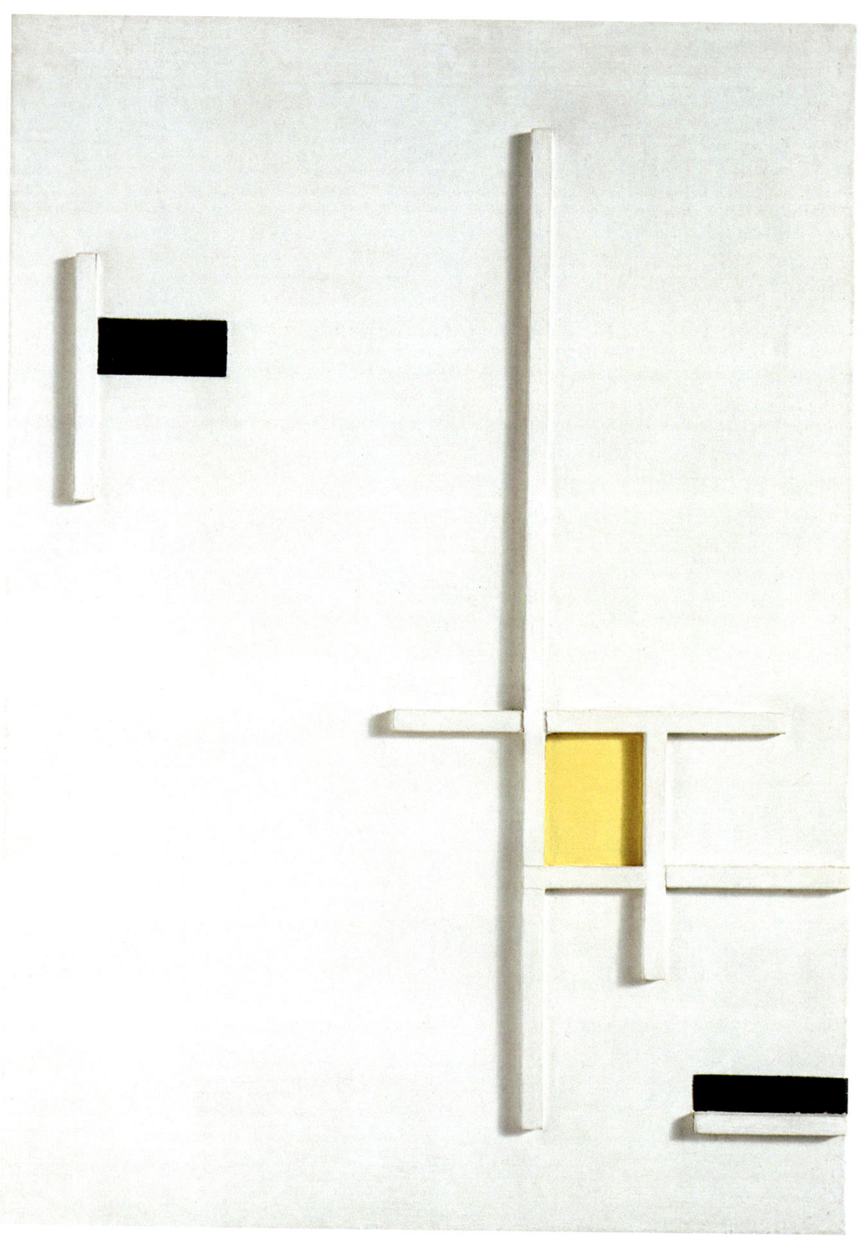

Marlow Moss
*Composition in Yellow,
Black and White*, 1949
Oil and wood on canvas,
50.8 x 35.6 x 0.6 cm
(20 x 14⅛ x ¼ in.)
Tate Collection, UK

**This painting assumes
a three-dimensional
aspect with its system
of low-relief linear wood
elements, creating
defined shadows that
counterbalance the
bright white expanse of
the canvas surface and its
vivid yellow focal point.**

British Constructivist artist Marlow Moss was born Marjorie Jewel Moss in London. She later adopted the first name Marlow, possibly in an attempt to undermine assumptions about her gender. She moved to Paris in 1927 to study with the renowned Cubist painter Fernand Léger at the Académie Moderne. Meeting Piet Mondrian in 1929 had a profound impact on her artistic development, as she subsequently renounced all but the three primary colours. In 1931 Moss was invited to become a founding member of Abstraction-Création, alongside another forty abstract artists. She developed a good working knowledge of mathematics and geometry, which she applied to her paintings, low reliefs and sculptures that sought to express 'space, movement and light'.

In 1941, following the German occupation of France that put her at risk as a Jewish lesbian woman, Moss swiftly relocated to a remote village in Cornwall, England. She retained contact with her European network of artists, rather than forging close ties with the St Ives School of artists based nearby, including Ben Nicholson and Barbara Hepworth. Her isolation in Cornwall was circumstantial rather than intentional, but as a result, the legacy of Moss's early role in geometric abstraction has been obscured, also because most of her artistic output prior to the Second World War was lost during the war. Her innovation in 1931 of the double line (two closely set parallel lines) within rectilinear compositions is often credited to Mondrian, who later adopted it in his own paintings. This contribution, amongst many others, is testament to her vitality and centrality to the Parisian scene of abstract artists in the interwar period.

KEY EVENTS

1937: Moss's work is included in the major group exhibition 'The Constructivists' at Kunsthalle Basel, Basel.

1962: A posthumous solo exhibition is organized by the Stedelijk Museum, Amsterdam.

EMMA KUNZ
1892–1963

Emma Kunz's artworks were never exhibited during her lifetime.
Born into a family of weavers in Brittnau, German-speaking
Switzerland, at eighteen she began to explore her prophetic and
telepathic abilities. Kunz did not train as an artist, but rather
understood her drawings to play a role in assisting her work as
a natural healer and researcher. She developed remedies based
on minerals and plants sourced from her rural environment to
promote the healing of her patients.

In 1938, Kunz began to make large-scale abstract drawings
on graph paper. She described these works as 'shape and form
expressed as measurement, rhythm, symbol and transformation
of figure and principle'. Numbering around four hundred drawings
in total, these works are a visual manifestation of her research.
To produce these geometric works on paper, Kunz used a divining
pendulum to plot the linear designs, in a technique called
radiesthesia. She used her drawings to help diagnose her patients.
Kunz conceived of them as 'energy fields' in which each geometric
shape, line and colour corresponded to a specific meaning that
cumulatively helped her to reach towards a holistic understanding
of the world (in both its spiritual and philosophical dimensions).

In the early 1940s, during the course of her research, Kunz
discovered a healing rock in a Roman quarry. She claimed its anti-
inflammatory properties were derived from its mineral composition
and biodynamic energies. Kunz named the rock AION A, meaning
'without limitation' in Greek. Her drawings were often produced
during intensive sessions that could last up to forty-eight hours
without breaking for rest or food. Anticipating that her works
would only fully be appreciated after her death, Kunz asserted:
'My drawings are designed for the 21st century.'

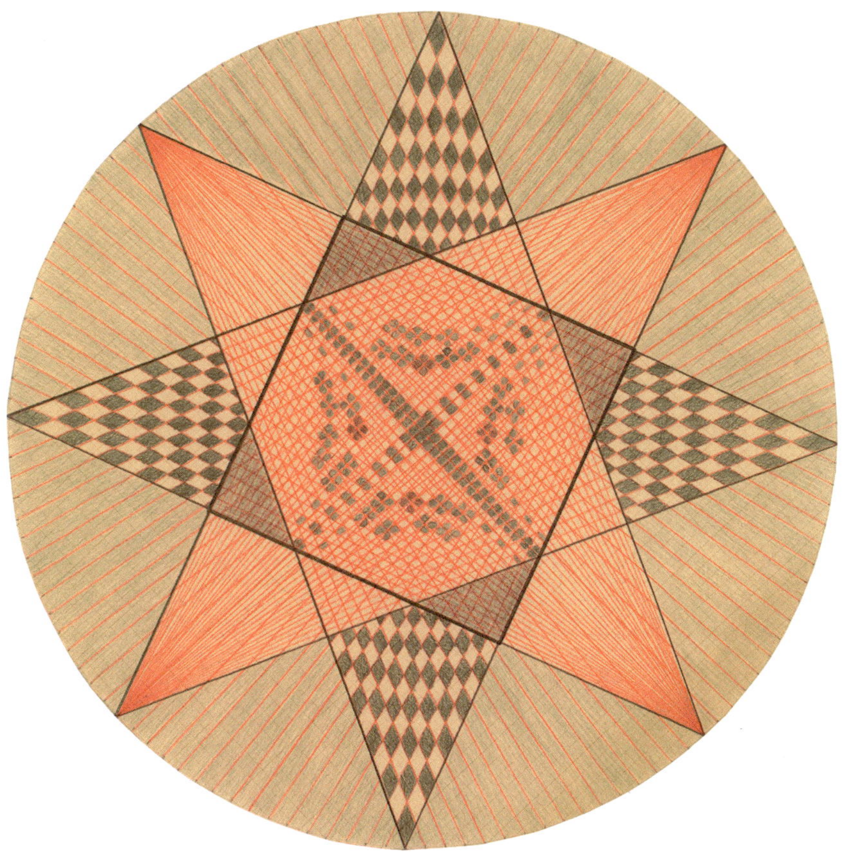

Emma Kunz
Werk Nr-483, undated
Pencil, crayon and oil
crayon on graph paper,
diameter 60 cm (23⅝ in.)
Emma Kunz Zentrum,
Würenlos

**Kunz's compositions are
both arithmetical and
reminiscent of weaving
grids, suggesting the
repetitive movement of
her divining pendulum.**

KEY EVENTS

1973: Kunz's drawings are first exhibited posthumously at
Aargauer Kunsthaus.

1986: The Emma Kunz Centre opens in a stone grotto in Würenlos,
Switzerland, to preserve the artist's legacy and to continue
extraction of AION A. An exhibition space opens in 1991 to
show seventy of her drawings on permanent display.

2005–6: '3 x Abstraction: New Methods of Drawing – Emma Kunz,
Hilma af Klint, and Agnes Martin', a major exhibition tour of
her artwork, is organized by The Drawing Center, New York, NY,
displaying her drawings alongside works by two major figures
of twentieth-century abstraction.

PAULE VÉZELAY
1892–1984

Vézelay was a British abstract pioneer, born in Bristol as Marjorie Watson-Williams. She trained at the Slade and the London School of Art, developing a reputation initially as a figurative painter. Like many artists of her generation she moved to Paris in the 1920s, where she adopted the more continental and perhaps also more androgynous name of Paule Vézelay.

Around 1928 she abandoned representational art to commit herself fully to abstraction. She was associated with Surrealism for a time, particularly in relation to her use of biomorphic forms (which we could understand as Surrealist Abstraction), but she also experimented with geometric and linear relief styles of working, later using wire and thread to produce her series *Lines in Space*. In 1929 she met the painter André Masson, who was renowned for his dreamlike approach to Surrealist chance effects and automatic drawing. They spent four years together, at a time when Vézelay was an increasingly central figure within Parisian avant-garde circles. She developed a close friendship with Sophie Taeuber-Arp and Hans (Jean) Arp, amongst many other connections and dialogues. Vézelay was admitted to the Abstraction-Création association of artists in 1934 and subsequently took part in many important exhibitions of abstract art held across Europe.

She returned to the UK at the outbreak of the Second World War in 1939. In post-war London she found that her abstract work was not in demand, and so supplemented her painting practice with a career in the applied arts as a textile designer and illustrator.

Paule Vézelay
Forms, 1936
Charcoal on canvas,
73 x 54 cm
(28¾ x 21⅜ in.)
Tate Collection, UK

Commenting on her visual vocabulary of this period, Vézelay stated that: 'I am sure the forms in my non-figurative works are invented forms and do not have their origins in natural forms.'

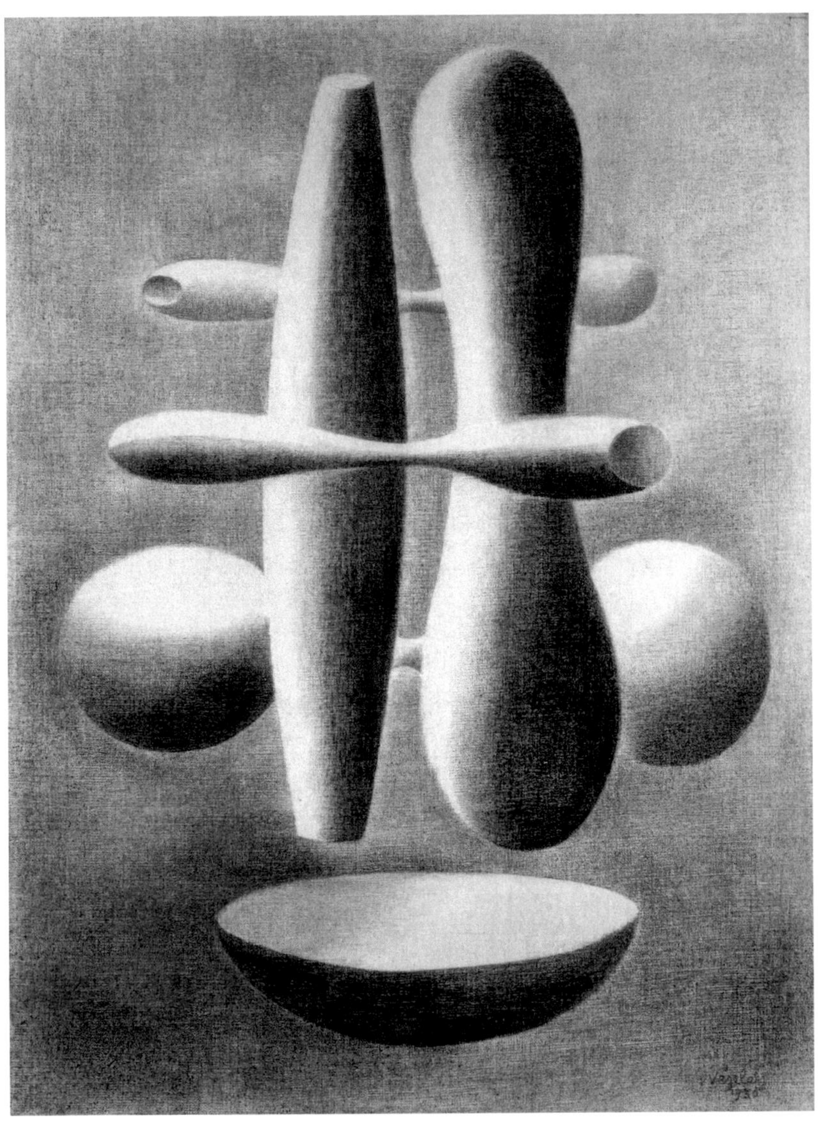

KEY EVENTS

1952: Invited by André Bloc to form a London branch of Le
Groupe Espace, a Parisian-based group of architects and
artists committed to promoting geometric abstraction.

1983: A retrospective of Vézelay's work is staged at the Tate
Gallery, London, in the year before her death at the age of
ninety-one.

BEN NICHOLSON

1894–1982

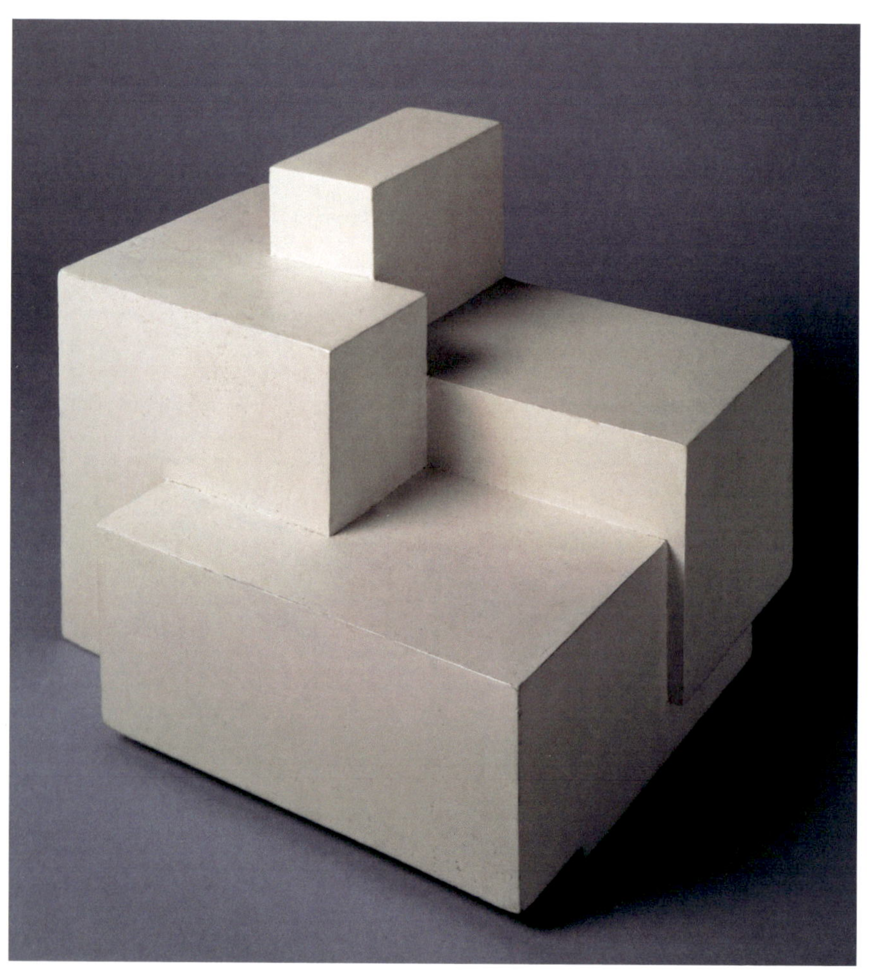

Ben Nicholson
c. 1936 (sculpture), c.1936
Painted wood,
22.8 x 30.5 x 24.1 cm
(9 x 12⅛ x 9½ in.)
Tate Collection, UK

Simplicity was a virtue for Nicholson. He relished the ease and speed with which he could cut, plane and sand this block of hardwood. His painted white sculpture recalls 1930s modernist architecture and the influential De Stijl movement.

The eldest son of artists Sir William Nicholson and Mabel Pryde, who were known for their portraits and still-life paintings, Ben Nicholson grew up in a bohemian, creative environment in Bloomsbury, London, surrounded by artists and writers.

Having first trained briefly at the Slade School of Art, London, where he met the British Surrealist and abstract artist Paul Nash, Nicholson went on to travel throughout Italy, France and the United States. He saw Cubist paintings for the first time in 1921, which had an enormous impact on his own approach to still life at the time. Nicholson undertook several trips to Paris around 1932 to visit the studios of artists including Arp, Brâncuși, Braque, Mondrian and Picasso, before settling in London from 1932 to 1939. He produced his first abstract geometric reliefs in 1933, the same year he joined Unit One alongside its founder Paul Nash and his future wife, the British sculptor Barbara Hepworth. Unit One was a short-lived artist group that embraced the full spectrum of modern art from abstraction to Surrealism, and from architecture and design to painting and sculpture. The group organized an important touring exhibition of their works in 1934–5, before disbanding abruptly after two years.

In 1937 Nicholson, along with Naum Gabo and the architect Leslie Martin, edited the publication *Circle: International Survey of Constructivist Art*, which aimed to connect the British art scene with a global perspective on modern art. Writing in 1941, Nicholson described his fundamental belief that when viewing a work of abstract art: 'There is no need to concentrate; it becomes a part of living. I think that so far from being a limited expression, understood by a few, abstract art is a powerful, unlimited and universal language.'

KEY EVENTS

1939–58: Nicholson lives in Cornwall, England, where the coastal landscape has a major impact on his artistic practice.

1956: Nicholson is awarded the first Guggenheim International Painting prize.

1957: The artist wins the international prize for painting at the São Paulo Biennial, Brazil.

HENRYK STAŻEWSKI
1894–1988

Polish artist Henryk Stażewski had a long and distinguished international career lasting more than sixty years. He was committed to advocating for the shared global language of abstract art that created a community across a diverse range of countries.

From 1913 to 1919 Stażewski studied at the School of Fine Arts in Warsaw under the renowned painter Stanisław Lentz. He joined the Polish Expressionists, the first avant-garde group based in Poland, founded in 1917. They later changed their name to the Formists, indicating a new preference for Suprematist-inspired geometric abstraction. Shortly afterwards Stażewski participated in two major shows in 1923 – 'The International Exhibition of New Art' in Łódź and 'The New Art Exhibition' in Vilnius.

The influence of both Cubism and De Stijl was apparent in his early works of the 1920s and 1930s, particularly in their reliance on grid formats and a limited palette of the primary colours in tandem with black, grey and white. In 1923 he turned his hand to designing both interiors and stage sets, and throughout his life he continued to balance his painting and reliefs with the applied arts, especially ceramics and poster design. Stażewski was a founding member of the Blok group (Block Group of Cubists, Constructivists and Suprematists) in Poland between 1924 and 1926, while often travelling to Paris, where he developed a friendship with Mondrian. He later joined Cercle et Carré (from 1929) and Abstraction-Création (from 1931) – two Parisian abstract art groups.

In 1931, along with Katarzyna Kobro and Władysław Strzemiński, Stażewski was part of the group of artists who established the founding collection of the public Museum of Modern Art in Łódź, clearly favouring abstraction. During the Second World War, the vast majority of Stażewski's pre-war artworks were destroyed or lost.

In 1966 he co-founded the Foksal Gallery, a new artist-led non-commercial gallery space in Warsaw. It quickly became the focal point for the Polish avant-garde in the 1960s and 1970s,

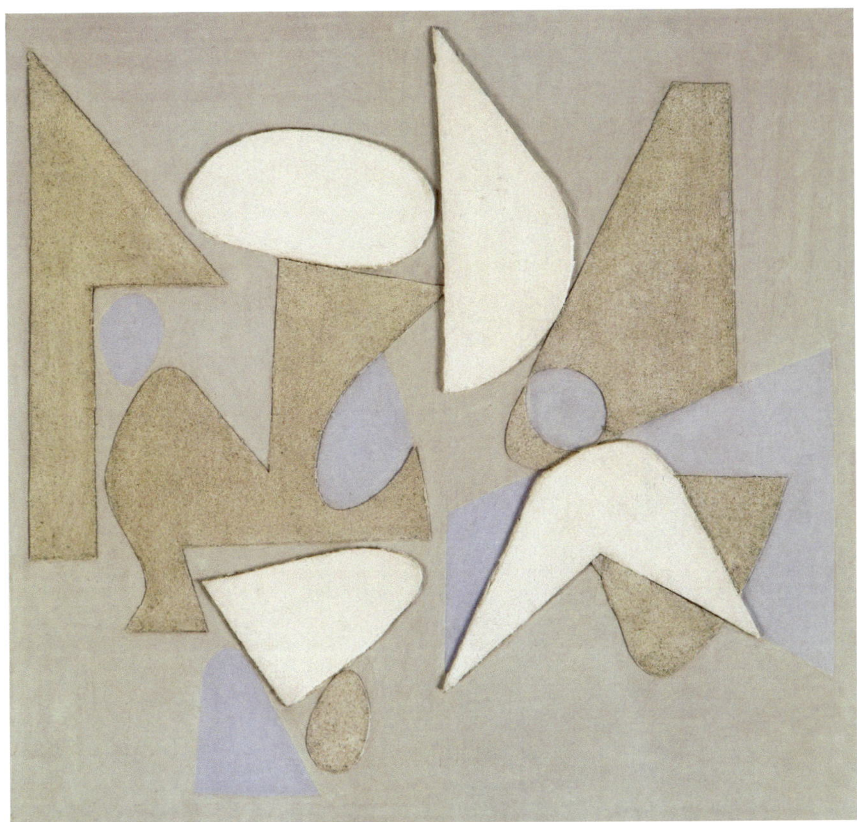

Henryk Stażewski
Abstract Composition
(*Kompozycja Abstrakcyjna*)
– *Relief*, 1958
Mixed media on
fibreboard, 34.5 x 37 cm
(13⅝ x 14⅝ in.)
Zachęta – National
Gallery of Art, Warsaw

The second half of the 1950s was dominated by Stażewski's exploration of the low-relief format, supplanting oil painting as his preferred method of production.

hosting many artists from overseas. In later life Stażewski continued to cultivate links amongst artists operating in different countries, overcoming political difficulties to institute an exchange between communist Poland and capitalist United States at the height of the Cold War. He continued to promote geometry as the underlying constant linking art and science throughout history.

KEY EVENTS

1970: Younger artist Edward Krasiński moves into Stażewski's apartment and studio in Warsaw, where together they create an experimental and social art space, characterized by Stażewski's brightly coloured Constructivist paintings and Krasiński's installations of blue Scotch tape.

1982: Stażewski's Polish–US exchange culminates in a major group exhibition at the Musée d'Art Moderne de la Ville de Paris.

LÁSZLÓ MOHOLY-NAGY
1895–1946

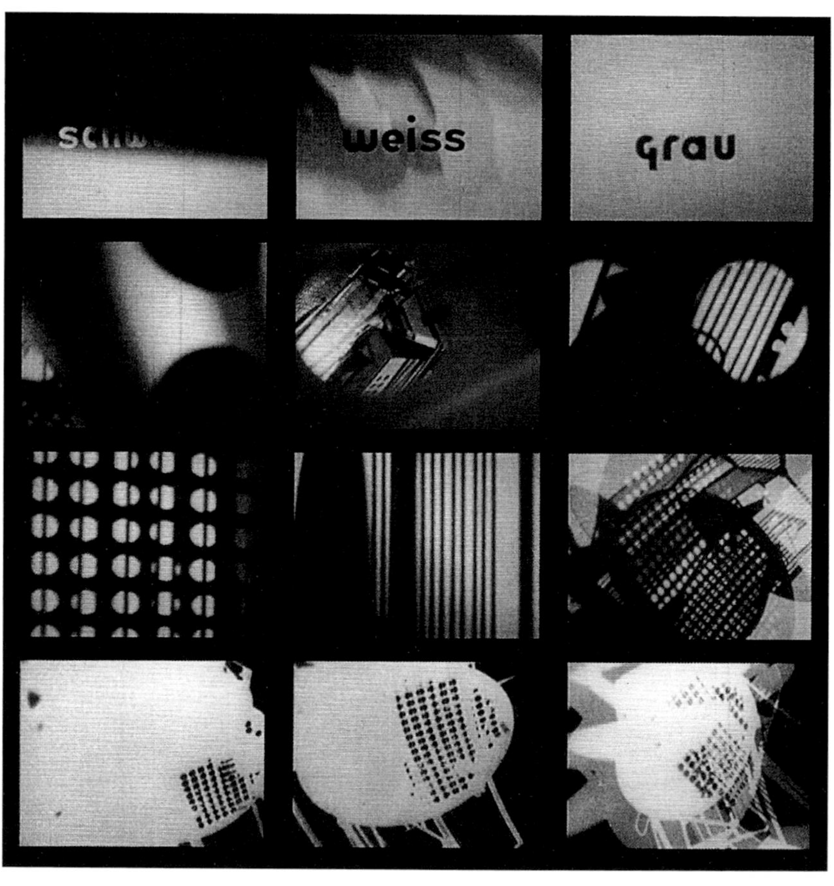

László Moholy-Nagy was an early innovator in experiments that distanced the artist's hand from the means of production. Early in his career he made a series of austere abstract works known as the 'Telephone Paintings'. Moholy later looked back on this important moment:

> In 1922, I ordered by telephone from a sign factory five paintings in porcelain enamel. I had the factory's colour chart before me and I sketched my painting on graph paper. At the other end of the telephone the factory supervisor had the same kind of paper, divided into squares. He took down the dictated shapes in the correct position. (It was like playing chess by correspondence.)

The industrial fabrication of these geometric works anticipates many aspects of Minimal and Conceptual Art in the 1960s.

Moholy was a nearly self-taught artist who ranged freely across a vast number of materials and mediums. He did not distinguish between fine art and commercial art, and spent many years working as a freelance designer on advertising and typographic projects. Like many artists of his generation, he believed in the marriage of artistic and scientific progress and strived to produce art that reflected the times in which he lived. His forward-looking approach to testing the boundaries of new technologies such as film and photography made him a skilful and influential teacher, and in 1923 he was invited by founder Walter Gropius to teach at the Bauhaus in Weimar and Dessau, Germany. After five years, and following Gropius's resignation, Moholy left for Berlin, where he set up his own design studio. Short stays in Amsterdam and London followed Hitler's rise to power in 1933. Moholy's final relocation was to the United States in 1937, where he would once again have a substantial impact through his commitment to teaching.

László Moholy-Nagy
A Light Play, Black White Grey (Ein Lichtspiel schwarz weiss grau), 1930
16-mm black-and-white film, 6 mins
Moholy-Nagy Foundation, Ann Arbor

Moholy described this pioneering abstract film as a 'moving painting'. The effects were created using the artist's *Light Prop for an Electric Stage* (1930), the first motorized kinetic sculpture, whose metal and glass moving parts are captured in the film's close-ups.

KEY EVENTS

1925: Publishes *Painting, Photography and Film* in the Bauhaus Books series. It includes many of the artist's camera-less photograms and his thoughts on communication technologies.

1937: On Gropius's recommendation moves to Chicago to establish the New Bauhaus: American School of Design. Although it is forced to close after little more than a year, it forms the blueprint for the city's Institute of Design.

LUCIO FONTANA
1899–1968

Lucio Fontana was born in the Argentinian port city of Rosario de Santa Fé to Italian parents. He was sent to Milan at the age of eight to receive an Italian education, returning to Argentina as a young man in 1922. Fontana established his own workshop three years later, dedicated to investigating new forms of sculpture. In 1927 Fontana left once more for Italy, to study classical sculptural techniques at Milan's Brera Academy of Fine Arts. His first solo exhibition took place at the city's Milione Gallery in 1930. Around this time Fontana's sculpture focused on abstracting the human body into blocky geometric profiles. He produced his first fully abstract sculptures in 1934, which proved highly controversial.

Returning to Argentina at an opportune moment, he spent the years 1940 to 1947 in Buenos Aires, escaping the carnage of the Second World War. Here Fontana established the Altamira Academy in 1946, which provided the most fertile ground for his growth into abstraction. Fontana published *The White Manifesto* (1946), which was written collectively with his students. In it they proclaimed: 'We demand an art which is free from all aesthetic artifice . . . All artistic concepts are due to the workings of the subconscious.' Fontana's later concept of Spatialism (Spazialismo) evolved from this manifesto's ideas. By rejecting the rational basis of much abstract art, Fontana moved towards a more organic form of spatial expression, equally grounded in nature and technology.

He succeeded in regenerating painting by using many of the techniques of his sculptural training, such as modelling. By the late 1940s Fontana was advancing his Spatialist abstract vocabulary,

Lucio Fontana
*Spatial Concept, The End
of God (Concetto Spaziale,
La Fine di Dio)*, 1964
Oil paint on canvas, cuts,
holes, 178 x 123 cm
(70⅛ x 48½ in.)
Rachofsky Collection,
Dallas

***The End of God* series
was produced in the
final decade of Fontana's
life. The oval-shaped
canvases are each painted
in a single bright colour
(monochromes), with
random clusters of holes
puncturing their surfaces,
and some with the
addition of glitter. The
title alludes to Fontana's
promotion of a visual art
that transcends human
belief systems.**

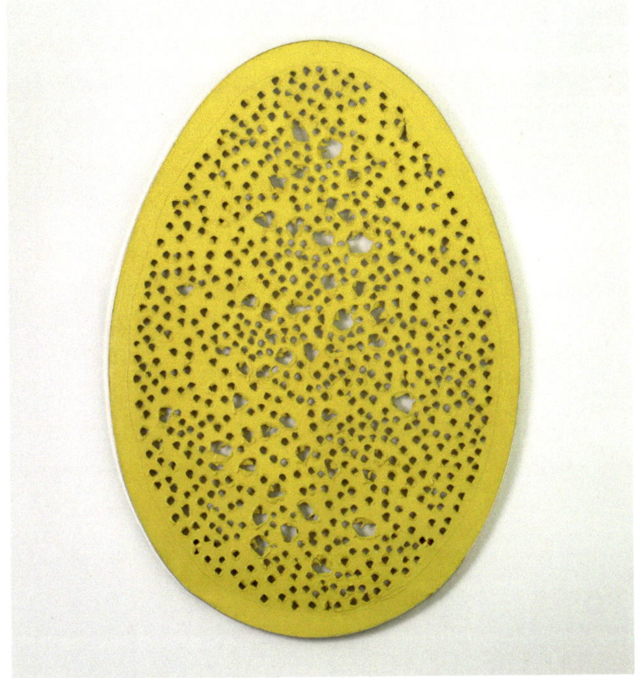

first consisting of the *Holes (Buchi)*; these works were joined in the
1950s by the *Stones (Pietre)*, *Impastos (Gessi)*, *Nature Sculptures* and
most famously his *Slashes (Tagli)*, which appeared in 1958. Of these
iconic works, Fontana commented: 'I managed with this formula to
give the spectator an impression of spatial calm, of cosmic rigour,
of serenity in infinity.'

KEY EVENTS

1947: The first *Manifesto of Spatialism* is published, signed by
Fontana alongside writer Milena Milani, philosopher Beniamino
Joppolo and critic Giorgio Kaisserlian.

1949: Fontana creates *Spatial Environment in Black Light* for the
Naviglio Gallery in Milan: an experiment using phosphorescent
light elements suspended from the ceiling to create an
immersive spatial abstraction.

1966: Fontana is awarded a prize at the Venice Biennale for his
series of white paintings, each with a single slash, situated
within an oval-shaped, maze-like environment, designed in
collaboration with the architect Carlo Scarpa.

MARY MARTIN
1907–69

Mary Martin (née Balmford) was born in Folkestone, England,
and trained at Goldsmiths College and the Royal College of Art,
London. At the RCA she met the artist Kenneth Martin, whom
she married in 1930. Initially her work focused on the still-life and
landscape-painting genres, and prior to the Second World War she
exhibited regularly under her maiden name, most notably as part
of the Artists International Association (AIA), a London-based
exhibiting society without a unifying style that supported various
left-wing political causes.

During the war Martin taught various courses at Chelmsford
School of Art, including drawing, design and weaving. It was only
in the late 1940s that both Kenneth and Mary Martin looked to
develop their work towards an abstract style, recuperating many
references to Constructivism, the geometric abstract movement
that had dominated Europe earlier in the twentieth century. Martin
made her first totally abstract painting in 1950, swiftly followed
by her first low-relief work in 1951 – a technique with which she
would become closely associated. First working in plaster, she
quickly began to favour transparent and reflective materials such
as Plexiglass and metal. These enabled the introduction of optical
effects into the surface of her works, which were based on cubes
and squares in sequential mathematical variations.

By the mid-1950s Martin was making large-scale structural
works that integrated with their intended sites. She believed that
artists were required to 'have an understanding of, and a capacity

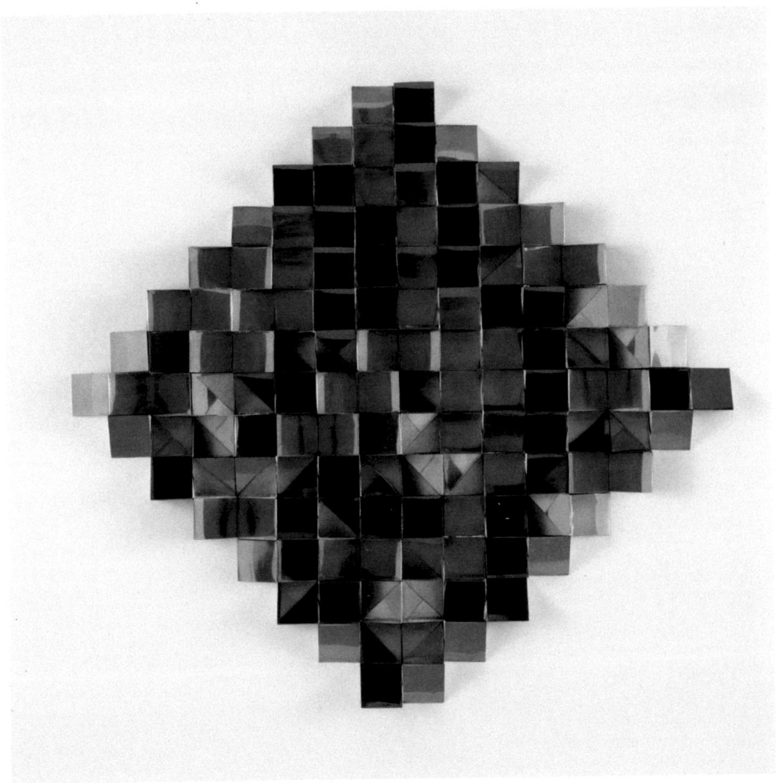

Mary Martin
*Compound Rhythms
with Blue*, 1966
Steel, aluminium, paint,
wood and Formica,
107.4 x 108 x 7.6 cm
(42³⁄₈ x 42⁵⁄₈ x 3 in.)
Arts Council
Collection, UK

**The symmetry,
proportions and
numerical permutations
that determine the
layout of this relief all
work in tandem with
its reflective surface to
allow its viewers to be
incorporated into the
ever-changing space
of the work itself.**

to enter into, architecture, without destroying it, or dominating it, or distracting from it'. This relational understanding led to many public art commissions including relief screens for the interior of the ocean liner SS *Oriana* (1960), and a major work, *Wall Construction*, for the University of Stirling in the year of her untimely death, 1969.

KEY EVENTS

1956: Mary and Kenneth Martin collaborate with designer John Weeks on the 'Environment' section of the experimental group exhibition 'This is Tomorrow', staged by the Whitechapel Gallery, London, in collaboration with the Independent Group.

1969: Joint first prize winner (with Richard Hamilton) of the John Moores Painting Prize at Walker Art Gallery, Liverpool, for her relief *Cross*, 1969, which is purchased by the museum. Martin is the first woman ever to win the prestigious award, but sadly dies before the exhibition opens.

SALOUA RAOUDA CHOUCAIR
1916–2017

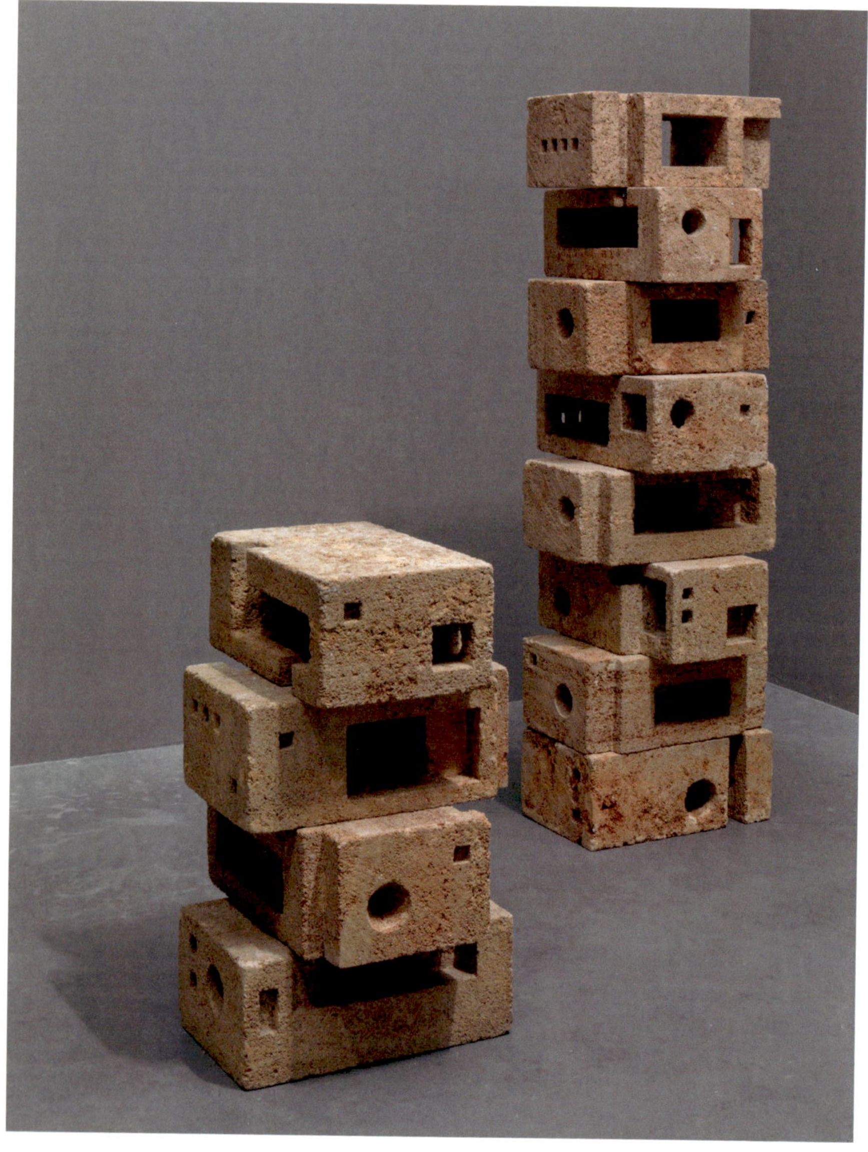

Saloua Raouda Choucair
Infinite Structure, 1963–5
Tufa stone, 240 x
48 x 30 cm (94½ x
19 x 11⅞ in.)
Tate Collection, UK

**This stack of twelve
individual stone blocks
partly references
Constantin Brâncuși's
Endless Column sculptural
project. Each block
is incised with both
rectangular and circular
forms. This interlocking
structure is inspired
by Islamic and Sufi
poetry, in which
individual stanzas can
have a standalone
existence outside
the poem's context.**

Choucair burst onto the art scene of her hometown Beirut in the 1940s, after studying with renowned Lebanese landscape artists Omar Onsi and Moustafa Farroukh, who worked in Impressionist and realist styles. A trip to Egypt in 1943 gave her a grounding in the history of Islamic art and architecture, despite her tutors' clear preference for European art. She then took a degree in philosophy at the American University of Beirut, followed by three years in Paris that transformed Choucair's artistic approach. She studied printmaking, sculpture and fresco techniques at the Ecole Nationale Supérieure des Beaux-Arts, while also attending the studio of Cubist painter Fernand Léger.

This broad base of artistic training enabled Choucair to arrive at her favoured vehicle of expression by the early 1950s: an abstraction based on modular units and sinuous curved forms, realized in both two and three dimensions. It was through her passion for geometry and mathematics that Choucair was able to synthesize a distinctive abstract language that achieved an equilibrium of visual references from both East and West. In 1951 she published her manifesto-like text, 'How the Arab Understood Visual Art', in which she writes: 'Arabs are the most sensitively sophisticated of peoples in understanding art, and that is why they broached the subject at its abstract essence.'

From the 1960s onwards Choucair increasingly devoted her energies towards sculpture, producing important series of works known as the 'Interforms' and 'Poems' based on stacking units, carved in wood or stone, and the 'Duals' based on two interlocking forms – often executed in aluminium or fibreglass. Rather than overemphasize the importance of her studies in Europe, Choucair stressed that: 'What I experience, everyone in the world experiences, and, in fact, all of the rules I apply to my sculpture are derived from Islamic geometric design.'

KEY EVENTS

1950: During her time in Paris shows a series of small geometric paintings at the Salon des Réalités Nouvelles, an exhibiting society dedicated to pure abstraction founded by Sonia Delaunay-Terk and dancer and musician Nelly van Doesburg.

2013: Tate Modern, London, stages the solo exhibition 'Saloua Raouda Choucair', enabling international audiences to see a comprehensive range of the artist's work for the first time outside of Choucair's native Lebanon.

YVES KLEIN

1928–62

Born in the city of Nice on the French Riviera, Yves Klein only committed to working as an artist in 1954, eight years prior to his untimely death at thirty-four. After several commercially and critically unsuccessful shows in Paris that presented a range of monochrome paintings in various sizes and colours including pink, orange, green, yellow and violet, Klein decided that a more dramatic statement was required – and dedicated himself to achieving an immaterial, limitless realization of the colour blue. He sought out a method by which to produce the most vivid and intense pigment possible. Utilizing a new chemical compound, this synthetic resin sold by a paint dealer in Paris allowed Klein to develop a new paint that he named and trademarked as 'International Klein Blue' (IKB).

In a 1959 lecture at the Sorbonne, 'The Evolution of Art towards the Immaterial', Klein explained his decision to privilege this colour over all others: 'Blue has no dimensions, it is beyond dimensions, whereas the other colours are not. . . . All colours arouse specific associative ideas, psychologically, material or tangible, while blue suggests at most the sea and sky, and they, after all, are in actual, visible nature what is most abstract.' Klein would extend his experiments with IKB into the 'Sponge Reliefs and Sculptures', soaking pigment into the natural textures of the sponges; and the 'Anthropometries', where he used female models as 'living paintbrushes', their naked bodies dipped in blue paint to make a series of transfers and impressions on canvas during public performances with live musicians. In 1961 Klein made a series of abstract 'Fire Paintings' using a flame thrower in a highly exaggerated performance documented for the camera, designed to accentuate his interest in natural phenomena and elemental forces.

Yves Klein
Untitled Blue Monochrome (IKB 181), 1956
Dry pigment and synthetic resin on gauze mounted on panel, 73.7 x 55.9 cm (29⅛ x 22⅛ in.)
Museo Nacional Centro de Arte Reina Sofia, Madrid

The artist created almost 200 paintings using his powerful ultramarine pigment, International Klein Blue. The completely abstract focus on the colour blue is suggestive of the void or the cosmos in its rich, deep emptiness.

KEY EVENTS

1954: Klein announces his practice with his artist's book *Yves Peintures* (*Yves Paintings*), documenting a set of monochrome paintings, prior to their exhibition and in some cases their actual fabrication.

April–May 1958: Klein's solo exhibition at Galerie Iris Clert, Paris, 'Le Vide' (The Void), presents only the totally empty gallery, painted white.

27 October 1960: The manifesto of Nouveau Réalisme (New Realism), a French art movement founded by the critic Pierre Restany, is signed at Klein's home. His interest in staging live happenings and performances connects him to this group of artists, who often utilize everyday objects in their work.

PIERO MANZONI
1933–63

Raised in Milan, Italy, Manzoni's earliest artworks were based on
silhouettes of the body or imprints of everyday objects. In 1957
the artist exhibited the first of his *Achromes* – completely white
paintings made by dipping canvas into glue and kaolin, a mineral slip
used in pottery also known as China clay. He later experimented
with kaolin-coating three-dimensional objects and textures
including polystyrene, cotton wool, straw, plastic, rabbit fur and
even bread rolls. He invented 'achrome' in order to distinguish his
work from the 'monochrome' – particularly Yves Klein's use of
that term. Manzoni went one step further than Klein's use of pure,
unadulterated blue by suggesting that the removal of colour in its
entirety would be his end goal: 'Infinity is strictly monochromatic,
or better still, colourless . . . Here, the artist has achieved total
freedom: pure matter is transformed into pure energy.'

The following year, Manzoni exhibited with Lucio Fontana as
well as Enrico Baj, the influential co-founder of the Milan-based
Nuclear Movement art group. The avant-garde circles in which
Manzoni moved often sought to define art in the post-war period
as a reaction against the new consumer culture of excess. By 1959
Manzoni had begun another series of works, in parallel with his
ongoing *Achromes*. These were the *Lines* (*Linee*), which debuted as
the inaugural exhibition at Azimut Gallery, co-founded by Manzoni
with Enrico Castellani. The *Lines* were displayed as scrolls of single-
line drawings in canisters, with typed labels indicating the length of
the line sealed within. They continued Manzoni's interest in pushing
against undefinable limits. Manzoni was only twenty-nine years old

Piero Manzoni
Achrome, 1959
Kaolin on
pleated canvas,
140 x 120.5 cm
(55⅛ x 47½ in.)
Centre Pompidou, Paris

**In his 1960 article
'Free Dimension',
Manzoni avowed that
he strove to achieve
'a white that is not a
polar landscape, an
evocative or beautiful
material, a sensation or
a symbol, or anything
else: a white surface that
is a white surface and
nothing more'.**

when he died in his studio of a heart attack. His friend, artist
Ben Vautier, signed his death certificate, declaring it to be
a final work of art.

KEY EVENTS

4 July 1960: Produces the longest *Line* in black ink on a
7,200-metre (7,874-yard) roll of newsprint, in Herning,
Denmark, using a mechanical spool to support the giant surface.

May 1961: Creates his notorious work *Artist's Shit*, an editioned
set of ninety small cans each purportedly containing 30g of
Manzoni's dried faeces. Later that year he wrote to artist Ben
Vautier: 'If collectors want something intimate, really personal
to the artist, there's the artist's own shit, that is really his.'
Manzoni sold the cans for the price of their equivalent weight
in gold.

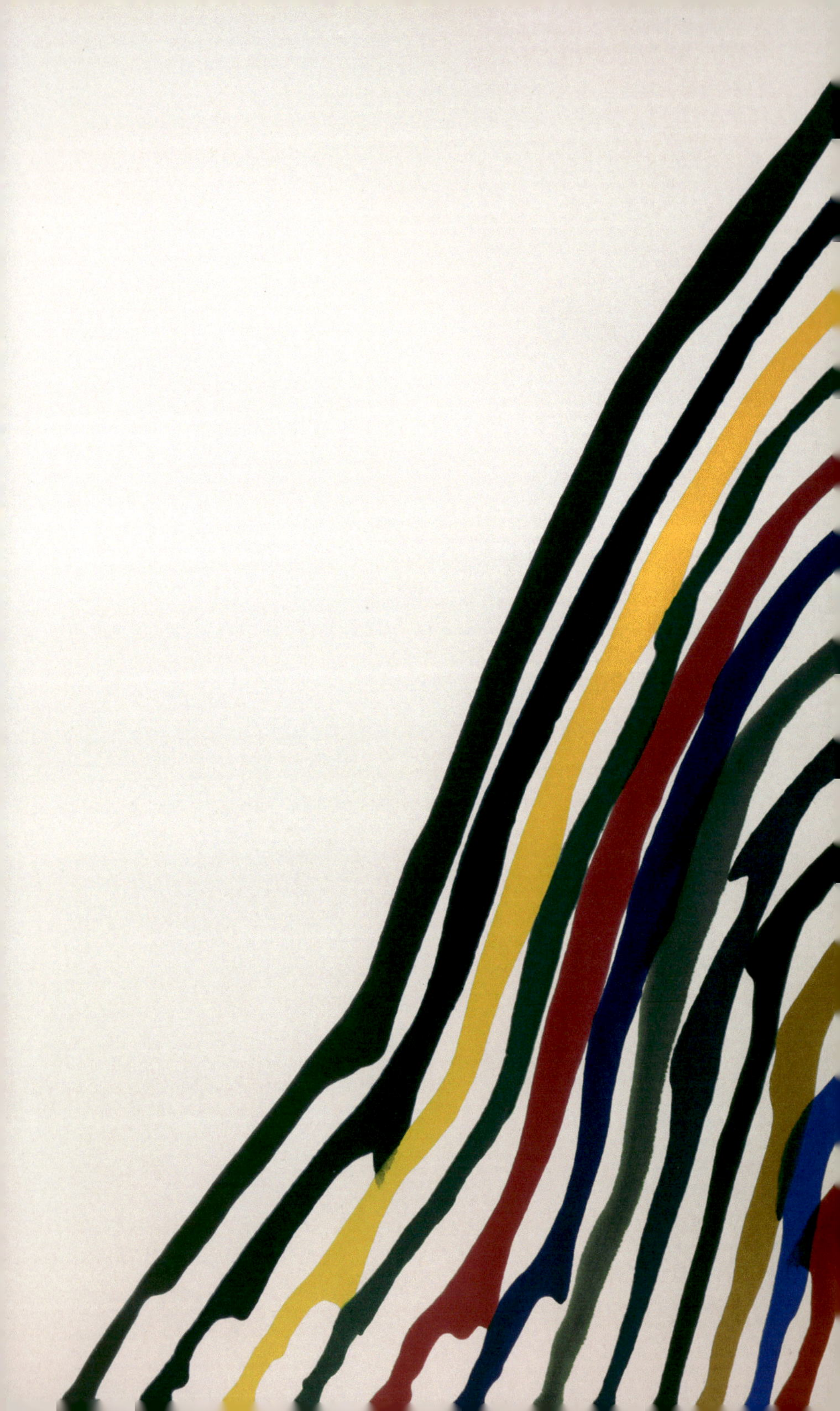

ABSTRACT EXPRESSIONISM AND ITS LEGACIES

-

We are freeing ourselves of the impediments of
memory, association, nostalgia, legend, myth or what
have you, that have been the devices of Western
European painting. Instead of making cathedrals
out of Christ, man or 'life', we are making it out
of ourselves, out of our own feelings

-

Barnett Newman
1943–5

MARK ROTHKO
1903–70

Markus Rothkowitz was born in Dvinsk, Russia (now Latvia), in 1903. At the age of ten, his family relocated to Portland, Oregon, in the United States. Gaining a scholarship to Yale University in 1921, Rothko left for New York after two years without graduating, finding it a stiflingly conservative atmosphere. Rothko took classes at the Art Students League and the New School of Design under the renowned Armenian-born painter Arshile Gorky, who shaped the development of Rothko's painting practice, in particular his understanding of European Surrealism. Rothko's paintings of the early 1940s are characterized by references to classical mythology and floating biomorphic forms that show the influence of Gorky.

In 1947 Rothko finally embraced a fully abstract approach with no figurative allusions or descriptive intentions. He developed the 'Multiforms' with irregular areas of soaked paint that would define his mature career. A further refinement of technique in 1949 achieved his final works later known as 'Sectionals', in reference to the large fields of colour that glow with light, soft at their edges, blended and overlapped in a complex layering of hues.

Rothko once said: 'I paint big to be intimate.' The 'Sectionals' elicit an emotional and even quasi-spiritual power. Often substantial in size, the paintings were always meant to be experienced at close range. The canvases were often hung very near the floor, to create an equivalency with the people in the room. Rothko addressed his viewers by stating: 'If you are only moved by colour relationships, you are missing the point. I am interested in expressing the big emotions – tragedy, ecstasy, doom.' The artist took his own life in 1970.

Mark Rothko
Untitled, 1949
Oil and acrylic
with powdered
pigments on canvas,
142.2 x 83.8 cm
(56 x 33 in.)
The Metropolitan
Museum of Art,
New York

This work, from the crucial transitional year of 1949, demonstrates the energetic brushwork and intensified colour tones of Rothko's most fully accomplished phase. The overlaid rectangular forms that structure the composition are strengthened by the carefully positioned dark rectangle in the bottom third of the painting. Rothko would in later years develop an even more sombre colour palette.

KEY EVENTS

1964: Rothko is commissioned by the Houston-based art patrons and collectors John and Dominique de Menil to work on a building now known as the Rothko Chapel, containing a set of fourteen of his paintings in an austere, contemplative space.

1971: Rothko Chapel finally opens to the public, following the artist's death, as a non-denominational space for reflection.

BARNETT NEWMAN
1905–70

Barnett Newman
Onement III, 1949
Oil on canvas,
182.5 x 84.9 cm
(71⅞ x 33½ in.)
The Museum of Modern
Art, New York

**Onement as a term is
an archaic derivation of
'atonement' and as such
refers to Judeo-Christian
processes of spiritual
reconciliation, as well
as to a broader sense of
renewal, regeneration and
wholeness. The rich rust-
orange hue is cleaved by
the bleeding paint edge
of the 'zip' that gathers
the surface together as
a unified whole.**

New Yorker Barnett Newman was a relative latecomer to the artistic profession, embarking on his painting career aged around thirty after teaching and working in his father's clothing business. His intellectual rigour and demanding standards meant that he kept very little of his early work, destroying most of what he produced before 1944. The artist's horror at the human suffering inflicted by the rise of Nazism in Europe, the Holocaust and the atomic bomb shaped his decision to commit to abstraction, as he believed that it was the only possible visual solution in such barbaric times.

Newman once said that he wanted 'to start from scratch, to paint as if painting never existed before'. In 1948 he produced a painting (later titled *Onement I*) that was the first realization of what would become his signature 'zip' composition: a narrow band created using masking tape running lengthways down the painting to unify it as a single, indivisible space. Of this decisive moment in his practice, Newman later reflected: 'I remove myself from nature, but I do not remove myself from life.'

His first solo exhibition took place in 1950 at the renowned Betty Parsons Gallery, New York. It was met with incomprehension, sarcasm and even downright aggression by the art world of the time. Newman wrote a statement to accompany the exhibition, in which he explained his paintings were 'specific and separate embodiments of feeling, to be experienced, each picture for itself'. After the overwhelmingly negative reception, he withdrew for a period of four years in which he continued working but did not show or sell anything. Nevertheless, Newman's austere refinement would slowly have a profound influence on many other painters, particularly the intense abstractions of Ad Reinhardt and Clyfford Still.

KEY EVENTS

1948: Alongside fellow painters William Baziotes, Robert Motherwell and Mark Rothko, Newman establishes a New York art school called Subject of the Artist that hosts lectures and seminars, contributing to the intellectual climate around Abstract Expressionism.

1966: Newman exhibits his cycle of fourteen paintings titled *The Stations of the Cross* (1958–66) at the Solomon R. Guggenheim Museum, New York, to critical acclaim. Of the work's spiritual intensity, he explained: 'I tried to project something I felt was very real in relation to the Passion and I feel that kind of suffering has gotten almost universal.'

LEN LYE
1901–80

Born in Christchurch, New Zealand, in 1901, Len Lye's creative vision and quest to achieve an 'art of movement' forged an experimental path throughout the twentieth century. He spent time in various places around New Zealand during his difficult childhood and travelled to Australia and Samoa as a young adult to study Aboriginal and Samoan visual cultures. Lye eventually settled in London in 1926. His innovations in animation, filmmaking and photography soon followed, with the premiere of his first experimental film, *Tusalava*, held at the London Film Society in 1929. Subsequently, Lye began to refine his direct filmmaking technique, in which no camera is used, and imagery is applied directly to the celluloid film stock, often by painting or scraping into the coloured emulsion.

A *Colour Box* (1935) was Lye's first foray into a fully abstract art of animated colours and shapes. It was commissioned by the UK's General Post Office and became the first 'camera-less' film to be screened to cinema audiences across Britain. Lye's three-minute film concludes with advertisement text for parcel postage. This striking combination of avant-garde abstraction and commercial marketing would permeate much of his career. Lye moved from London to New York in 1944, lured by a filmmaking opportunity and the chance to immerse himself in a key centre for experimental film. He made newsreels for Time, Inc. as his day job, and socialized with Abstract Expressionists at the Eighth Street Club at night, where he often screened his short films. By the early 1960s Lye committed himself to another art of movement: large-scale kinetic sculptures that danced like bodies in space.

Len Lye
Color Cry, 1952–3
16-mm film, colour,
3 mins
Ngā Taonga Sound &
Vision, Stills collection,
Wellington

As his first noteworthy experimental film made in the United States, *Color Cry* is clearly in dialogue with Abstract Expressionism, the lush planes of Color Field Painting specifically. Various stencils and fabrics are arranged on top of filmstrips to produce the 'cast shadow' abstract effects, the same technique used in direct-exposure photograms.

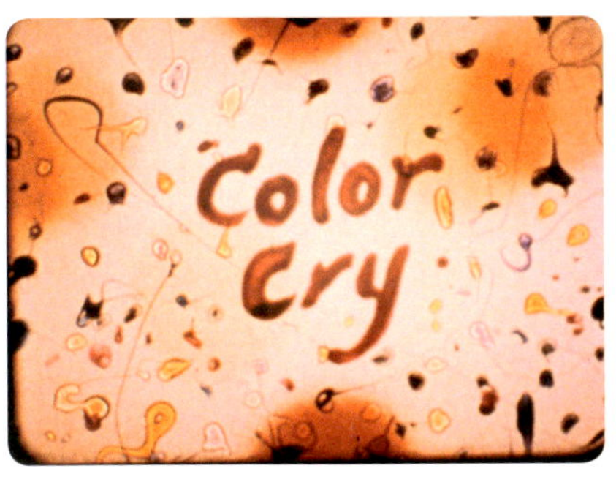

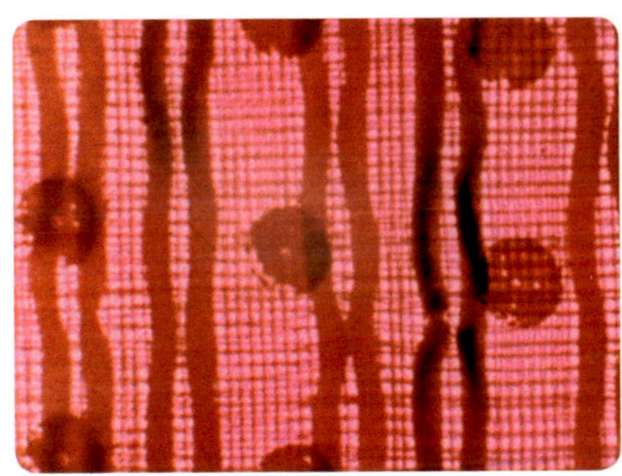

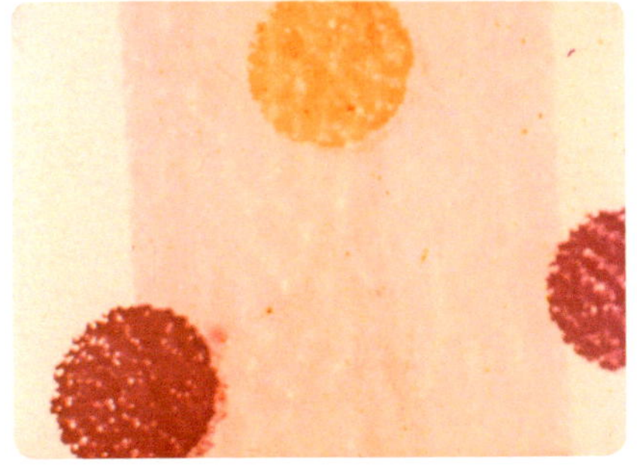

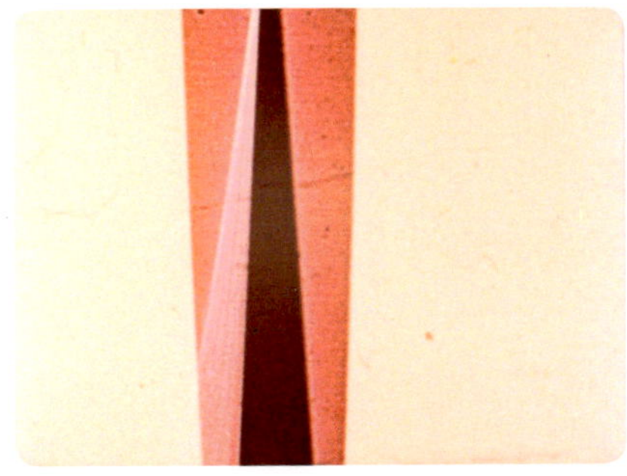

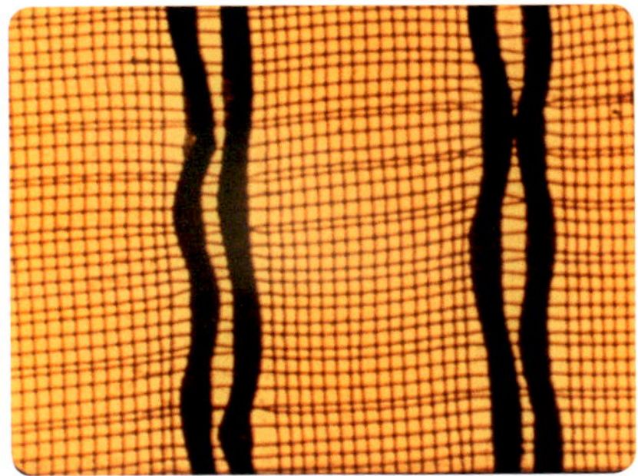

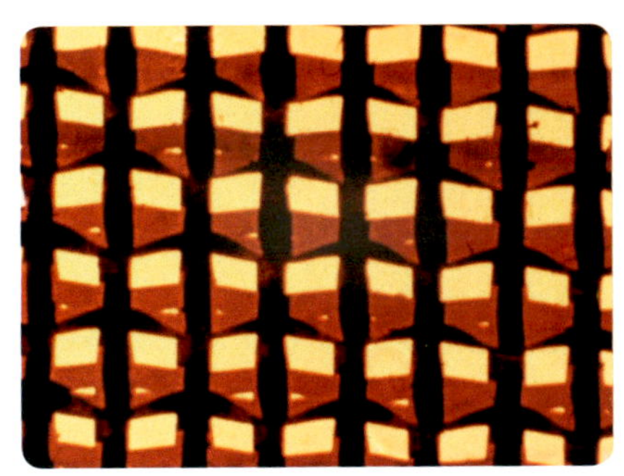

KEY EVENTS

1928: Lye joins The Seven and Five Society, a British artists'
group founded in 1919 and now led by a pioneering group of
modernist artists including Ben Nicholson, Barbara Hepworth
and Henry Moore. In 1935 it stages the first 'all abstract'
exhibition in London.

1936: Lye is included in the historic 'International Surrealist
Exhibition' at the New Burlington Galleries, London.

5 April 1961: Lye performs *An Evening of Tangible Motion
Sculpture* at the Museum of Modern Art, New York.

LEE KRASNER
1908–84

Krasner was one of the earliest American artists to commit to abstraction and a renowned first-generation Abstract Expressionist painter. She was born and raised in New York City in a Russian Jewish *émigré* family. From the age of seventeen, she underwent extensive artistic training in several esteemed institutions, including Cooper Union and the National Academy of Design. It was during her studies at the second organization that she made the switch from her given first name Lena to the more gender ambiguous 'Lee'.

From 1937 to 1940 Krasner received a scholarship to attend classes at the Hans Hofmann School of Fine Arts. Hofmann was a leading German abstract painter and widely regarded as an important influence – primarily through his rigorous teaching based on analytical Cubism – on the development of Abstract Expressionism in the United States, where he was based from 1933 until his death. Charcoal studies made during Hofmann's life drawing classes mark Krasner's shift away from a reliance on direct observational studies towards an abstract vocabulary rooted in Cubism's fractured planes and multiple perspectives on the body's movement in space. It is recorded that Hofmann commented on a work done by Krasner during this time: 'This is so good you would not know that it was done by a woman.' The artist had to fight such overt sexism, and indeed anti-Semitism, throughout her long career. Krasner was even suspected of being a spy by the FBI during the Cold War, in all probability simply because she was Jewish.

Almost forty years later, in 1974, Krasner came across a set of her old drawings from Hofmann's classes, hidden away in her studio. She began to use them, precisely sliced into angular shards, as the basis for a new body of collage paintings, titled *Eleven Ways to Use the Words to See*. Of the source material, Krasner observed: 'I experienced the need not just to examine these drawings, but a peremptory desire to change them: a command as it were, to make them anew.'

Krasner never committed to a singular, definable style, but rather created visually distinctive groups of abstract drawings, collages and paintings across her long career. Her artworks varied in size from tiny watercolours on handmade paper to mosaic tables and vast oil

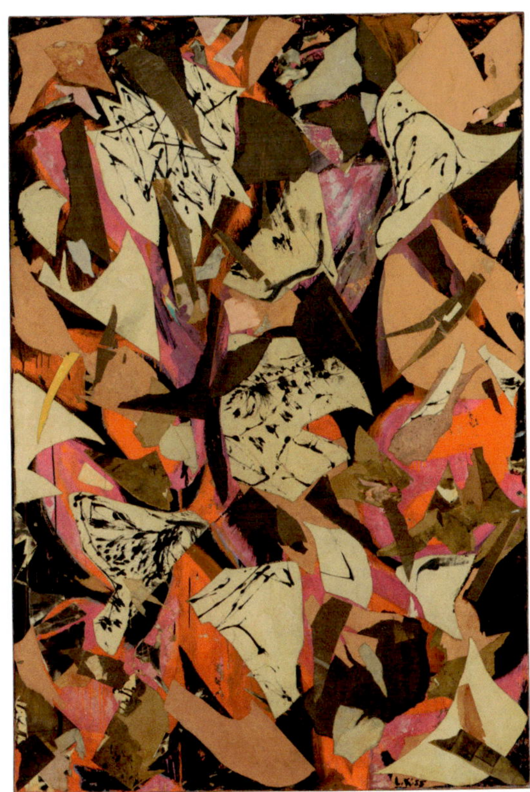

Lee Krasner
Bald Eagle, 1955
Oil, paper and canvas
collage on linen,
195.6 x 130.8 cm
(77⅛ x 51½ in.)
Collection of Audrey
Irmas, Los Angeles

Bald Eagle belongs to
the group of collage
paintings that Krasner
first exhibited at the
Stable Gallery, New York,
in 1955. The composite
surface combines canvas,
torn up newspapers
and even fragments
of destroyed drawings
and paintings by both
herself and Pollock –
all recombined into a
pulsating, dynamic whole.

paintings 20 feet (approximately 6 metres) in length – something
that was only possible after her husband Jackson Pollock's death in
1956. The following year, Krasner moved into his large, light-filled
studio, where she could, for the first time, work on a scale to match
her boundless ambitions as a painter.

KEY EVENTS

1942: Views the work of Jackson Pollock for the first time when
both artists are included in the group exhibition 'American and
French Painting' at the McMillen Gallery alongside other major
figures of Abstract Expressionism including Willem de Kooning.
Krasner and Pollock marry in 1945.

1942: Leads a major artistic commission to produce War Service
Window Displays across New York, for war training courses.

1965: Krasner is afforded a major solo survey exhibition by the
Whitechapel Gallery, London – her first show to take place in
Europe as well as in a public institution.

NORMAN LEWIS
1909–79

An African-American artist of Bermudian heritage, Lewis studied at
Columbia University in his hometown of New York City in the early
1930s. In this decade his painting was representational, working in
a Social Realist style to capture everyday experiences of African
Americans, from social injustice and poverty to violence at the
hands of the police.

A teacher and academic throughout his painting career, Lewis's
turn towards abstraction occurred around 1946, prompted by his
growing concern that representational painting 'that merely mirrors
some of the social conditions' was not capable of bringing about
political change. From this point onwards, Lewis's art cultivated a
more oblique relationship to the fraught socio-political fault lines
of post-war America. His painting remained concerned with politics:
however abstract his approach became, his unionism, commitment
to civil rights and political activism were never wholly separate from
his art.

Lewis's abstract works of the mid-1940s to mid-1970s often
showcase his calligraphy skills, as well as integrating other visual
sources from Chinese and Japanese art, and architectural forms,
improvisational music and poetry techniques. The paintings
frequently retain ghostly figurative presences that hint at the
complexities of abstract art's role in the fabric of society.

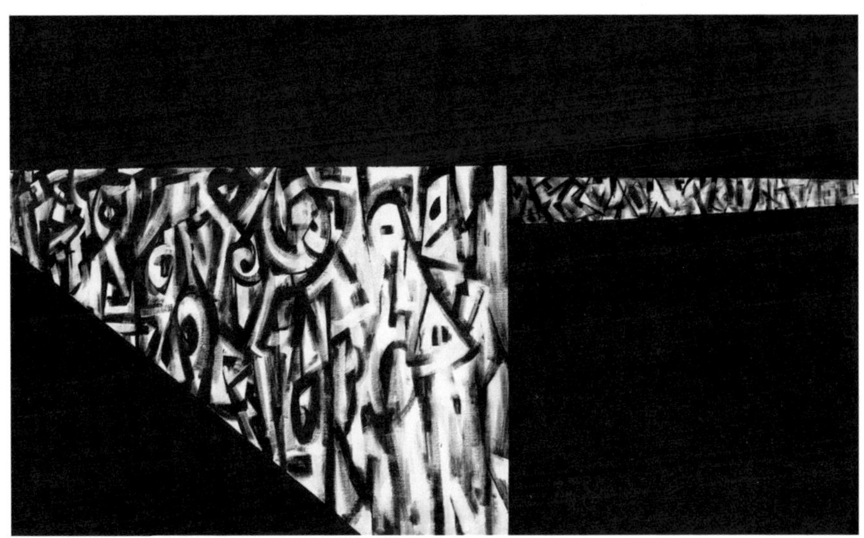

Norman Lewis
Untitled (Alabama), 1967
Oil on canvas,
114.9 x 186.7 cm
(45¼ x 73½ in.)
National Gallery of Art,
Washington, DC

The angular shape that contains Lewis's rhythmic geometric abstraction is an exaggerated version of the state of Alabama. The abstract black and white strokes contained within could be seen as referencing the crosses and hoods of the Ku Klux Klan; this idea is made more potent when considering the painting's creation at the height of the Civil Rights Movement.

KEY EVENTS

1950: Lewis participates in the Artists Sessions at Studio 35, New York, alongside numerous leading abstract artists, including Barnett Newman and Hedda Sterne. The two sessions ultimately led to an agreement to privilege 'Abstract Expressionism' as a shared term for their approaches to art making.

5 July 1963: Alongside Romare Bearden and others, Lewis is a founding member of Spiral, an African-American collective of both figurative and abstract artists that emerges from preparations to attend the historic March on Washington for Jobs and Freedom on 28 August that year.

JACKSON POLLOCK
1912–56

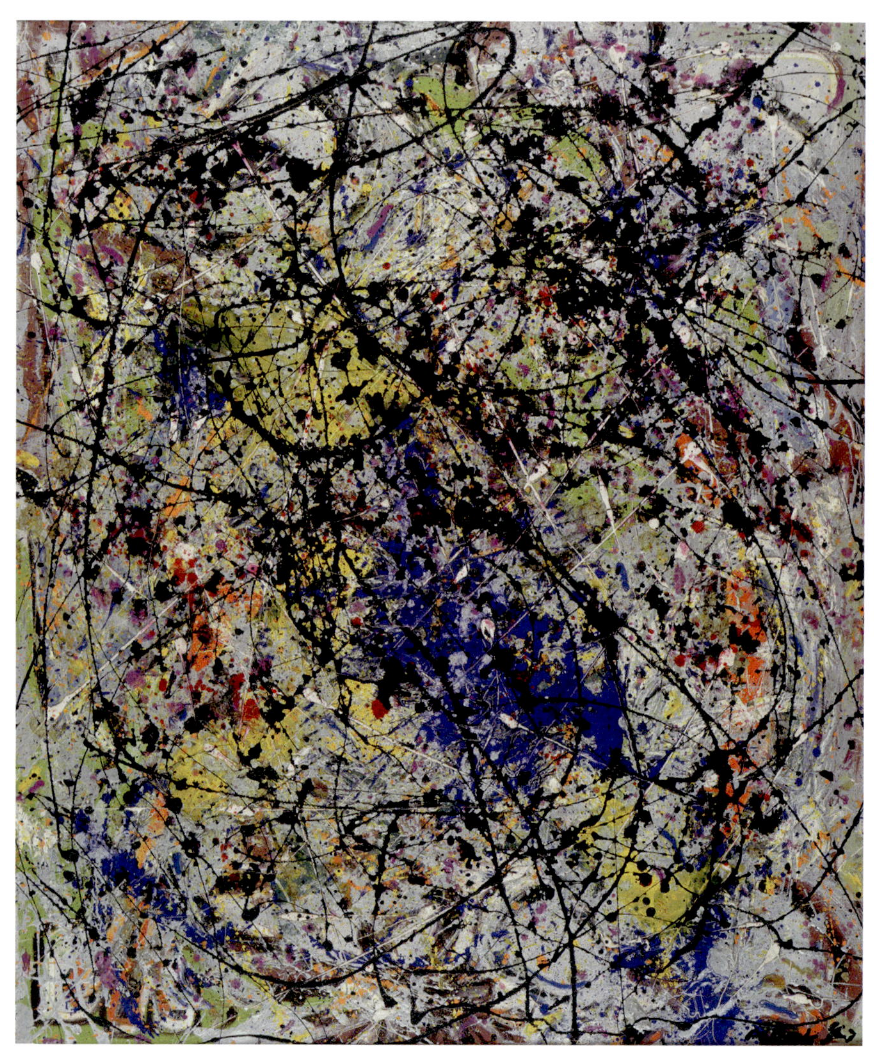

Jackson Pollock
*Reflection of the Big
Dipper*, 1947
Paint on canvas,
91.5 x 111 cm
(36⅛ x 43¾ in.)
Stedelijk Museum,
Amsterdam

**One of Pollock's earliest
'drip' paintings, the
title of this completely
abstract image references
the Big Dipper: seven
stars within the
constellation Ursa
Major. A year later
Pollock abandoned such
evocations of natural
phenomena and began
titling his paintings only
using numbers.**

Born in Cody, Wyoming, to a ranching family that moved frequently
across Arizona and California during his childhood, Jackson Pollock's
journey from a Social Realist painter forged in the Great Depression
to one of the defining abstract artists of the post-war era would
rapidly assume the status of an American legend both ambitious
and tragic. He first studied art at the Manual Arts High School of
Los Angeles, before moving to New York in 1930 to enrol at the Art
Students League under teacher Thomas Hart Benton, renowned
for his murals depicting everyday life in rural America.

Pollock's signature 'drip' technique first appeared in paintings
of 1947; before this year his quasi-representational work was
deeply influenced by Surrealism and Pablo Picasso in equal measure.
The iconic photographs by Hans Namuth document Pollock's
emphatic gestures as he parries and thrusts towards an immense
canvas on the floor of his studio. The term 'action painting', first
used in 1952, places emphasis on the role of the unconscious in
bringing forth the abstract webs and laced skeins of paint that
are submitted to the forces of gravity. Pollock used industrial
house paints often poured straight from the can or flung onto the
canvas by way of sticks or knives. In later years figurative images
such as human faces and forms from nature began to reappear
in his *Black Paintings*, begun in 1951, but he remained invested in
the possibilities of abstraction to the end of his life. Pollock was
killed in a car accident near his East Hampton home in 1956, after
many years battling with alcohol addiction. His widow Lee Krasner
devoted many years of her own career to securing his posthumous
international legacy.

KEY EVENTS

1943: Paints the epic *Mural* for his patron Peggy Guggenheim's
    townhouse in New York – Pollock's largest work at nearly
    6 metres (20 feet) in length. In the same year, Pollock's first
    solo exhibition takes place at Guggenheim's Art of This
    Century gallery.

August 1949: An illustrated feature on Pollock in *LIFE* magazine
    asks the question: 'Is he the greatest living painter in the
    United States?' The article helps cement Pollock's fame and
    reputation.

1950: Solo exhibition at New York's Betty Parsons Gallery
    achieves widespread critical acclaim.

MORRIS LOUIS
1912–62

Baltimore-born Morris Louis Bernstein was the son of Russian *émigrés* to the United States. At the age of fifteen he won a scholarship to the Maryland Institute of Fine and Applied Arts (1927–32). He was elected president of the Baltimore Artists' Union in 1935, and in 1938 registered with the Works Progress Administration, a New Deal-era initiative of public works projects for jobseekers including visual artists, musicians and writers.

Louis's full embrace of abstract art coincided with his relocation to Washington, DC, in 1952. In April 1953, along with the prominent art critic Clement Greenberg and Color Field painter Kenneth Noland, Louis visited the studio of Helen Frankenthaler. The visitors were particularly struck by her majestic poured and stained abstract painting *Mountains and Sea*, 1952.

Louis was plagued by doubts about his painting. He destroyed probably hundreds of canvases from the latter half of the 1950s. Nevertheless, the signature technique that he developed, in part inspired by Frankenthaler's soak/stain method, proved deeply influential for many abstract artists. Using only unprimed raw canvas, Louis would pour thin-consistency acrylic paint directly onto the canvas, creating bands of pure colour without the use of paintbrushes – thereby minimizing the artist's gesture and emphasizing the porous texture of the paint-soaked canvas.

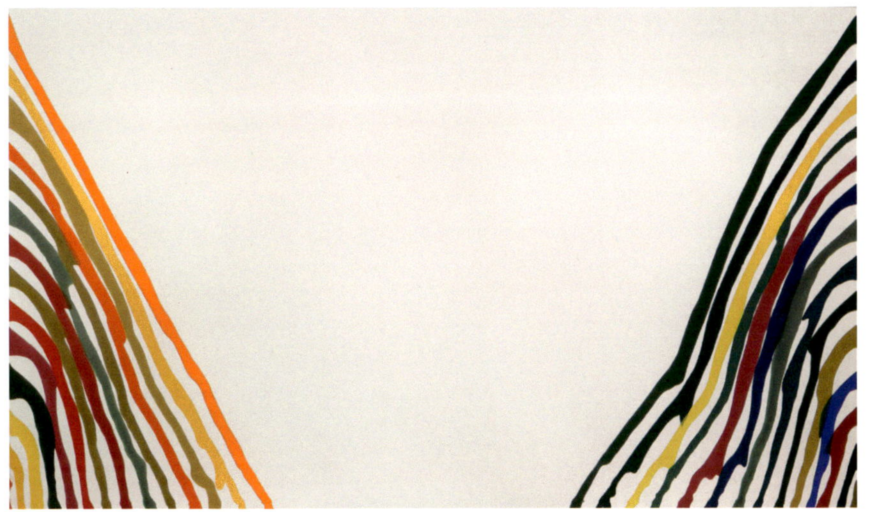

Morris Louis
Beta Kappa, 1961
Acrylic on canvas,
262.3 x 439.4 cm
(103¼ x 173 in.)
National Gallery of Art,
Washington, DC

**Only two paintings from
Louis's *Unfurled* series
of nearly 150 works
were titled and shown
before his death. The vast
expanse of unpainted
canvas forms a roughly
V-shaped wedge of
empty space, as the
unmixed paint colours
flow from the sides to
the bottom edge of
the canvas in diagonal
rivulets.**

KEY EVENTS

1948: Louis begins painting with Magna, a new acrylic-based resin
paint, which he uses devotedly for the rest of his career. In 1960
the paint's manufacturers develop a new formula specifically for
Louis and Noland.

1963: 'Morris Louis 1912–1962: A Memorial Exhibition of Paintings
from 1954–1960' opens at the Solomon R. Guggenheim Museum,
New York, one year after Louis's death from lung cancer.

1965: 'The Washington Color Painters' at the Washington Gallery
of Modern Art, Washington, DC, gives the DC-based abstract
artists including Louis and Alma Thomas their own category of
second-generation Abstract Expressionism.

AGNES MARTIN
1912–2004

Canadian-born American artist Agnes Martin's decades-long
painting practice demonstrates the profound entanglement of
abstract art and nature in poetic and clear-headed terms. She first
began experimenting with abstraction as a response to the shifting
patterns of the desert floor during her time in New Mexico in the
1940s. The early works were biomorphic in character, with some
similarities to Mark Rothko's 1940s paintings.

In 1957 Martin relocated to Coenties Slip in lower Manhattan,
where she was surrounded by a community of artists that included
Ellsworth Kelly and the abstract fabric artist Lenore Tawney,
who gifted Martin's painting illustrated here to the Guggenheim.
Martin committed to her signature grid format around 1960,
and for the next five decades explored its endless varieties across
drawing, printmaking and painting – first using a six-foot square
canvas format, later reduced to five-foot square. Her approach
to grids, stripes and serial progressions is not precise or rigid, like
other systematic work made in the 1960s based on mathematical
permutations. Her lines waver and shudder in their honest, hand-
drawn variation, and her bands of colour create atmospheric veils
across the canvas.

Martin resettled in New Mexico in 1968, and for many years
lived and worked in the remote region of Galisteo. In a 1993
interview Martin gave some insight into her approach to abstract
painting: 'I think that personal feelings, sentimentality and those
sorts of emotions, are not art but that universal emotions like
happiness *are* art. I am particularly interested in the abstract
emotions that we feel when we listen to music.' Her titles of the

Agnes Martin
White Flower, 1960
Oil on canvas, 182.6 x
182.9 cm (71⅞ x 72 in.)
Solomon R. Guggenheim
Museum, New York, Gift
of Lenore Tawney, 1963

**Like many of Martin's
works from this period,
the title *White Flower*
refers to a plant found
in nature, in contrast to
the painting's strictly
abstract manifestation of
a gridded arrangement
of rhythmic white lines
and dashes against a deep
grey background.**

1990s make reference to blissful emotional states, such as *Happy Holiday* and *Faraway Love* (1999). The artist died in Taos, New Mexico, in 2004, at the age of ninety-two.

KEY EVENTS

1958: The artist's first exhibition is held at Section Eleven, an offshoot of Betty Parsons Gallery in New York, and includes her first geometric abstract works of the late 1950s.

1966: Martin is included in the group exhibition 'Systemic Painting' at the Solomon R. Guggenheim Museum, New York, alongside many artists associated with the Minimalist Art movement in the United States.

1997: Martin is awarded the Golden Lion for Lifetime Achievement at the Venice Biennale.

ZAO WOU-KI
1920–2013

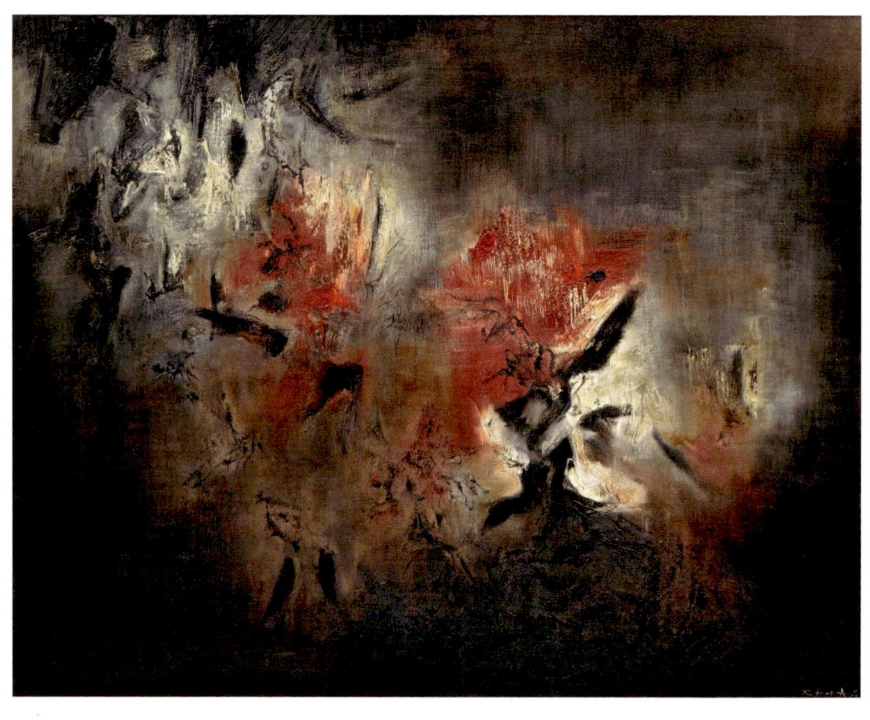

Zao Wou-Ki
Untitled, 1958
Oil on canvas,
130 x 162 cm
(51¼ x 63¾ in.)
Private collection

This work is from Zao's important 'oracle bone period'. The artist once said that: 'I want to convey the sense of movement – be it intricately tender, or be it swift and soaring. For me, a boisterous uproar is more attractive than quietness and silence.'

Born in Peking (now Beijing) in 1920, Zao was only fifteen when he began training at the prestigious National Academy of Fine Arts in Hangzhou in calligraphy, landscape painting and other classical Chinese techniques. Zao immigrated to Paris in 1948 and based himself there for the rest of his long life. This was a heady period of creative flourishing for abstract art in the French capital, where many artists were gathered under the heading of Art Informel, including the French painter Pierre Soulages and American Sam Francis. In 1956 Zao painted *Crossing Appearances*, which began his abstract exploration of landscape, not by referencing western painters, but by returning to sources in Chinese visual culture, particularly calligraphy and Shang-dynasty oracle bone script (the earliest writing in China). A visit to his brother in New Jersey in 1957 provided Zao with an opportunity to meet many of the major figures associated with Abstract Expressionism in New York, including Rothko, Franz Kline and Adolph Gottlieb.

After his New York experience, the scale of Zao's canvases increased substantially. Two years later, in 1959, the artist stopped giving descriptive titles to his works, and instead titled them with the date of their completion. This desire to avoid specific associations was another consolidation of his abstraction. Zao's work in the 1960s grew ever more non-representational. In 1961 he explained his position negotiating both Chinese and European art histories: 'Everybody is bound by tradition. I am bound by two.' He moved away from landscape abstractions and towards evocations of diaphanous space without horizontal or vertical distinction. His void-like treatment of the canvas became more atmospheric than land-bound, suggesting his growing interest in cosmology and other elemental forces. Throughout his career, the artist preferred the term nature to landscape, perhaps indicating his more expansive perspective.

KEY EVENTS

1951: Meets the architect I. M. Pei in Paris, and they sustain
   a lifelong friendship and collaboration.

1959–60: Zao returns to New York for his exhibition at Samuel
   Kootz Gallery.

2003: The first major French retrospective of his work is held
   at the Jeu de Paume, Paris.

2006: Zao is promoted to Grand Officer of the Légion d'Honneur
   by French President Jacques Chirac.

ELLSWORTH KELLY
1923–2015

Born in Newburgh, New York, Ellsworth Kelly's art studies were interrupted by active US military service from 1943 to 1945 in a specialist camouflage design unit. During this time, he first visited Paris, returning on the GI Bill in 1949 to live and study in the city for a five-year period that proved formative for his artistic career. He met many abstract artists in Paris, including Hans (Jean) Arp and Constantin Brâncuși, and began to experiment with chance procedures and automatic drawing as a result of these encounters. In Europe Kelly also experienced the patterns of Byzantine and Romanesque art and architecture, which would influence his approach to abstraction.

A single event in 1949 prompted his pivot to abstract art. Visiting an island off the coast of Brittany, Kelly noted the clear structure of a cottage window, and made an abstracted version of this motif in black against white. So began his lifelong commitment to clean, sharp geometric shapes. Even at its most severe, Kelly's practice was always rooted in an encounter with the real world, and a simplification of its forms.

Inspired by magazine accounts of Ad Reinhardt's success, Kelly returned to New York in 1954, hoping to relieve his precarious financial situation. His work's dissimilarity from the grand gestures of Abstract Expressionism meant that he did not achieve success until the 1960s, and the more austere era of Minimal and Conceptual Art. The artist considered his hard-edged monochromatic, shaped canvases (first produced in 1966) to

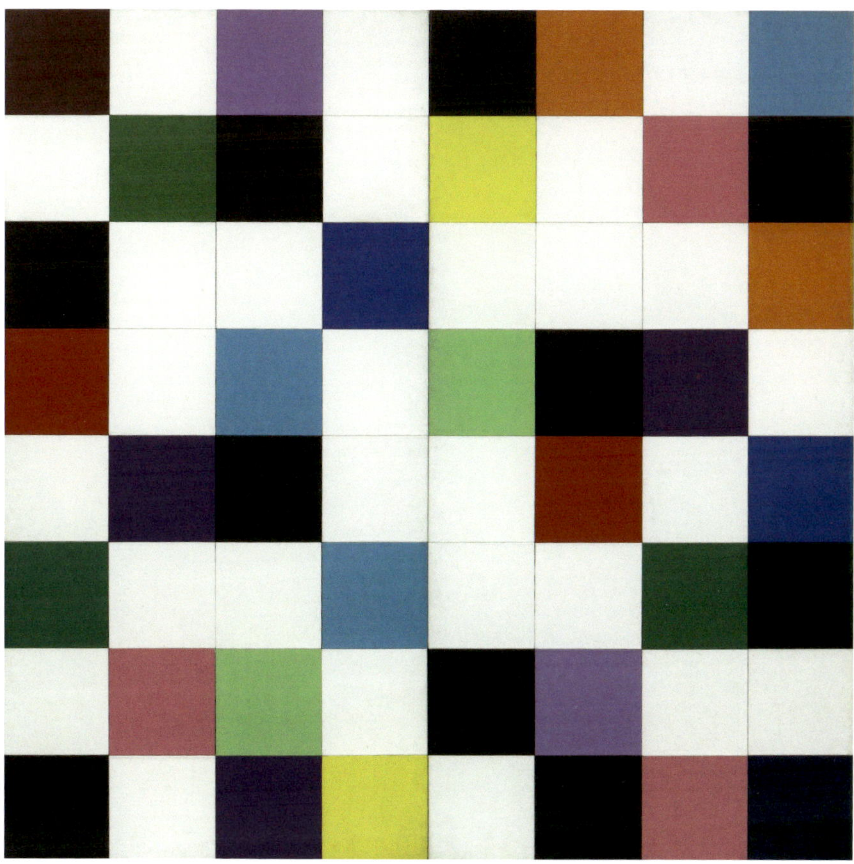

Ellsworth Kelly
*Colors for a
Large Wall*, 1951
Oil on canvas, sixty-four
panels, 240 x 240 cm
(94½ x 94½ in.)
The Museum of Modern
Art, New York

**This is a combination
of sixty-four separate
single-colour panels,
randomly arranged
according to the laws
of chance, going against
the very idea that a
painting's appearance is
decided by the artist.**

be things in the world, rather than paintings as such. In 1996 he explained: 'My paintings don't represent objects. They are objects themselves and fragmented perceptions of things.'

KEY EVENTS

1959: The artist is included in the legendary MoMA group exhibition 'Sixteen Americans', alongside artists including Jasper Johns and Louise Nevelson.

2018: Three years after his death, the Blanton Museum of Art at the University of Texas unveils Kelly's final project, *Austin,* a non-religious chapel-like building based on Romanesque architecture, with stained glass, marble paintings and sculpture by the artist.

HELEN FRANKENTHALER

1928–2011

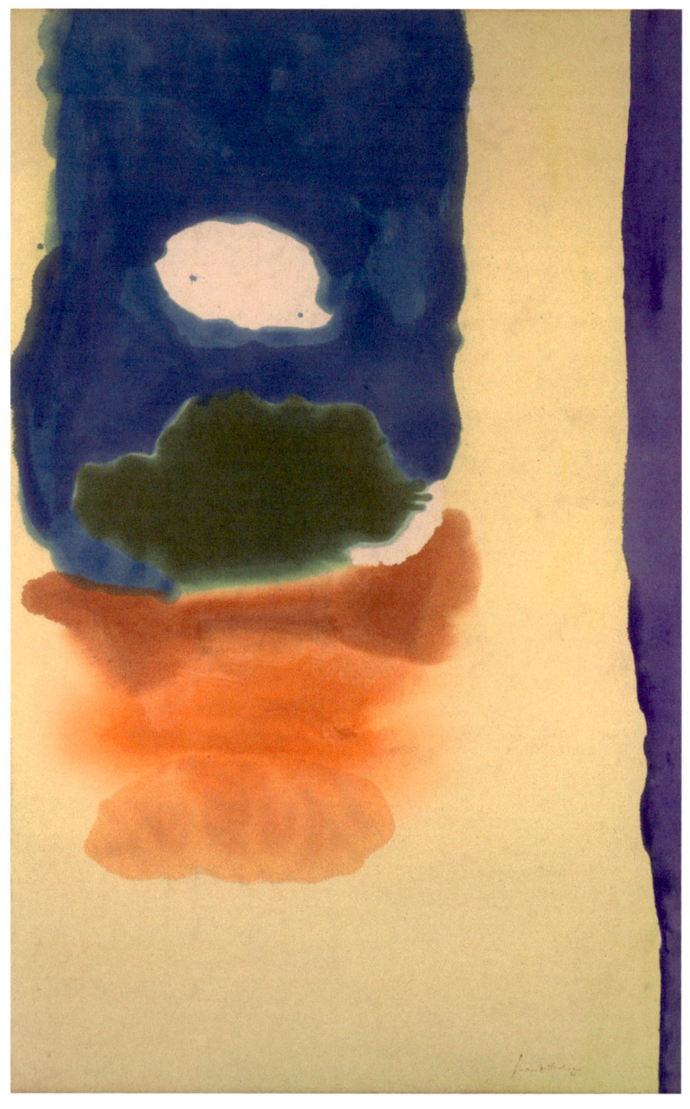

Helen Frankenthaler
Island Weather II, 1963
Acrylic on canvas,
236.2 x 147.3 x 2.5 cm
(93 x 58 x 1 in.)
Yale University Art
Gallery, New Haven

The artist said in 1962: 'The light touch is often the strongest gesture of all.' She replaced her oil paints with synthetic acrylic because 'it fights painterliness'. One year later she executed this sizeable painting, leaving more than half of the canvas untouched by paint.

New York-born Helen Frankenthaler played a crucial role within the second generation of American artists who developed the impassioned gestures of Abstract Expressionism into the serene spaces of Color Field Painting. After graduating from Bennington College in Vermont, Frankenthaler was briefly taught by Hans Hofmann. Her painting *Beach* (1950) was chosen by Adolph Gottlieb for inclusion in the group show 'Fifteen Unknowns: Selected by Artists of the Kootz Gallery', which kickstarted her exhibiting career. In the early 1950s she invented what became known as the soak-stain technique, widely adopted by artists including Morris Louis and Kenneth Noland. This was epitomized by what came to be regarded as her masterpiece: *Mountains and Sea* (1952), a purely abstract work of art that saw no need to distance its relationship to landscape painting.

To achieve her soak-stain effects, Frankenthaler thinned oil paint before pouring it directly onto unprimed raw canvas, laid flat on the studio floor. She moved around the vast canvas, adding paint from all sides, to build up hovering fields of edgeless colour. Her first museum retrospective took place at the Jewish Museum, New York, only a decade after her first show. Her friendships with other important second-generation female Abstract Expressionist painters, including Grace Hartigan and Joan Mitchell, offered a counterpoint to the excessive masculine focus of the New York School, and they fought to achieve equality amid the gender imbalance of the art world. Frankenthaler's creation of the stain technique has implications for the body, its sexuality and psychological states that shape the social history of mid-century abstract painting.

KEY EVENTS

1964: Frankenthaler is included in the ‹Post-Painterly Abstraction' group exhibition curated by critic Clement Greenberg that consolidates the group of artists he gathered under Color Field Painting, the term he coined in 1955.

1966: Alongside Ellsworth Kelly, Jules Olitski and Roy Lichtenstein, Frankenthaler represents the United States at the 33rd Venice Biennale.

2001: The artist is awarded the US government's National Medal of Arts.

CY TWOMBLY
1928–2011

Edwin Parker Twombly inherited his father's baseball nickname 'Cy', after the baseball player Cyclone Young. He began his training at Boston's School of the Museum of Fine Arts, followed by a scholarship to the Art Students League, New York, in 1950. This gave Twombly the opportunity to see many important Abstract Expressionist exhibitions and meet fellow student Robert Rauschenberg, and they became friends. His studies culminated in two intensive semesters at Black Mountain College in 1951–2, where he was taught by first-generation Abstract Expressionists Franz Kline and Robert Motherwell.

Together with Rauschenberg, Twombly embarked on a grand tour of Europe and North Africa in autumn 1952, during which time he made tapestries in Morocco, exhibiting them in Florence. On his return to the United States, Twombly was swiftly drafted into the army to work as a cryptologist. During his weekends off, he started to produce drawings in the dark, a process intended to eliminate any residue of skilled draughtsmanship. Twombly's career trajectory was profoundly altered by his decision to move to Rome in 1957, at the height of Abstract Expressionism's influence in the United States. He was inspired by the ancient graffiti found across Rome, as well as the artworks and writings of both classical Rome and the Italian Renaissance. Twombly lived between Italy and the United States for the rest of his life, while travelling extensively across the world.

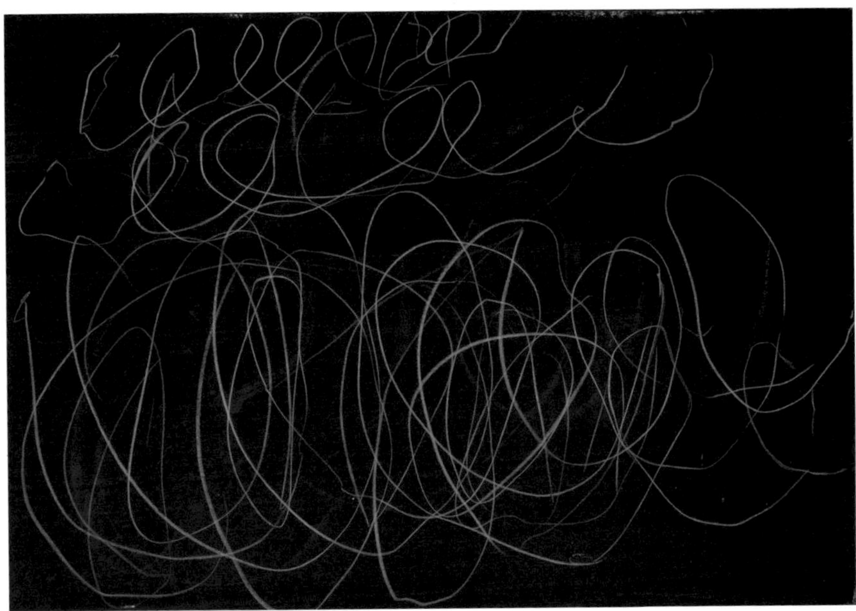

Cy Twombly
Untitled, 1970
Oil paint and wax crayon,
70.5 x 100 cm
(27¾ x 39⅜ in.)
Collection Cy Twombly
Foundation, Rome

Perhaps Twombly's most recognizable contribution to the lexicon of post-war abstraction was his de-skilled calligraphic scrawls, rendering logic and writing meaningless, and formless. Working on surfaces often reminiscent of blackboards, his paintings and drawings distort any clear boundary between the written and drawn mark.

Various periods within Twombly's long career focus on allusions to landscape and the flora and fauna of the natural world; graffiti and scribbled writing; and antiquity, classicism, history and poetry. At all times, he continued to promote a dissolving type of abstraction that recognizes its many links with language, myth and the imprecise space of clouds and other elemental forces.

KEY EVENTS

1965: His first large museum exhibition opens at the Museum Haus Lange, Krefeld, and travels to venues in Brussels and Amsterdam.

1994: The Museum of Modern Art in New York presents a major retrospective of Twombly's work; it marks a shift in the reception of his practice in his home country, largely deemed to be 'too European' until that point.

SAM GILLIAM
b.1933

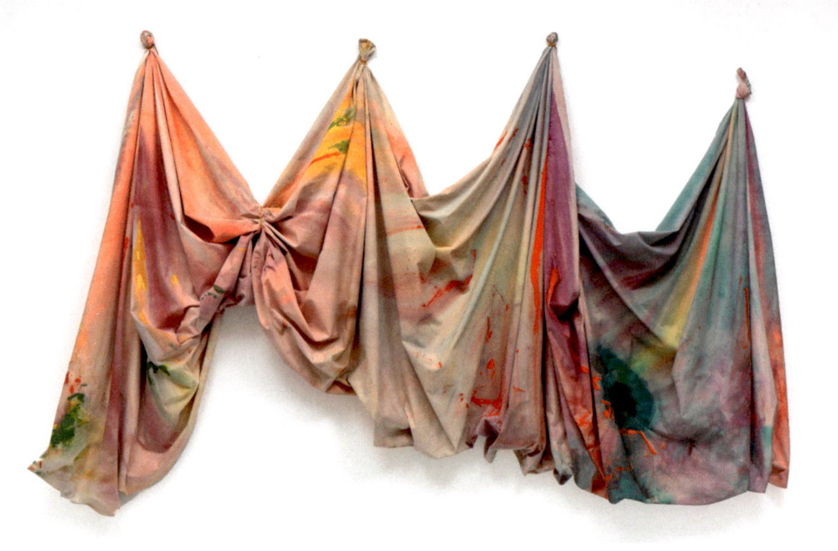

Sam Gilliam
Relative, 1968
Acrylic on canvas, overall
(suspended [installed]
canvas): 304.8 x
411.48 cm (120 x 162 in.)
overall (full canvas):
304.8 x 1341.1 cm
(120 x 528 in.)
National Gallery of Art,
Washington, DC

**There is no set way to
exhibit Gilliam's works
such as *Relative*: the
artist, his assistants and
curators must decide
how best to arrange
the canvas folds for
the given space. The
drape paintings change
each time, becoming
sculptural – even
architectural – in their
occupation of space.**

Mississippi-born Gilliam completed his undergraduate and master's
degrees at the University of Louisville, where his professors favoured
the Bay Area painters, a group including Richard Diebenkorn.
Gilliam moved to Washington, DC, in 1962, and as a result became
associated with the city's Color Field painters. Around 1965 Gilliam
made the decision that would transform his painting career. He
abandoned the wooden bars, known as stretchers, that define a
painting's surface area. Now, his vast paintings moved and shifted
as loose, billowing swirls of suspended canvas, knotted and gathered
at various points to create dramatic draperies that extended from
ceilings and walls, and sometimes even swallowed up floors. While he
credited the influence of Jackson Pollock and Barnett Newman in
reaching this innovation, Gilliam also revealed in 1973 that 'what was
most personal to me were the things I saw in my own environment
– such as clotheslines filled with clothes with so much weight that
they had to be propped up . . . That was a pertinent clue.' Key to his
technique is Gilliam's decision to fold, pleat and drape the canvas
before the paint dries, creating kaleidoscopic tie-dye effects.

As an African-American artist making abstract works, Gilliam
was often called on to make explicit the political intentions behind
his painting, especially at the height of the Civil Rights movement.
While he never wavered from his commitment to abstraction, he
titled many works in relation to the activism of the era, such as his
Martin Luther King series. He later said of *Double Merge* (1968) and
related works that: 'They came out of uniting Color Field with the
March on Washington [for Jobs and Freedom].' Over the course of
his impressive career, Gilliam's belief in the importance of teaching
art at both high school and university has never wavered.

KEY EVENTS

1971: Gilliam co-organizes 'The DeLuxe Show', a group exhibition
in Houston that may have been the first time that contemporary
black and white artists were shown together.

2005: The Corcoran Gallery of Art in Washington, DC, stages a
major travelling retrospective of Gilliam's career.

FRANK BOWLING

b.1934

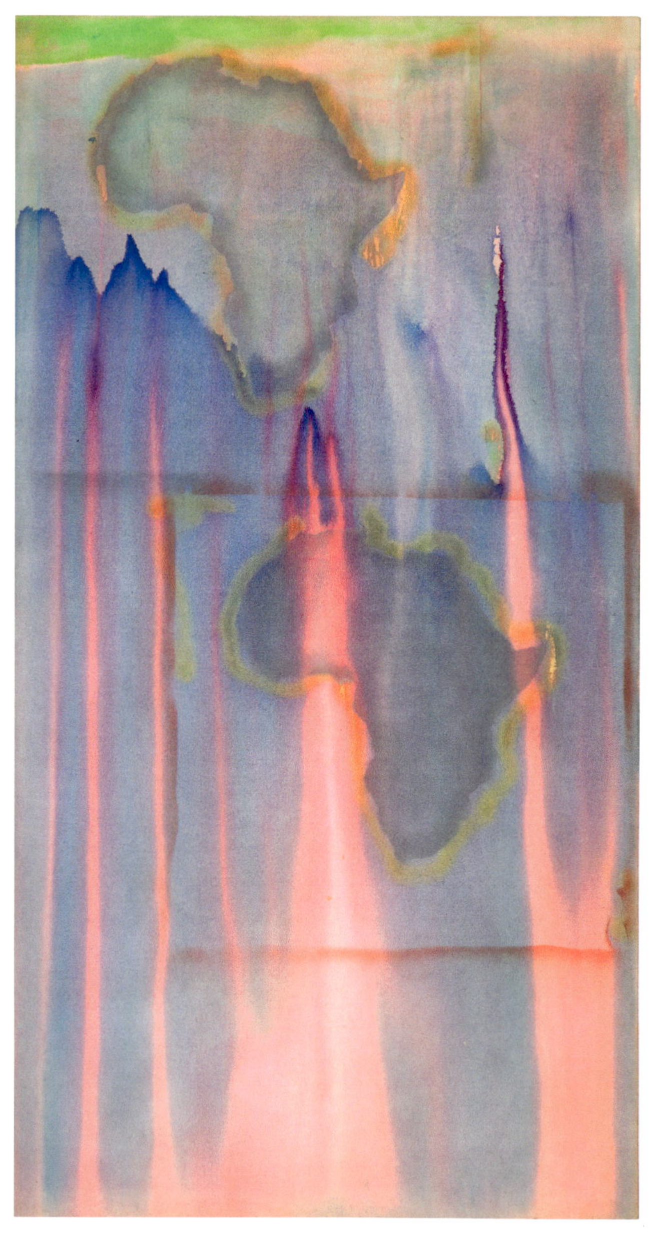

Frank Bowling
Barticaborn I, 1967
Acrylic paint, spray paint
and oil wax on canvas,
234 x 122.4 cm
(92¼ x 48¼ in.)
Lowinger Family
Collection

**This works belongs to
Bowling's important
series of *Map Paintings*,
dating from 1967 to 1971
and shown at his Whitney
Museum exhibition.
Their lush and luminous
poured and sprayed
colour fields are
combined with stencilled
maps, mainly of the
southern hemisphere,
implying the artist's
rejection of western-
centric art history
and cartography, and
the coexistence of
representation and
abstraction.**

Bowling is one of abstract art's greatest living colourists, endlessly pushing the limits of what paint can do on canvas without the aid of a brush. His improvisatory gestures bristle with the energy of both control and chance. Born in colonial-era British Guiana, South America, Bowling took up the free passage offered by the UK to their colonial 'subjects' when he was nineteen, in May 1953. He trained at the Royal College of Art in London from 1959 to 1962, as part of an exciting cohort of fellow students including David Hockney and R. B. Kitaj. Bowling's early paintings centred on expressive figure studies, with some reference to the bodily contortions of Francis Bacon's practice. He began to introduce external elements to the painting surface, such as stencils and silkscreen printing, which aided his exploration of abstraction.

Bowling moved to New York in 1966, and almost immediately stopped representing the human body. His new artistic colleagues in the city included the abstract painter Jack Whitten and sculptor Melvin Edwards. As well as painting in his Brooklyn studio, Bowling wrote for contemporary journals including *Arts Magazine*, where between 1969 and 1971 he published an important series of six articles on the complexities of 'black art' as a terminology. He also developed a friendship with the art critic Clement Greenberg, champion of Abstract Expressionism, with whom he engaged in a series of debates about the abstract, formal qualities specific to the medium itself, such as flatness and pigment.

His ability to synthesize an abstract visual language with references to the culturally hybrid identities and histories of the global black diaspora reflects Bowling's standing as a truly transatlantic artist, maintaining studios in both London and New York. He refuses specific or singular meanings, instead preferring his paintings to occupy an open-ended space that welcomes multiple interpretations.

KEY EVENTS

1971: Bowling has a solo exhibition at the Whitney Museum of American Art, New York, as part of their strategy to exhibit more black artists in response to the political activism of the BECC (Black Emergency Cultural Coalition) formed in 1969.

2005: Bowling is the first black artist to become a Royal Academician, 200 years after the art institution's founding in London.

2019: Frank Bowling's first full retrospective exhibition opens at Tate Britain, London.

GLOBAL GEOMETRIES

-

There is nothing I love more than to make
a straight line. How can I explain it?
It's the beginning of all structures, really

-

Carmen Herrera

2010

FAHRELNISSA ZEID
1901–91

Zeid's turn towards abstraction occurred in the mid-1940s, after an already significant career as a figurative painter. In 1947 she painted a work titled *Fight Against Abstraction* which articulated the complex tensions at the heart of her evolving style: clenched fists and human faces battle for space against a mosaic-inspired abstract geometric field. Her eventful life took her to many countries, as she synthesized a visual language that combined elements from Byzantine art, Islamic art and modern European influences.

Born into an aristocratic Ottoman family in Turkey, Zeld was one of the first women to attend art school in Istanbul, later training in Paris at the Académie Ranson. Her marriage into the Hashemite royal family of Iraq in the 1930s resulted in a move to Berlin in 1935, as her husband Prince Zeid bin Hussein took up his role as the first Iraqi ambassador to Germany. By 1941 Zeid was back in Istanbul concentrating on her painting practice. Her short-lived association with the Turkish avant-garde D Group developed her confidence and she began to stage solo exhibitions from her home. While in London from 1946, she also rented a studio in Paris, dividing her time between the two cities and developing a network of international abstract artist colleagues.

Zeid's life was shattered in 1958 by the military coup and assassination of the entire Iraqi royal family – except her husband. They were ordered to depart the embassy in London within 24 hours. Of this traumatic time, Zeid said: 'Instead of the brilliant kaleidoscope that once seemed to surround me, I can only perceive, all around me, a winding labyrinth of hard and heavy black lines.' Later in life she returned to portrait painting and set up an art school in Amman, Jordan, to mentor young female artists.

Fahrelnissa Zeid
Resolved Problems, 1948
Oil on canvas,
130 x 97 cm
(51¼ x 38¼ in.)
Istanbul Museum of
Modern Art Collection,
Eczacıbaşı Group
Donation

Zeid revealed one source of her kaleidoscopic art of interlocking abstract shapes: 'I did not "intend" to become an abstract painter; I was a person working very conventionally with forms and values. But flying by plane transformed me . . . The world is upside down. A whole city could be held in your hand: the world seen from above.'

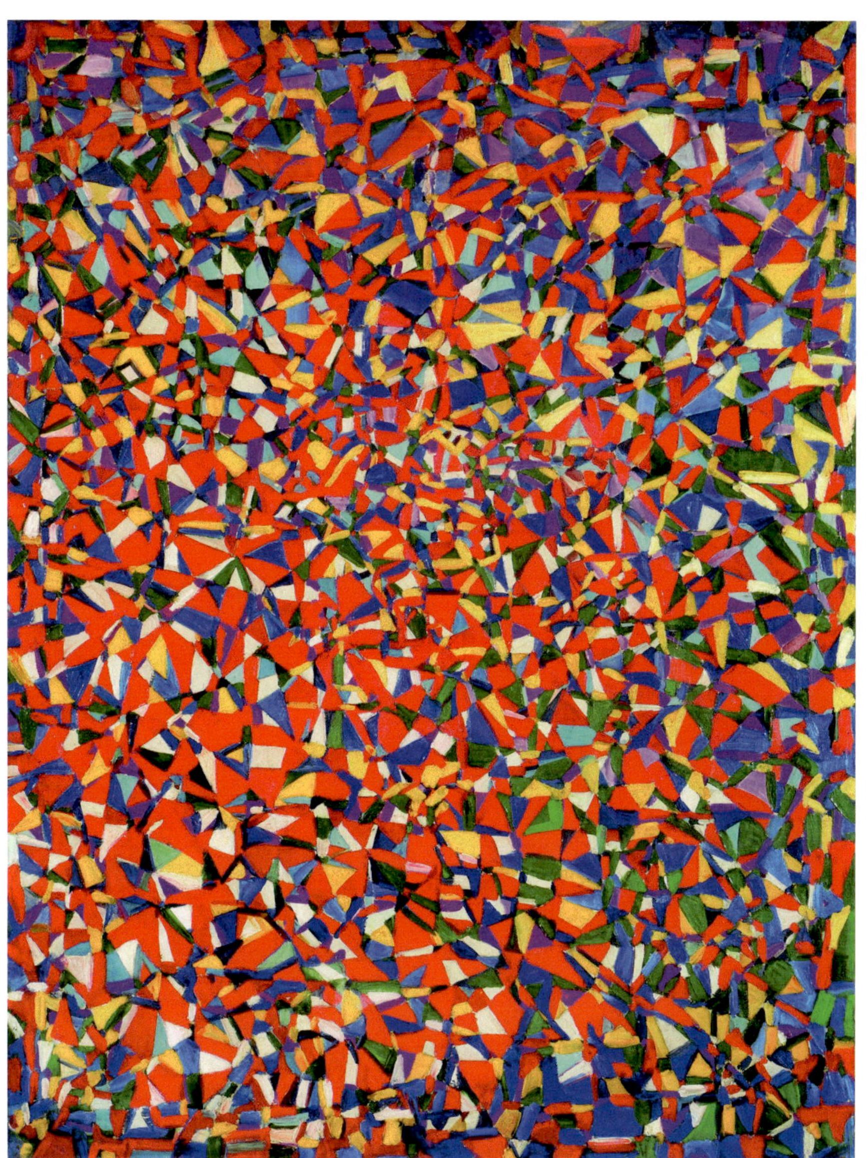

KEY EVENTS

1954: A solo exhibition of Zeid's work is held by the Institute
of Contemporary Art, London.

2017: Tate Modern stages a major retrospective of Zeid's
paintings and sculptures, both abstract and figurative.

CARMEN HERRERA
b.1915

Born in Havana, the Cuban-American artist Carmen Herrera has been based in New York since the mid-1950s. The daughter of two journalists (her father established the Cuban newspaper *El Mundo*), she began drawing and painting lessons at a young age, before being sent to a Parisian finishing school at fourteen, where she first took art history classes. In 1938 Herrera studied architecture for one year at the University of Havana: a brief interlude that nevertheless had a profound impact on her trajectory towards a precise form of geometric abstraction. She later said of this time that 'an extraordinary world opened up to me that never closed: the world of straight lines, which has interested me until this very day'.

Herrera won a scholarship to the Art Students League in 1941, two years after moving to New York, although she bristled at the emphasis on figurative art. It was only when she moved to Paris in 1948 that Herrera found herself part of a dynamic, avant-garde art scene that she had sought for so long. In the French capital she exhibited her works at the Salon des Réalités Nouvelles, founded by Sonia Delaunay-Terk, forging a link with earlier Constructivist and Concrete Abstraction. She began limiting her palette to three then two colours per painting. Herrera returned to New York in 1954, at the apex of Abstract Expressionism's flourishing in the city, when she befriended many artists including Mark Rothko and Barnett Newman. She maintained her commitment to hard-edged abstraction in the face of gestural painting.

Herrera was long ignored by the art world, critics and historians, as well as the art market. She sold her first painting only at the age of eighty-nine, in 2004. Since then, she continues to paint, and her work has been enthusiastically collected and exhibited by museums internationally.

Carmen Herrera
Cerulean, 1965
Acrylic on canvas,
175.6 x 173.4 x 4.1 cm
(69⅛ x 68¼ x 1⅝ in.)
Crystal Bridges Museum
of American Art,
Bentonville

Herrera considers her paintings as objects in the world, affected by their spatial orientation, rhythmic tension and architectural setting. In 2012 she stated: 'My quest is for the simplest of pictorial resolutions.'

KEY EVENTS

2016: The Whitney Museum of American Art, New York, opens
'Lines of Sight', a solo retrospective covering Herrera's work
in the formative years 1948 to 1978.

2019: 'Estructuras Monumentales', Herrera's first major show
of her outdoor sculptures (initially conceived as drawings in
the 1960s), is staged by the Public Art Fund outside City Hall,
New York.

RUBEM VALENTIM
1922–91

Born in Salvador da Bahia, the Afro-Brazilian artist Rubem
Valentim's first profession was dentistry, before he became a painter
in 1948. He travelled extensively across Latin America, Africa and
Europe. Valentim moved to Rio de Janeiro in 1957 for six years,
and became part of the city's artist networks centred around the
abstract collectives of Concrete and subsequently Neo-Concrete
Art. He made vertical arrangements of abstract symbols and shapes,
rooted in this shared modern language of geometric abstraction but
also combined with allusions to his own Bahian heritage and culture.

In 1962 he participated in the Brazilian national exhibition at
the Venice Biennale, showcasing a range of paintings with a dark
colour palette and simplified geometric shapes, alongside Lygia
Clark, Alfredo Volpi and others. A shift in Valentim's colour
scheme occurred around 1964 – an expansion into reds, yellows
and blues – perhaps partly as a result of his visit to that year's
Venice Biennale, with its brightly coloured Pop Art. During his time
in Rome (1964–5), Valentim began to make works that referenced
the African collections he had visited at the British Museum in
London, particularly statuary from Benin and Nigerian antiquities
that featured a double-headed axe symbol. The artist also
incorporated stylized symbolism and iconography that had roots
in the Yoruba religion and the Afro-Brazilian religion of Candomblé,
practised mainly in his home state of Bahia, as a fusion of Catholic
and Yoruba religious practices.

In 1966 Valentim visited Dakar, Senegal, to show twelve paintings
in the First World Festival of Negro Arts, which included exhibitions
of traditional African sculpture and contemporary art of the African
diaspora. Valentim's vertical stacks often recall the structure of
altars, while his codex of signs drew inspiration from Uruguayan
artist Joaquín Torres García, who was instrumental in bringing
Concrete Art from Europe to Latin America, synthesized with his
interest in the archaic symbols of Pre-Columbian visual cultures.

Rubem Valentim
Composição 12, 1962
Oil on canvas, 100 x
70 cm (39⅜ x 27⅝ in.)
Museu de arte de São
Paulo (MASP), São Paulo

**It was Valentim's
intention to construct
a universal abstract
language that connected
the many points of the
African diaspora network
and its visual cultures,
both in Brazil and
internationally.**

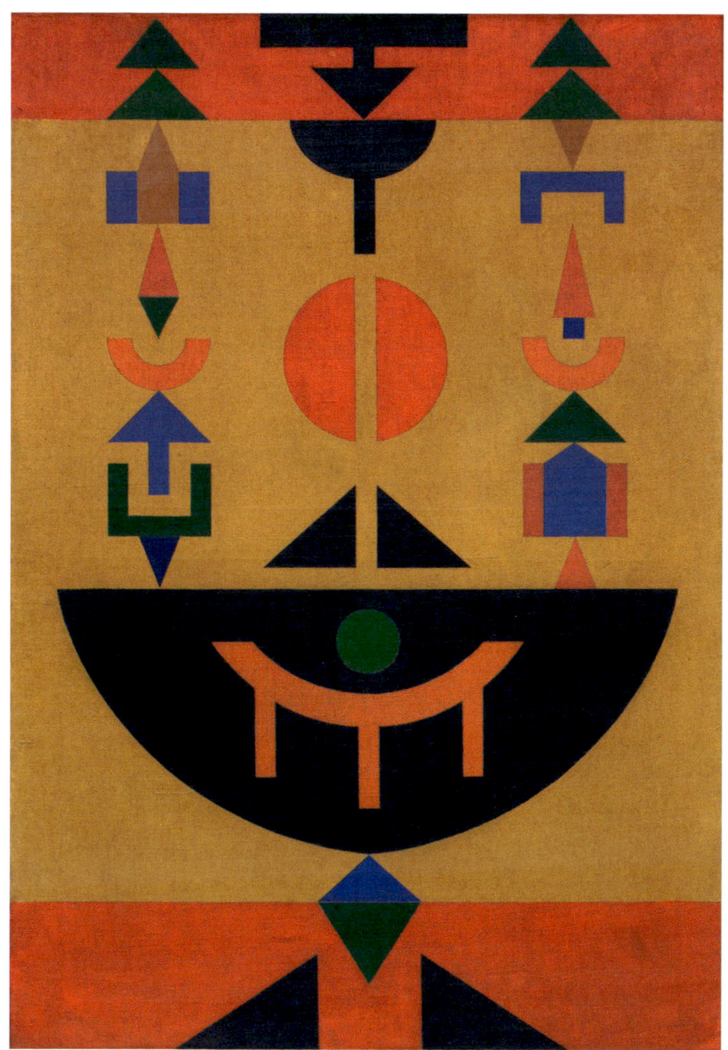

KEY EVENTS

1955: Participates in the third São Paulo Biennial alongside
abstract artists including Lygia Pape and Alfredo Volpi.

1959: Valentim joins the board of the International Association
of Plastic Artists together with major figures of Brazilian art
including Lygia Clark.

1961: Solo exhibition at Museu de arte de São Paulo, São Paulo.

1963: Travels to Barcelona, after winning a prize for foreign
travel for Brazilian artists.

MONIR SHAROUDY FARMANFARMAIAN
1922–2019

A native of Qazvin, Iran, Monir Sharoudy Farmanfarmaian studied at Tehran's Fine Arts College before moving to New York in 1945, to become one of the first Iranians to study in the United States following the end of the Second World War. After graduating from Parsons School of Design in 1949, the artist spent three years at the renowned Art Students League. Farmanfarmaian's later career evolution towards abstract art would be informed by many other artists working in New York at this time, such as Louise Nevelson and Jackson Pollock. Monir returned to Iran in 1957.

One important place would deeply affect Farmanfarmaian's artistic development. On a trip to Shiraz with the American Minimal artists Robert Morris and Marcia Hafif, Monir returned to visit the Shah Cheragh, a mosque and funerary monument with a dazzling domed hall of mirrors, tiles and cut-glass dating to the fourteenth century. In her memoir she described the scene: 'It was a universe unto itself, architecture transformed into performance, all movement and fluid light, all solids fractured and dissolved in brilliance in space, in prayer. I was overwhelmed.' Her work began to synthesize the principles of Islamic geometric design, the ancient Iranian decorative techniques of mirror mosaic (*aineh-kari*) and reverse-glass painting, with contemporary forms of geometric abstraction, inspired by New York artists such as Frank Stella. In a 2015 conversation, Stella commented: 'Monir took geometry off the surface of architecture, and made it into essentially its own surface.'

The Iranian Revolution of 1979 enforced another long period of exile in New York; Farmanfarmaian would not return to reopen her Tehran studio until 2004, in her eighties, when at last she was reunited with the craftsmen who could assist in the historic techniques underpinning her contemporary abstract transformations.

Monir Shahroudy Farmanfarmaian
Group 4 [Convertible Series], 2010
Mirror and reverse-glass painting on plaster and wood, dimensions variable
Museum of Contemporary Art Chicago, Chicago

Farmanfarmaian's works engage with external spatial elements including light sources and reflections, to create an ever-changing refracted surface texture, with the precise shapes of geometric patterns and constantly shifting colour sensations.

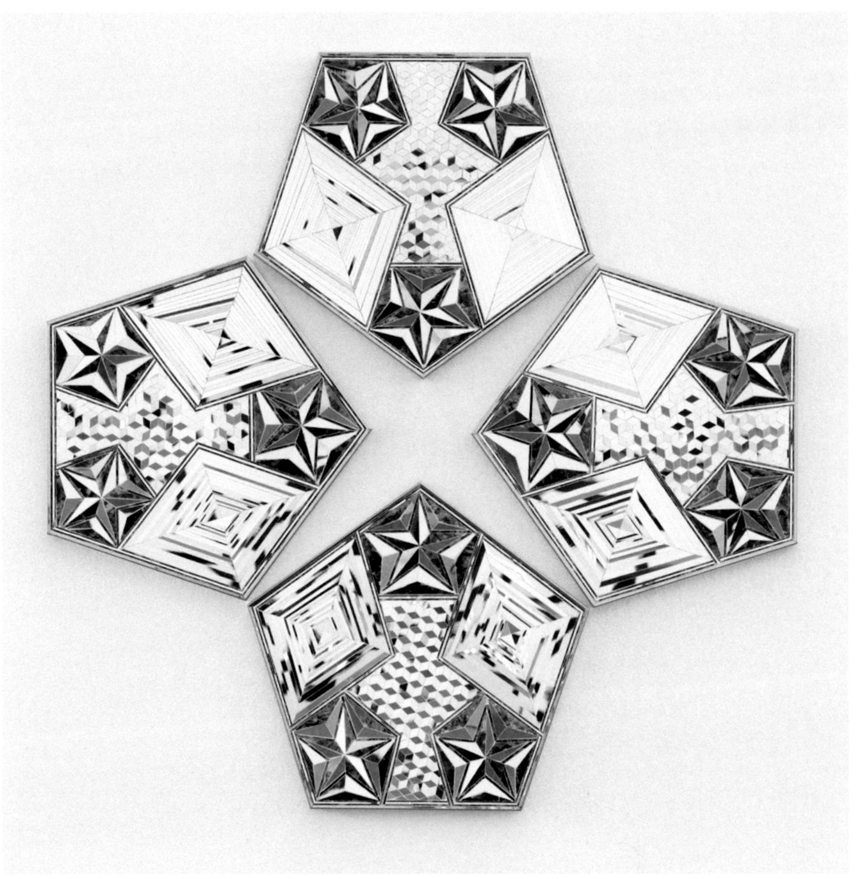

KEY EVENTS

1958, 1964 and 1966: Farmanfarmaian represents Iran at the prestigious Venice Biennale on three occasions.

2011: Publishes her memoir *Cosmic Geometry*.

2017: The Monir Museum opens at the University of Tehran with more than fifty works donated by the artist. It is Iran's first museum dedicated to a single female artist.

CARLOS CRUZ-DIEZ
1923–2019

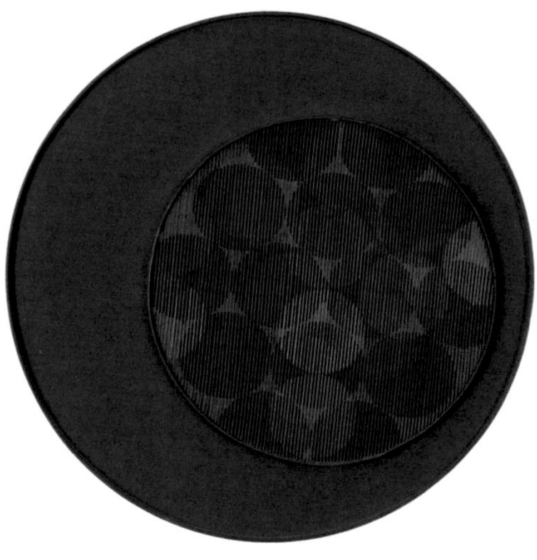

Franco-Venezuelan artist Carlos Cruz-Diez studied at Caracas's
School of Visual Arts and Applied Arts. Together with fellow
students Jesús Rafael Soto and Alejandro Otero, Cruz-Diez would
advance immersive geometric abstraction as Kinetic and Op Art
in Venezuela. Following his graduation, the artist worked as artistic
director of the Caracas outpost of global advertising agency
McCann-Erickson for five years (1946–51). Inspired by the colour
theories of Bauhaus artist-educator Josef Albers, in 1959 Cruz-
Diez created a new kind of polychromatic relief construction that
would completely alter his experiential understanding of colour
and movement. His *Physichromie* series engaged with the science
of optical perception by juxtaposing a series of coloured edges of
cardboard sheets that together produce on the viewer's retina the
image of colours not present in reality.

The artist settled with his family in Paris in 1960, where he
lived and worked for the rest of his long life. In Paris he debated
his perceptual colour theories with a host of international abstract
artists, including Alexander Calder, Sérgio de Camargo and François
Morellet. Cruz-Diez later wrote of this new-found artist community
that: 'We were all for the destruction of the sacred aura surrounding
the romantic artist, for we considered our research of the same
nature as that of a scientist. Art had to be in the streets, not only

Carlos Cruz-Diez
Physichromie 93, 1963
Acrylic on cardboard and
wood, diameter
50 cm x depth 6.4 cm
(19¾ x 2⅝ in.)
Cruz-Diez Art
Foundation, Houston

In 1975 Cruz-Diez stated:
'Colour is not simply
the colour of things or
the colour of form. It is
an evolving situation, a
reality which acts on the
human being with the
same intensity as cold,
heat, sound, etc.'

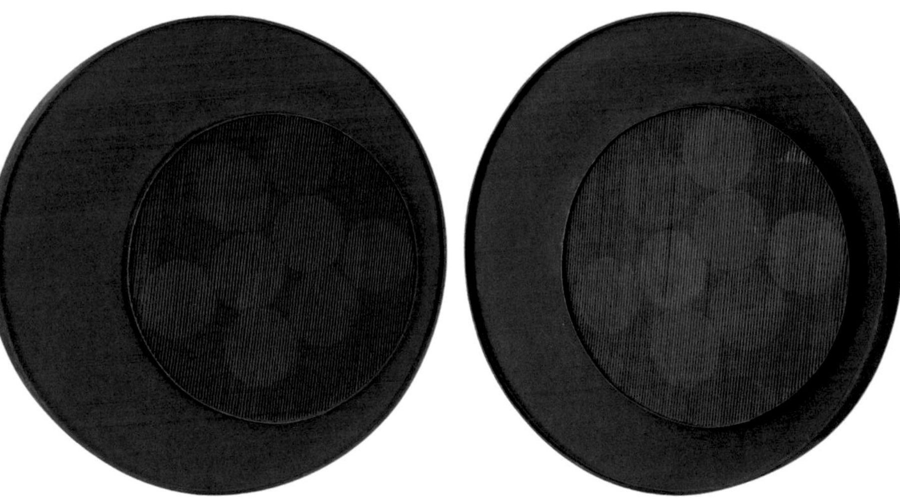

in museums.' This engagement of abstract art with public space
is something Cruz-Diez embarked upon on a vast scale. Many
of his works alter our experience of the public realm, such as the
Couleur Additive projects that transform pedestrian crosswalks
through slices of contrasting colours. He also produced room-filling
light installations infused with colour called *Chromosaturations*,
encouraging the viewer to become an active participant in the
space of colour.

KEY EVENTS

1956: Cruz-Diez returns to Venezuela after a year in Europe.

1957: The artist opens Estudio de Artes Visuales in Venezuela,
a graphic and industrial design and visual arts studio.

1965: Cruz-Diez's *Physichromie No. 116* (1964) is included in
'The Responsive Eye', the contentious and historic group
exhibition at MoMA, New York, alongside work by artists
including Bridget Riley and Frank Stella.

2014: The Cruz-Diez Art Foundation, Paris, publishes the artist's
memoir, *Vivir en Arte, recuerdos de lo que me acuerdo* (Living
in Art: Memories of What I Remember).

FRANÇOIS MORELLET
1926–2016

A native of Cholet, France, Morellet began painting at an early age and studied Russian literature in Paris before returning home to run the family business, a toy factory, which he continued to do until 1976. A trip to Brazil in 1950 proved momentous: he experienced first-hand the Concrete Art movement which espoused a rational geometry of simple coloured forms. Returning to France the next year, Morellet assumed a more analytic approach to his painting. Another crucial catalyst for his practice was a trip to the Alhambra palace in Granada, Spain, in 1952, where he saw its geometric Moorish tilework and architectural design schemes. In the very same year Morellet fully adopted a systems-based approach to the application of geometry, what he called a 'programmed experimental form of painting' where all elements of the work are pre-determined prior to execution.

Every aspect of Morellet's painting practice was organized according to mathematical formulae and impersonal chance factors (such as numbers in the phone book), ensuring no external meaning could be projected onto his colours, shapes or compositions. He divided his early work into formal categories: 'juxtaposition; superimposition; fragmentation; interference; randomization; and destabilization.' From 1963 onwards Morellet also began working with a neon fabricator to produce sculptural installations of lines and grids of neon tubing, gradually adopting an architectural dimension and sometimes even suspended in space. *No End Neon* (1990/2017) is the largest of the artist's neon installations, comprised of sixty-one tubes whose positions are adapted anew according to each space's requirements.

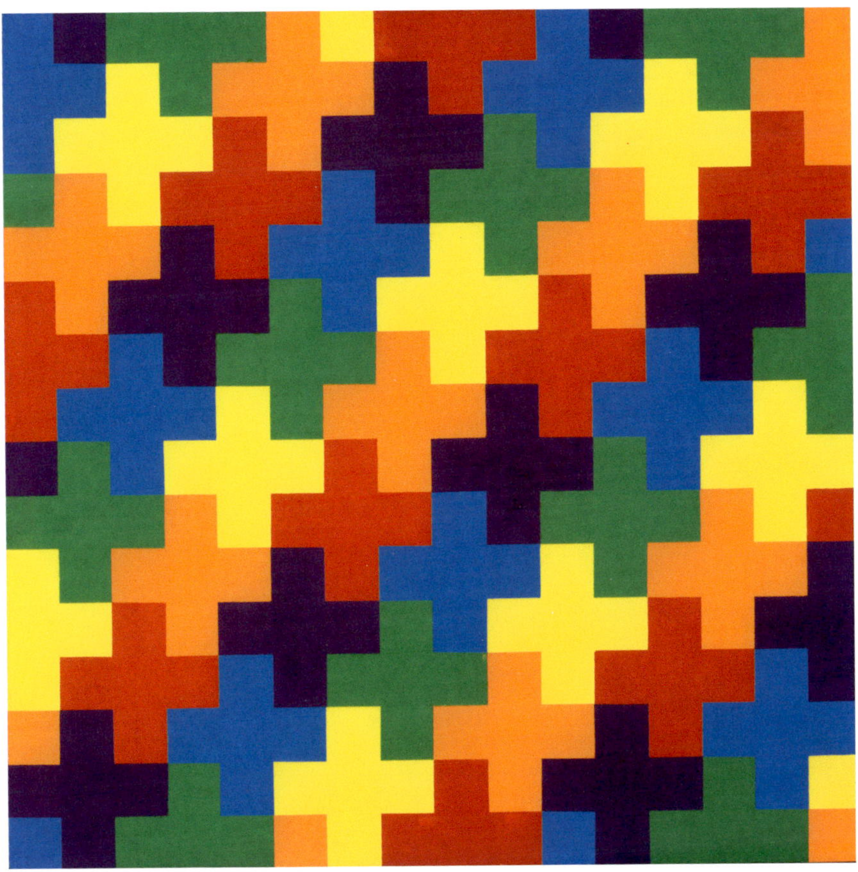

François Morellet
Violet, bleu, vert, jaune,
orange, rouge, 1953
Oil on wood, 80 x 80 cm
(31½ x 31½ in.)
Centre Pompidou, Paris

This painting of the six primary and secondary colours is created using a simple organizing principle, in which each unit is equal in a purely relational system. The repetitive, interlocking crosses create an optically dazzling pattern with no centre and no edges.

KEY EVENTS

1961: Morellet is a founding member of GRAV (Groupe
de Recherche d'Art Visuel), an experimental collective
dedicated to exploring the kinetic and optical effects
of immersive art installations.

1990: Unveils a site-specific neon installation, *30 néons
et 1 point du vue,* for the Abbey of Saint Philibert in
Tournus, France.

2010: Morellet becomes one of only three contemporary
artists to install a permanent artwork at the Louvre Museum,
L'Esprit d'escalier in the Lefuel Staircase.

LYGIA PAPE
1927–2004

The first São Paulo Biennial art exhibition in 1951 brought together a new wave of artists working with geometric abstraction, seen as the appropriate artistic expression of the new prosperity of Brazilian society and its architectural, economic and technological advancements. Lygia Pape was part of this movement, known as Concrete Art, and she also joined Grupo Frente, a more structured group of artists established in Rio de Janeiro, 1954, who were united in their rejection of the Brazilian nationalist style of figurative painting.

Produced around 1960, Pape's three book-based works, *Book of Architecture*, *Book of Creation* and *Book of Time*, are early instances of her Neo-Concrete approach, in which 'stories' are communicated across unbound pages through a sequence of abstract geometric shapes alluding to natural processes and systems. Of these works the artist explained: 'Through each person's experiences there is a process of open structure through which each structure can generate its own meaning.' This emphasis on variable meaning challenged the strict formalism of Concrete Art.

By the early 1990s Pape was able to realize her immersive installations based on drawings dating to the 1950s and a series of workshops in the late 1970s where the artist worked with her architecture students in Rio to make outdoor arrangements of string. These iconic installations are known as the *Ttéias*, a play on

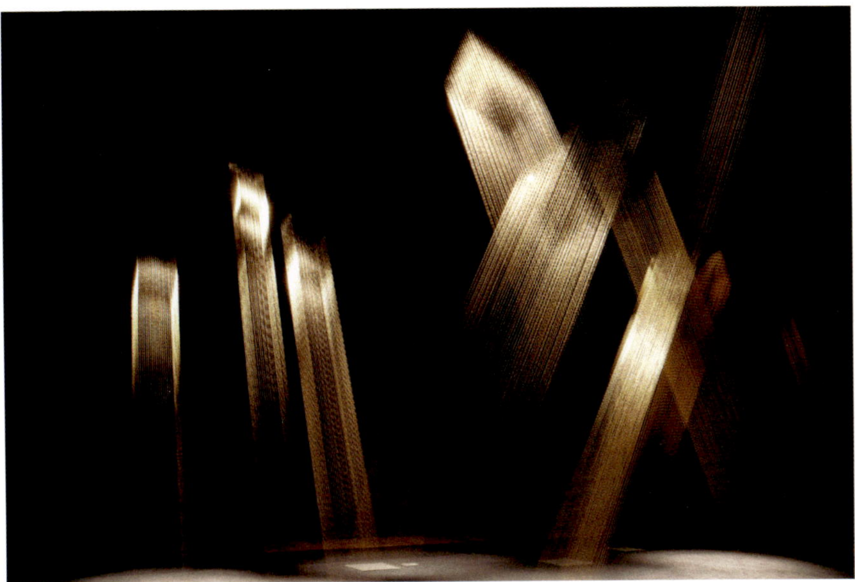

Lygia Pape
Ttéia 1,C, 2003/2012
Thread, wood, nails, light,
dimensions variable
Pinacoteca do Estado
de São Paulo, from
the exhibition '*Espaços
Imantados*/Magnetized
Space', 2012

**Dramatic lighting and
cast shadows play an
important role in Pape's
Ttéia installations: they
create imaginary lines
not present in reality,
tricking the perception
of the viewer, who
must negotiate their
rearticulation of space.**

the Portuguese words for 'web' and 'delicate object or person'.
They construct a dramatic space from silver and gold threads in
linear patterns that stretch from floor to ceiling or wall to wall, some
threads woven or staggered, creating plays on real and illusory space.
Across her investigations in drawing, printmaking and installation
art, Pape was concerned with articulating a 'magnetization' of space
– a physically charged sensation of energy from abstraction.

KEY EVENTS

1959: Pape signs the Neo-Concrete art manifesto, ushering
   in a new era of Brazilian neo-avant-garde art with a joint
   commitment to abstraction and the body (of the artist
   and spectator).

1960: Pape features in the monumental group exhibition
   'Konkrete Kunst', organized by artist Max Bill in Zurich.

2017: The Met Breuer, New York, opens 'Lygia Pape:
   A Multitude of Forms', the first large-scale survey of her
   work in the United States.

BRIDGET RILEY

b.1931

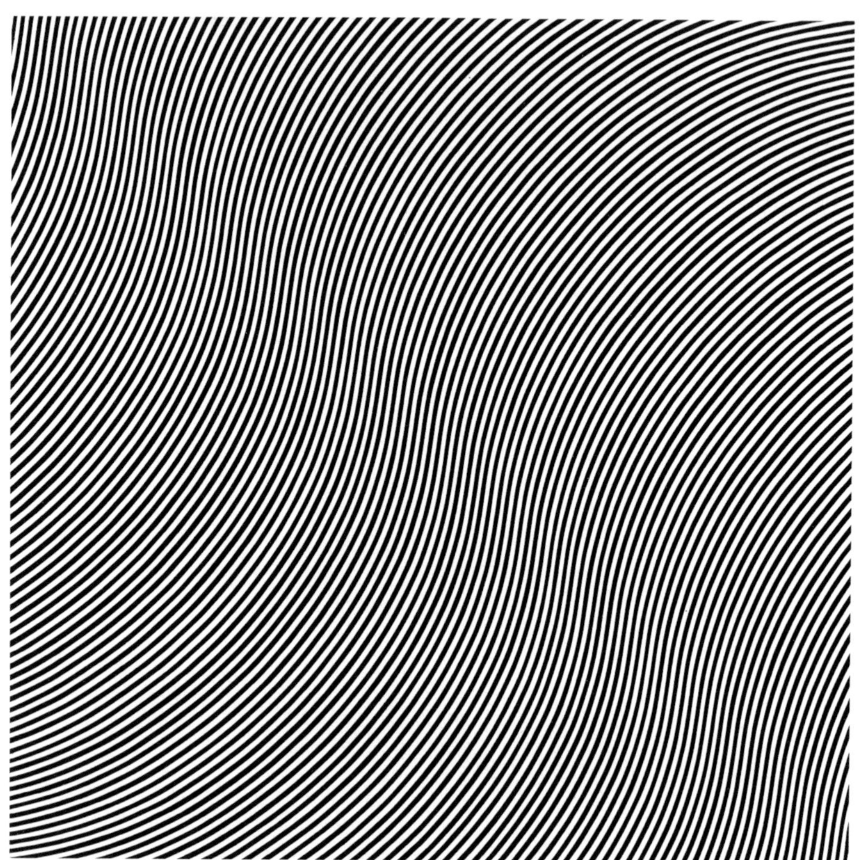

**In 2017 the artist
affirmed that:
'Looking is, I feel, a vital
aspect of existence.
Perception constitutes
our awareness of what it
is to be human, indeed
what it is to be alive.'**

British draughtsman, painter and printmaker Bridget Riley is one of the most influential abstract artists working today. She trained at Goldsmiths College (1949–52) and the Royal College of Art (1952–55) in London, where her early figure studies soon evolved into a landscape-based appreciation of the late-nineteenth century French art movement Pointillism, and in particular the artist who would become her greatest influence, Georges Seurat. Of Seurat's occasionally near-abstract paintings, Riley commented that 'his work gave me a sense of the viewer's importance as an active participant. Perception became the medium.'

At the start of the sixties Riley developed her interest in perception into a precise method of painting that investigated optical effects and visual phenomena, to produce the illusion of movement and rhythm through static geometric shapes on canvas. The phrase 'Op Art' – short for optical art – became attached to Riley's contrasting black-and-white works such as *Fall* (1963), whose undulating surface tension produces an almost physical response in the viewer. In 1965, she published a text, 'Perception is the Medium', in which she wrote that:

> It also surprises me that some people should see my work as a celebration of the marriage of art and science. I have never made any use of scientific theory or scientific data, though I am well aware that the contemporary psyche can manifest startling parallels on the frontier between the arts and the sciences.

Riley's staunch defence of abstract art's distinction from scientific exercise emphasizes her extreme focus on the painterly situation in her work, which developed into complex multicoloured arrangements of curves, diagonals, discs, rhomboids, stripes and triangles from the 1970s to the present day.

KEY EVENTS

1965: Riley takes part in the controversial group exhibition that defines Op Art, 'The Responsive Eye', at the Museum of Modern Art, New York.

1968: Riley becomes the first British artist and first woman to win the International Prize for Painting at the 34th Venice Biennale.

1983: The artist executes her first wall painting for the Royal Liverpool University Hospital.

FRANK STELLA
b.1936

Between 1959 and 1961 Frank Stella (a recent Princeton graduate)
produced in rapid succession a number of series that would cement
his startling contribution to the post-Abstract Expressionist
landscape of American painting: the *Black Paintings* and the *Copper*
and *Aluminum* series, all painted in the small West Broadway studio
Stella shared with Minimal sculptor Carl Andre and filmmaker Hollis
Frampton. These austere early works – the *Black Paintings* especially
– anticipate the beginnings of Minimalism in 1960s New York.

In summer 1961 Stella began work on a new group of paintings.
The *Benjamin Moore* series was named after a specific household
brand of alkyd paint designed to give a matte finish for interior
walls. Stella avoided pricey artists' colours, which he considered
'too sophisticated or something', and frequented instead the aisles
of the hardware store. He embraced the most systematic aspects
of commercial household paints, from the always consistent finish
offered by the alkyd paints, to his deliberately limited choice of
the three primary and three secondary colours from the paint
company's chart. This commercial aspect was so sympathetic to a
Pop Art sensibility that Andy Warhol would commission a set of six
Benjamin Moore paintings from Stella in a 12-inch format. As Stella
commented in a 1964 radio broadcast: 'I wanted to get the paint out
of the can and onto the canvas . . . I tried to keep the paint as good
as it was in the can.'

Stella's paintings are straightforward in their design and rules
for completion, while also provoking a dizzying sense of industrial
colour heading towards optical overload. This tension led the artist
to embrace the possibilities of computer-aided artistic production,
which Stella pioneered from the early 1990s onwards. He continues
to utilize the very latest materials and methods of three-dimensional
printing, modelling and production for his hybrid painting/objects
that interrogate colour, plane and surface.

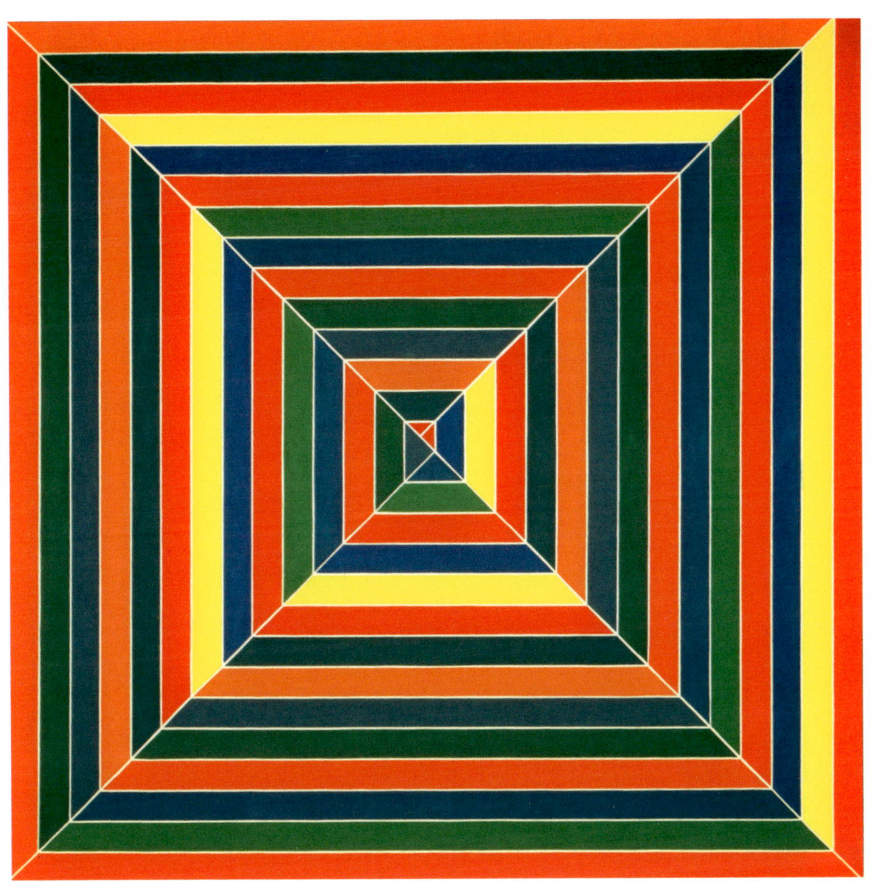

KEY EVENTS

1959–60: 'Sixteen Americans', a group exhibition at the Museum
of Modern Art, New York, includes four *Black Paintings* by
23-year-old Stella.

1963: Stella's first one-man exhibition opens at the Ferus Gallery
in Los Angeles.

1970: He becomes the youngest artist to have a retrospective
at the Museum of Modern Art (MoMA), New York, at age
thirty-three.

HÉLIO OITICICA
1937–80

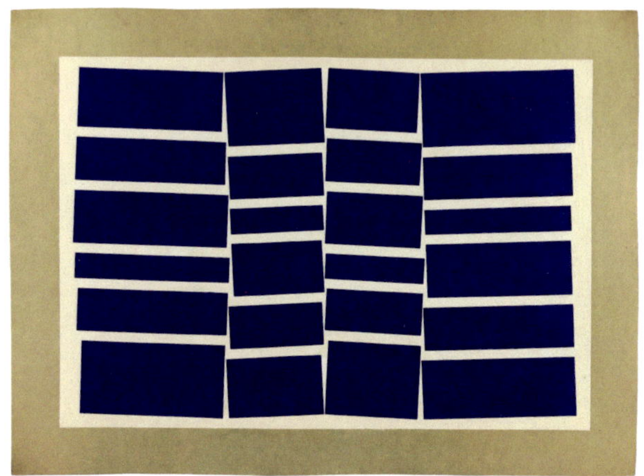

Brazilian artist Oiticica had a long-lasting impact on both the evolution of abstraction in Latin America in the 1950s and 1960s, and the global direction of contemporary art, especially in the development of installation art. His practice charts a transformation from geometric abstraction to immersive and participatory installations that activate the bodies and senses of their viewers.

Oiticica's artistic training came in the early 1950s from Ivan Serpa, a renowned abstract artist associated with Brazil's Concrete Art movement who taught at the newly opened Museum of Modern Art in Rio de Janeiro. Oiticica also joined Serpa's Grupo Frente alongside Lygia Pape and Lygia Clark. By the late 1950s Oiticica's experiments with colour, geometry and structure led to what he described as 'an obsessive dissection of space'. This progressed into all-white paintings and double-sided shaped paintings that were designed to hang from the ceiling, encouraging three-dimensional interactivity despite their flat surfaces.

The artist joined the Neo-Concrete movement in 1960, which was an attempt to retool Concrete Art into a more physically attuned and less rigid experience. The Brazilian military coup of 1964 dramatically altered everyday life in the country and galvanized a new artistic response to the oppressive social and

Hélio Oiticica
Metaesquema, 1958
Gouache on cardboard,
50.2 x 68 cm
(19⅞ x 26⅞ in.)
César and Claudio
Oiticica Collection

This series of more than 350 works utilizes a mirror effect to create dynamic compositions on a central axis. The Portuguese title of the work can be translated as 'meta-structure'.

Hélio Oiticica
*Filter Project – For Vergara
(Projeto Filtro – Para
Vergara)*, 1972
Nylon, acrylic, plastic
curtains, natural fibre
doormat, television set,
tape recorders, transistor
radio, orange juice
machine, fluorescent
lamps and fibreboard,
7.857 x 6.075 m
(25 ft 9⅜ in. x 19 ft
11¼ in.)
César and Claudio
Oiticica Collection

**Visitors wander
through this maze-
like structure of
multicoloured rooms,
to be met with a
sensory bombardment
from radio and TV sets
hidden within.**

political reality of life under a dictatorship. Oiticica's reaction was
to develop a series of collaborative, inhabitable artworks such as
his *Parangolés* – cape-like coloured structures intended to be worn
while dancing to samba music. The related *Penetrables* were room-
like assemblages of interlocking semi-transparent colour panels,
designed to be explored by the viewer, submerged in colour. In the
late 1970s Oiticica produced a series of maquettes collectively titled
The Invention of Colour, which intended to foster an experiential and
public understanding of colour on an architectural scale. In 1980 the
artist died prematurely at the age of forty-two in Rio de Janeiro.

KEY EVENTS

1960: Publishes his important theoretical text *Colour, Time and
  Structure*.
1967: Oiticica debuts his landmark *Tropicália* installation
  containing live parrots, poetry, recorded music and television
  sets. The term 'Tropicália' is subsequently used to describe a
  wider socio-cultural movement focused on music and dance.

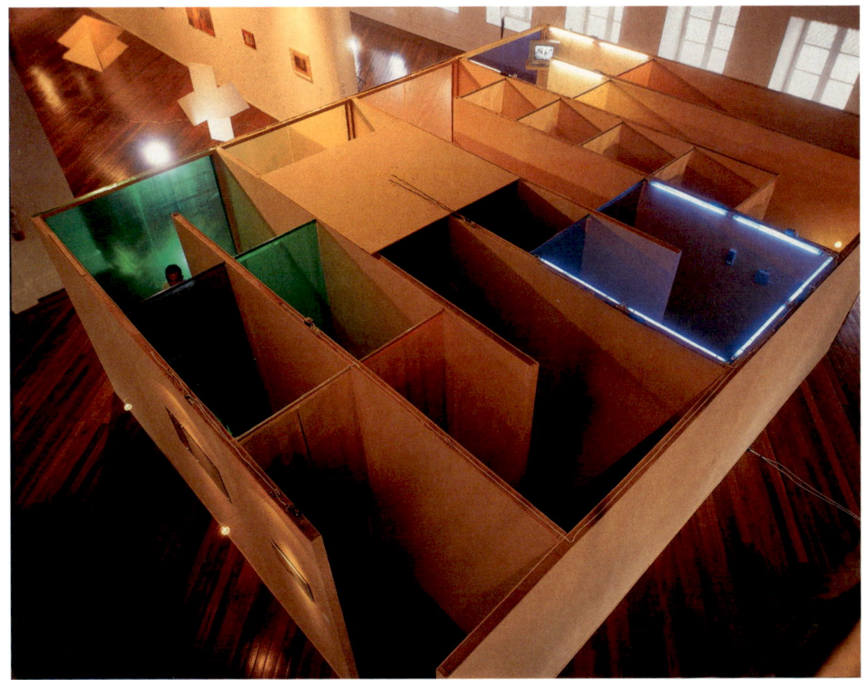

NASREEN MOHAMEDI
1937–90

Nasreen Mohamedi was born in Karachi, British India (now Pakistan), ten years before Partition. She was raised in Bombay (now Mumbai) and at the age of seventeen she left India for London to pursue her studies at the Central School of Arts and Crafts from 1954 to 1957, followed by a period in Paris studying printmaking in the early 1960s. In the interim Mohamedi relocated to Bahrain to work at her family business, which traded in Japanese camera equipment. This facilitated the artist's use of photography to develop her abstract compositions, making use of Bahrain's dramatic desert landscapes to create stark monochromatic studies.

Back in Bombay, Mohamedi set up a studio at the Bhulabhai Desai Institute, a cultural centre for the city's avant-garde. Established in the 1950s, it became a focal point for the consolidation of abstract art in India following the break-up of the Bombay Progressive Artists' Group in 1956. It was here that Mohamedi met the influential painter V. S. Gaitonde, whose calligraphy-inspired Zen Buddhist abstractions had a profound effect on Mohamedi's own biomorphic art, which at this time was partly inspired by Paul Klee.

After travelling extensively throughout the Middle East and South Asia, Mohamedi resettled in New Delhi in 1970. Around this time the artist established her signature style of hovering, parallel lines in ink on paper. She combined her knowledge of western modernism with inspiration from Islamic traditions in architecture, calligraphy (the Kufic script particularly) and geometry. Mohamedi worked at a large, horizontal architect's drawing table, set low to the floor. When showing her drawings to studio visitors, she always displayed them on the floor, never pinned to the wall.

Uniting discipline, precision and spirituality, Mohamedi's Minimal works embraced the rigour of repetition and she silently refused to allow the visual forms to come close to a communicative language. With a reduced palette of graphite, black and soft grey ink washes, she created tactile spaces and ethereal abstract compositions.

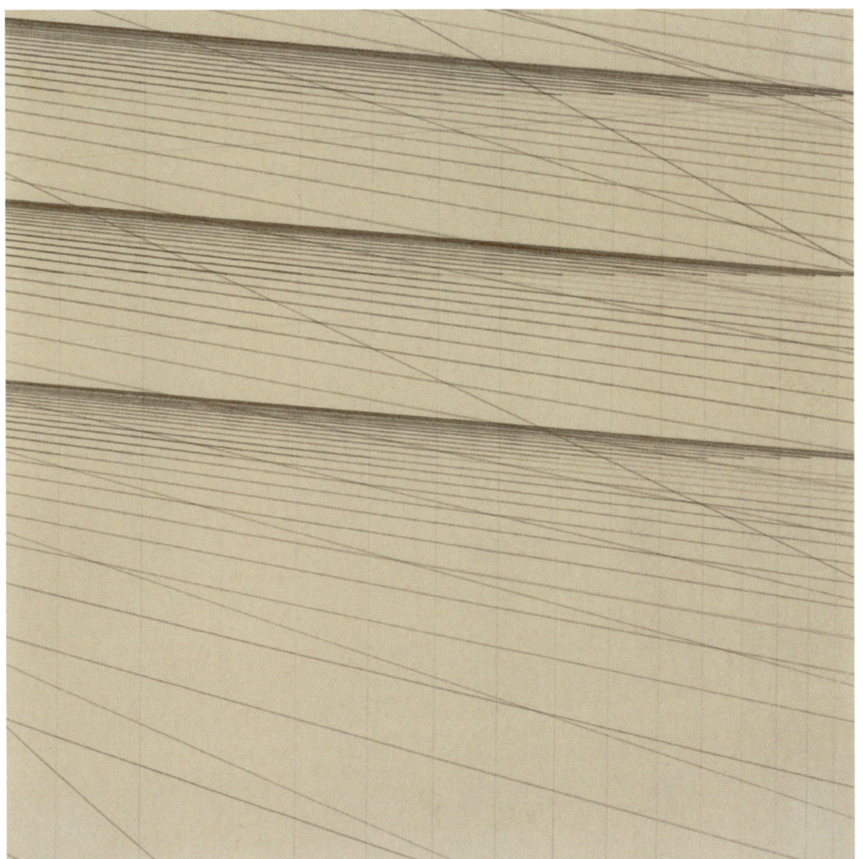

Nasreen Mohamedi
Untitled, c.1975
Ink and graphite on paper,
24 x 24 cm (9½ x 9½ in.)
Private collection

**The majority of
Mohamedi's drawings
are untitled and
undated. Here, the
receding perspective of
the gridded forms and
parallel diagonal lines
create the articulation of
three-dimensional space.**

KEY EVENTS

1972: Mohamedi is hired to teach drawing in the Department
of Fine Arts at Maharaja Sayajirao University, Baroda (now
Vadodara).

1991: The memorial exhibition 'Nasreen in Retrospect' is
presented by Jehangir Art Gallery, Bombay, shortly after her
death at the age of fifty-three.

2016: A major retrospective of Mohamedi's work is the inaugural
exhibition at the Met Breuer, New York.

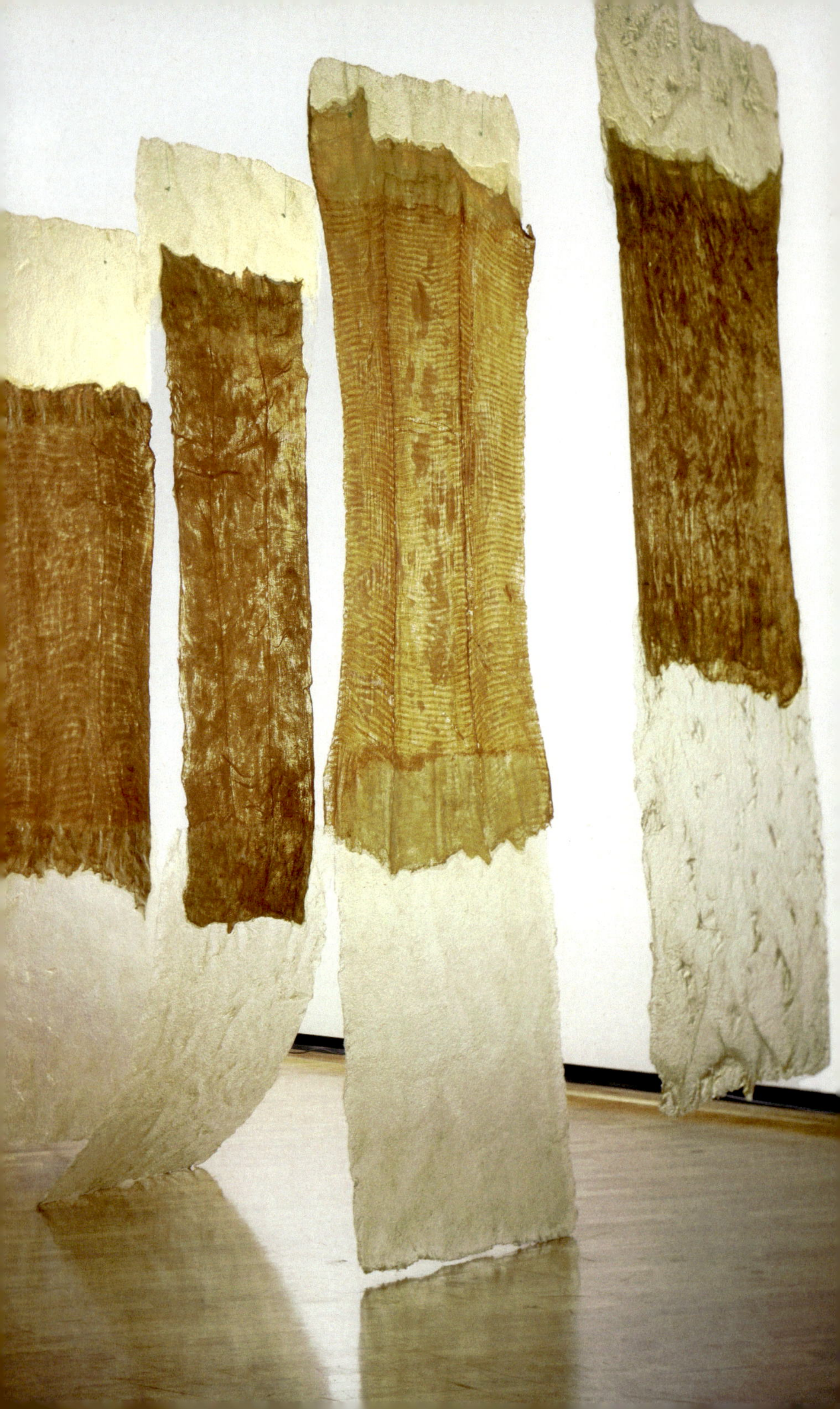

MINIMAL, CONCEPTUAL AND PROCESS ART

-

. . . not painting, not sculpture, it's there
though. I remember I wanted to get to non art,
non connotive, non anthropomorphic,
non geometric, non, nothing, everything,
but of another kind, vision, sort

-

Eva Hesse

1969

ANNE TRUITT
1921–2004

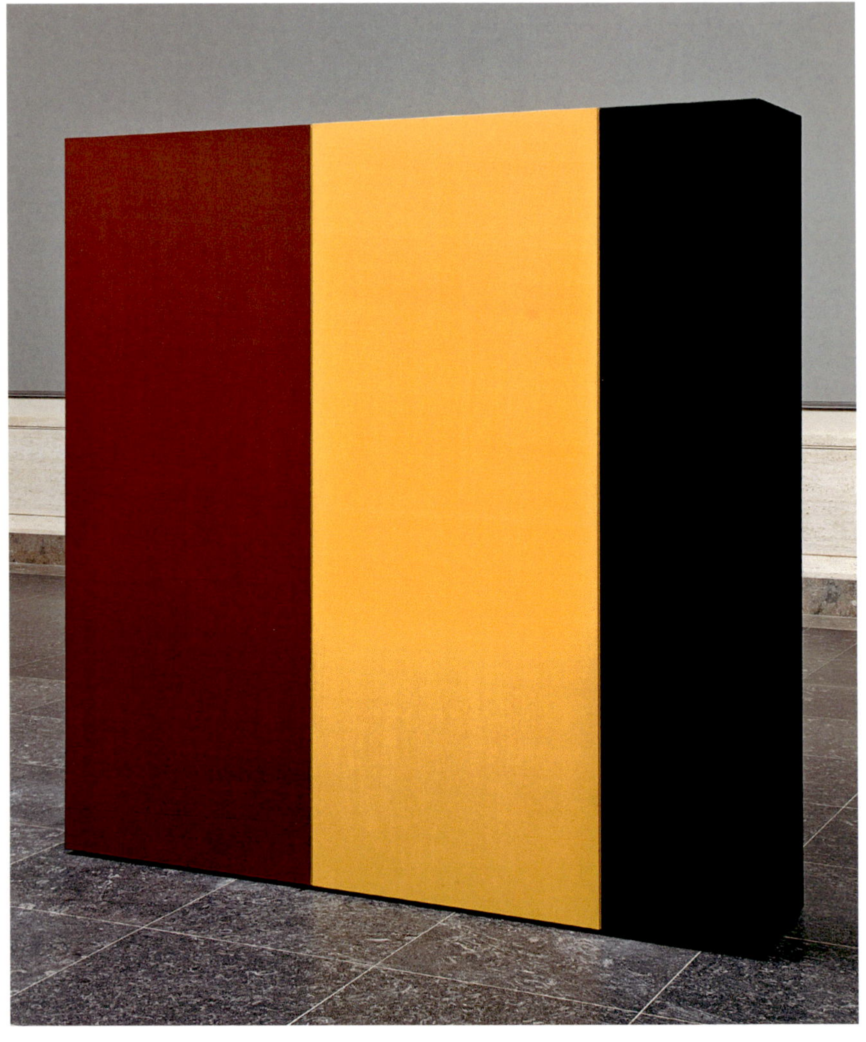

Anne Truitt
Knight's Heritage, 1963
Acrylic on wood, 153.35 x
153.35 x 30.48 cm
(60⅜ x 60⅜ x 12 in.)
National Gallery of Art,
Washington, DC

**The artist's acrylic
brushwork is visible on
the sculpture's wood
surface, which has
grooves delineating the
three sections painted
maroon, yellow and
black (similar but not
identical to the Belgian
and German flags). The
ambiguous title may
hint at the Kennedy
administration, known as
'Camelot', to which Truitt
was connected socially.**

Baltimore-born Anne Truitt's artistic training commenced in
September 1948, when she studied sculpture for one year at
Washington DC's Institute of Contemporary Art. For the next
decade she continued her material experimentation outside the
boundaries of formal art education, teaching herself steel welding,
plaster and cement casting, and many other sculptural techniques.
In 1961, at the age of forty, Truitt arrived at what would become her
signature style of abstract geometric sculptures, partly influenced
by seeing works by Barnett Newman and Ad Reinhardt in person.
Her painted wood units explore what she called 'the relationship
between shape and colour which feels to me like my experience.
To make what feels to me like reality.'

Her first solo exhibition took place in 1963 at the André
Emmerich Gallery, New York. From this point onwards Truitt
developed works in aluminium as well as painted wood and
utilized more complex shapes including polyhedrons. Just over a
decade after her first show she was recognized with a mid-career
retrospective at New York's Whitney Museum of American
Art in 1974.

In her memoir *Daybook*, Truitt wrote on 25 July 1974:

I am only just realizing how inorganic, unnatural, my work is.
Like the straight lines on the desert, what is clearest to me
bears no relation to what I see around me. This is paradoxical,
since everything I make in the studio is a distillation of direct
experience, sometimes even specific visual experience.

This statement underlines Truitt's nuanced understanding of
abstraction's relationship to everyday reality.

KEY EVENTS

1964–7: Truitt lives in Tokyo, Japan – an experience which proves
  influential to the development of her drawing and sculpture.

1982: Truitt publishes *Daybook: The Journal of an Artist*, based
  on seven years of diary entries that chart her balancing of
  creative artistic practice and the daily demands of motherhood,
  domesticity and financial pressures.

2009: A major retrospective of Truitt's work is staged by the
  Hirshhorn Museum and Sculpture Garden, Washington, DC.

RUTH ASAWA
1926–2013

Ruth Asawa's parents were Japanese immigrants to the United States who made their living as vegetable farmers in California. After the bombing of Pearl Harbor, Asawa's father was arrested and the family were incarcerated in Japanese-American internment camps, where Asawa studied landscape painting with a Disney animator, a fellow internee. In summer 1945 she travelled to Mexico and took a class with Cuban furniture and interior designer Clara Porset, who recommended the progressive Black Mountain College in North Carolina to Asawa. Studying there between 1946 and 1949 was a period of transformation through teaching from architect and designer R. Buckminster Fuller, dancer-choreographer Merce Cunningham, and Bauhaus *émigrés* Josef and Anni Albers. Asawa learnt colour and design theory alongside the value of simple materials from Josef Albers. On another trip to Mexico, in 1947, she observed a basket-weaving technique in Toluca that would influence the progression of her geometric and biomorphic drawings into three-dimensional sculpture.

In Asawa's suspended sculptures a single, continuous line of wire becomes a complex shape through accumulations of looping, creating forms both volumetric and transparent. While her abstract sculptures were based on highly skilled manipulations of metal

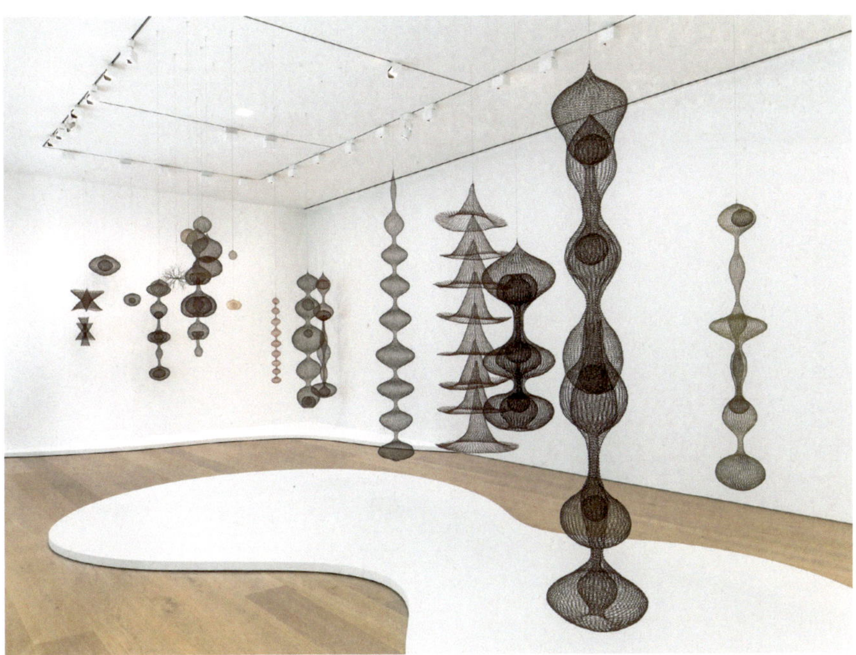

'Ruth Asawa'
Installation view of solo
exhibition at David
Zwirner, New York, 2017

**Of these works the artist
revealed: 'What I was
excited by was I could
make a shape that was
inside and outside at
the same time.' When
grouped together
the sculptures' visual
complexity of layered
positive and negative
space is heightened.**

wire, Asawa had no difficulty in switching to a more accessible
representational mode of working for her public commissions.
Her *San Francisco Fountain* (1973), involved 250 participants
of all ages who contributed scenes shaped in baker's clay, then
cast as bronze panels to form the fountain's circular panorama.
As Asawa stressed, 'it is the idea of bringing skills together that
interests me. We see this in science, in the space program, but
we have lost it in art.' Asawa had an inclusive vision of art's role in
society, and her practice jointly prioritized her singular abstract
artworks and collaborative approach to arts education.

KEY EVENTS

1954, 1956 and 1958: Solo exhibitions at Peridot Gallery,
New York.

1955: Asawa is included in the third São Paulo Biennial, Brazil.

1968: Together with neighbour Sally B. Woodbridge, Asawa founds
the Alvarado School Arts Workshop, San Francisco.

2006: 'The Sculpture of Ruth Asawa: Contours in the Air' opens
at the de Young Museum, San Francisco.

SOL LEWITT
1928–2007

Sol LeWitt is one of the key artists associated with Minimal and Conceptual Art in the United States: two related art movements which emerged in the 1960s, and which are often seen as more neutral correctives to the overt emotion and gestures associated with Abstract Expressionism. Minimalism extended a core principle of abstract art: namely, that art should not attempt to mimic the real world or visualize an experience, but rather describe its own reality, separate from the artist's personal expression. In the early 1960s, LeWitt concentrated on mathematical sequences of repeated geometric forms (primarily the cube) to develop an approach to modular seriality that would define Minimal sculpture.

In 1969 he suggested: 'Ideas can be works of art; they are in a chain of development that may eventually find some form. All ideas need not be made physical.' This diminished importance of the physical art object was termed 'dematerialization' by art critic and curator Lucy Lippard, who championed LeWitt's practice. While Conceptual Art is not necessarily abstract, LeWitt evolved a method of working that displaced his importance as the creator through abstracted systems of working. There is no spontaneous expression, instead schematic execution (often by people other than the artist) based on precise diagrams and written instructions.

The artist's first wall drawings starting in 1968 were completely monochromatic, often using only graphite pencil. In 1975 LeWitt introduced coloured grounds to his geometric wall drawings and in 1983 he began to employ bright ink washes. LeWitt has described his role in their production as akin to a composer, the works being 'like a musical score that could be redone by any or some people. I like the idea that the same work can exist in two or more places at the same time.'

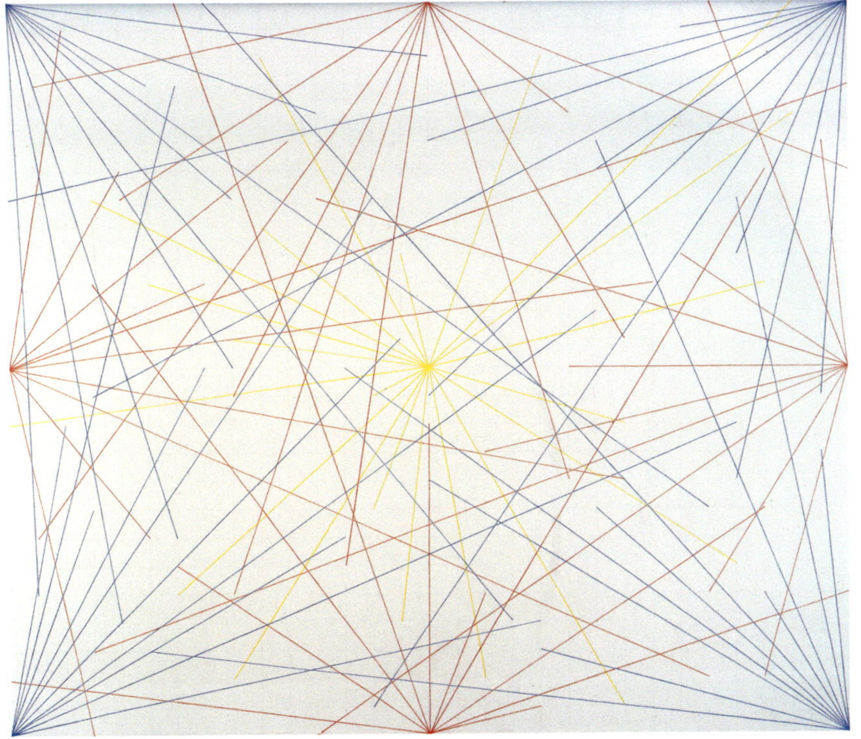

Sol LeWitt
Wall Drawing 273,
September 1975
Graphite and crayon on
seven walls, dimensions
variable
San Francisco Museum
of Modern Art, San
Francisco

**A barely visible pencil
grid is the armature
onto which are plotted
straight lines in blue,
red and yellow crayon,
radiating from points in
the corners, midpoints
and centre of the given
wall surface.**

KEY EVENTS

1966: LeWitt is included in the group exhibition 'Primary
Structures' at the Jewish Museum, New York, which is quickly
seen as one of the defining moments of Minimalism.

1968: LeWitt produces his first pencil wall drawing (based
on permutating square grids) at Paula Cooper Gallery,
New York.

2008: 'Sol LeWitt: A Wall Drawing Retrospective' opens at
Massachusetts Museum of Contemporary Art (MASS MoCA),
North Adams, including 105 of the artist's wall drawings from
1969 to 2007. The long-term exhibition will remain on view
until 2043.

DONALD JUDD
1928–94

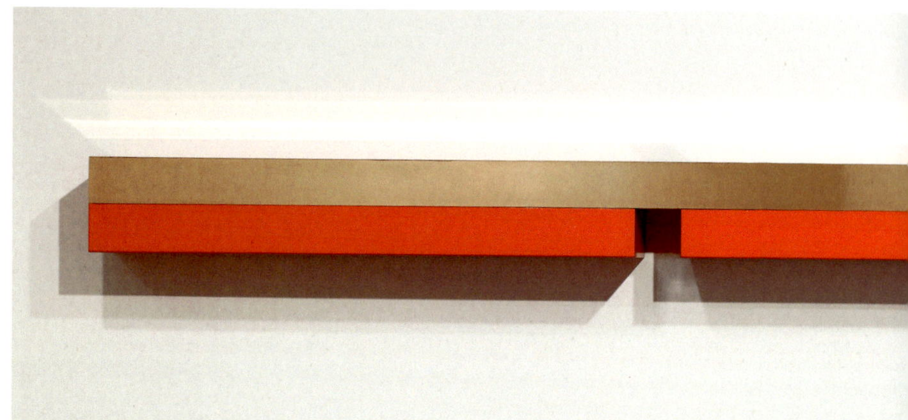

Donald Judd studied philosophy and art history at Columbia
University, New York. This academic grounding had a major impact
on his work as both an artist and art critic. He later studied painting
at the Art Students League, and by 1962 had made his first three-
dimensional object. Thereafter Judd refocused his efforts on the
articulation of what he described as 'specific objects', as opposed
to the more historically loaded categories of painting or sculpture.
He began to call his works 'floor pieces' (freestanding objects
without a pedestal) or 'wall pieces' (one or multiple modular units,
hung on the wall). Despite being one of the artists most closely
associated with Minimalism, he rejected the term, declaring:
'I don't think anyone's work is "reductive".'

For many years Judd worked part-time as an art reviewer. In his
criticism's clear, unadorned prose, we see the radical reduction of
formal flourishes also visible in his artwork. A note he wrote in about
1963 reveals some of Judd's insights into the category of abstract
art: 'The first thing to do is to dispel the reasonable expectation that
the term "abstract art" has a definite meaning . . . A primary thing
about abstraction is that it is open and changeable.' These emphatic
statements reveal Judd's philosophically inclined capacity to accept
ambiguity and experimentation in the development of new art.

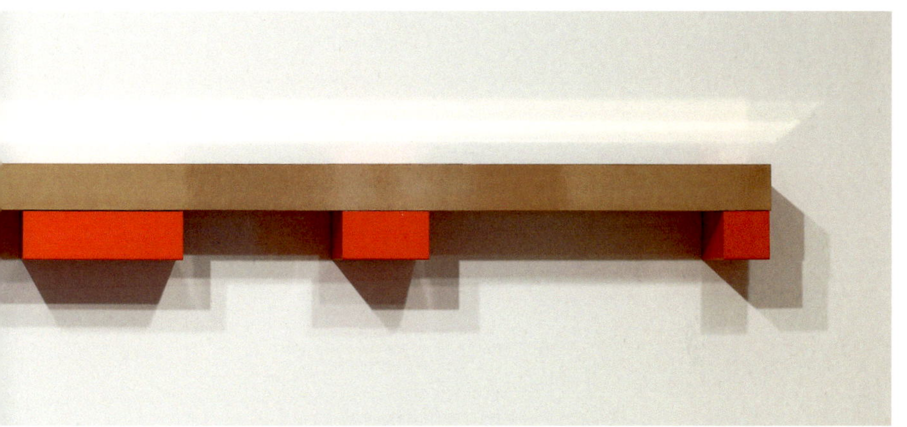

Donald Judd
Untitled, 1967
Painted steel boxes with
brass tube, 15.9 x 281.9 x
15.2 cm (6¼ x 111 x 6 in.)
Seattle Art Museum,
Seattle

**This wall piece juxtaposes
two horizontal structures:
an uninterrupted
brass top section and
a progression of red
steel boxes based
on mathematical
permutation. During
this period Judd worked
primarily with sheet
metal fabricators
Bernstein Brothers,
who produced his highly
polished objects from
diagrams.**

In 1968 Judd purchased a five-storey cast-iron building at
101 Spring Street, New York, where he would develop the ideal
conditions for the permanent installation of his objects, alongside
works by other artists. The interplay between three-dimensional
objects, architecture and design (including furniture design) would
remain fundamentally important to Judd's practice for the rest
of his career.

KEY EVENTS

1964: Judd writes the article 'Specific Objects', considered one
   of the key theoretical texts of Minimalism, which is published
   a year later in *Arts Yearbook 8*.
1977: The artist establishes the Judd Foundation to preserve
   the legacy of his artworks, archives, libraries and permanent
   installations of his large-scale works, particularly in his multi-
   building complex in Marfa.
2020: The Museum of Modern Art, New York, presents a major
   retrospective of the artist's work.

CHARLOTTE POSENENSKE
1930–85

Frankfurt-based Charlotte Posenenske was a crucial link between
Minimal and Conceptual artists working across the United States
and Germany. She studied with the renowned designer, typographer
and abstract painter Willi Baumeister in Stuttgart after the war,
and some of her earliest creative work was as a costume and stage
designer in Darmstadt, where she learnt the ideals of working
collaboratively and spatially. Her mature sculptural practice used
cheap industrial materials including corrugated cardboard, steel
and aluminium to produce large-scale modular units that had no
fixed arrangement or composition determined by the artist.

The *Square Tubes* series produced in 1967 are made up of
components formed by sheets of galvanized steel, industrially
produced and commercially available. The separate units (connector,
square, rectangular and T-brace pieces) could be bought by the
artist's collectors in any configuration they preferred and arranged
to their liking. In a radical anti-capitalist act, she sold these works to
her 'consumers' at the cost price of their materials. She described
her sculptures as 'components of a space, since they are like building
elements, they can always be rearranged into new combinations
or positions, thus, they alter the space . . . The simplicity of basic
geometric forms is beautiful.'

Inspired by the activism of the May 1968 student protests across
Europe, Posenenske stopped making work, believing that she had

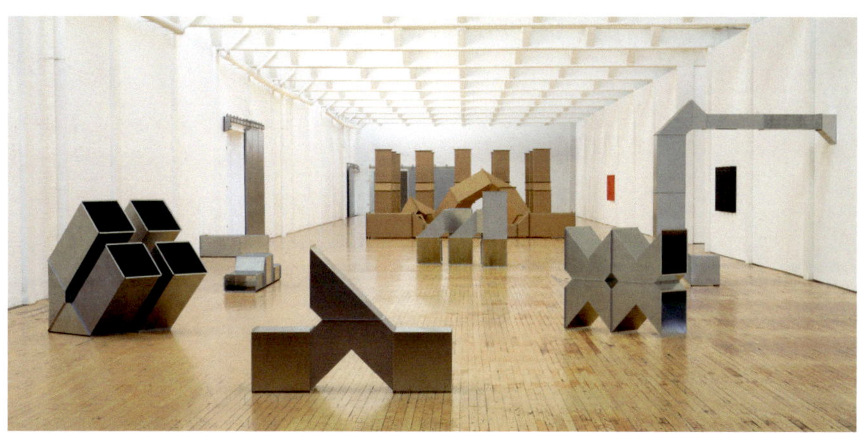

**'Charlotte Posenenske:
Work in Progress'**
Installation view of
exhibition at Dia:Beacon,
Beacon, New York, 2019

**This installation includes
various series, which
Posenenske described
as 'variable, as simple as
possible, reproducible'.
Over the course of
this exhibition the
arrangement of the Series
D steel units changed
twice, reflecting the
artist's commitment to
adaptation, cooperation
and teamwork.**

reached the end of what was possible through artistic practice, and wanting to have a more direct impact on issues such as social inequality. Her manifesto published in *Art International* that same month is essentially her farewell to the art world. She wrote that 'it is difficult for me to come to terms with the fact that art can contribute nothing to solving urgent social problems'. She became a sociologist specializing in industrial employment issues until her death in 1985.

KEY EVENTS

1967: Her works are included in the exhibition 'Serielle Formationen (Serial Formations)' at Frankfurt University alongside American artists Donald Judd, Sol LeWitt, Agnes Martin and Frank Stella, in the first German exhibition to explore Minimal Art.

2007: Posenenske's sculptures are featured in the twelfth edition of documenta, a five-yearly contemporary art exhibition in Kassel, Germany, introducing her work to a new generation.

2019: 'Charlotte Posenenske: Work in Progress', the first major retrospective of her work in the United States, opens at Dia:Beacon, New York.

ROBERT RYMAN
1930–2019

Nashville-born Robert Ryman is revered for his white-on-white Minimal paintings that over six decades explored the incredible range of permutations and variations within a painting's surface, support, fixtures, materials and textures. He began working with the square format in the 1950s, when he also worked as a security guard at the Museum of Modern Art, New York.

Ryman once said of his work that:

since I'm not working with illusion or narrative that allows me the freedom to explore . . . The painting can be very thin, very close to the wall. Sometimes it can come away from the wall. I think it's important that it stay connected to the wall; I think it needs the wall itself to be complete. But it opens up many possibilities.

This awareness of the spatial and material expansiveness of his painting – its ability to move beyond its physical confines to affect the room itself – is something shared by many other Minimal artists of the time. Ryman was meticulous in his approach to his paintings' installations, preferring natural daylight to illuminate his works.

Ryman believed that his formal restrictiveness led to limitless invention:

I'm not limited by a certain narrative that I want to get across. There's no symbolism or story that I need to tell or some kind of political project that I might want to do. I'm not limited by any of that. I don't have any of those things to stop me from experimenting and going forward.

Ryman considered himself a 'realist' painter rather than an 'abstract' one, because he focused on the physical reality of his paintings, and their spatial situation.

Robert Ryman
Untitled painting # 10,
1963
Oil paint, graphite, gesso
on unstretched raw linen
canvas, fabric irregular,
45.7 x 45.7 cm
(18 x 18 in.)
Xavier Hufkens, Brussels

Ryman once said: 'I don't think of my painting as abstract because I don't abstract from anything. It's involved with real visual aspects of what you are looking at – whether wood, paint, or metal – how it's put together, how it looks on the wall and works with the light.'

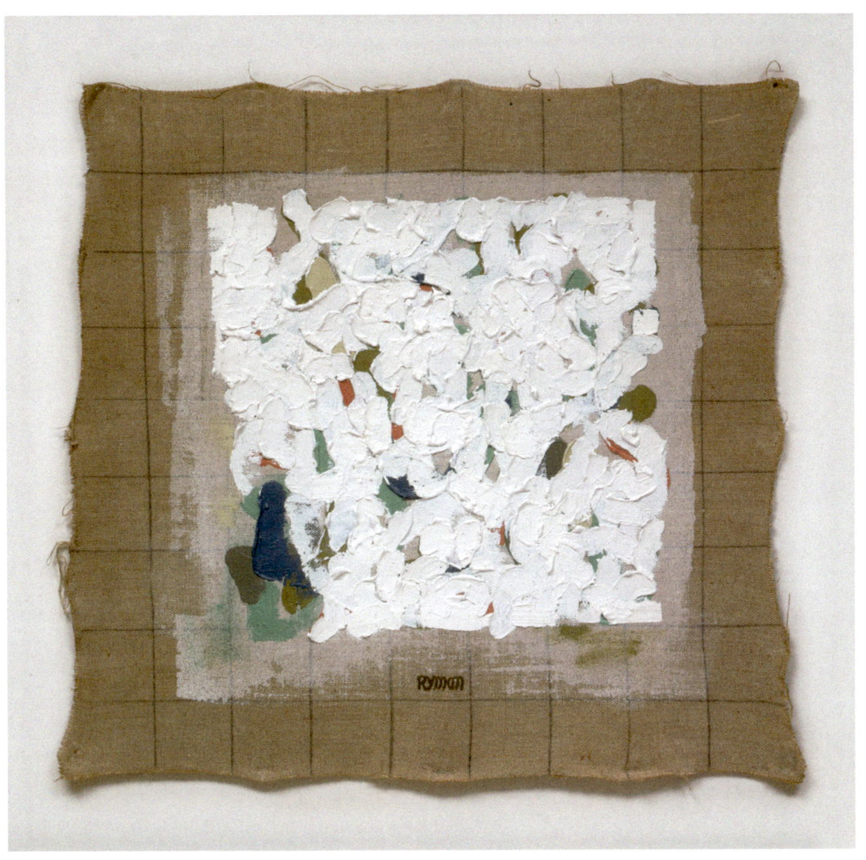

KEY EVENTS

1967: The artist's first solo exhibition takes place at Paul
Bianchini Gallery, New York.

1969: Ryman is included in the era-defining exhibition 'When
Attitudes Become Form' at the Kunsthalle Bern, curated by
Harald Szeemann.

1985: Ryman is awarded the Skowhegan Medal from the
Skowhegan School of Painting and Sculpture, Madison.

GERHARD RICHTER
b.1932

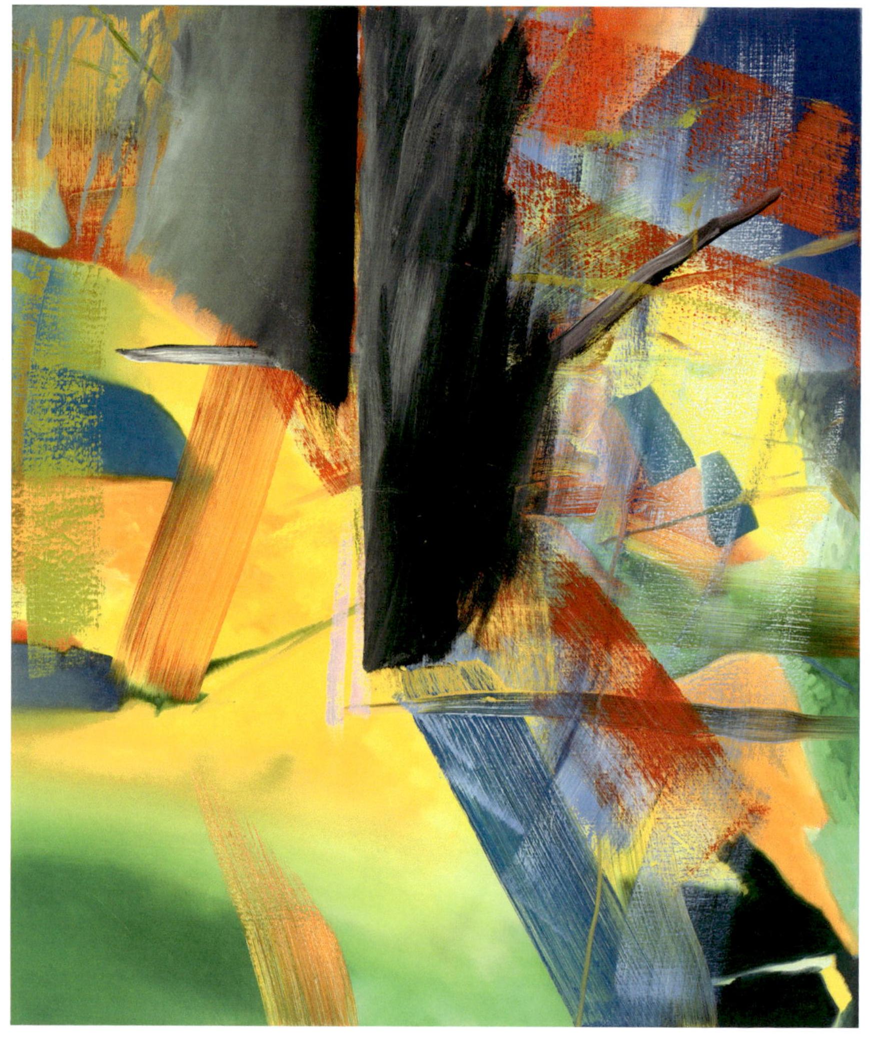

Gerhard Richter
Ingrid, 1984
Oil on canvas,
120 x 100 cm
(47¼ x 39⅜ in.)
Neues Museum,
Staatliches Museum
für Kunst und Design,
Nuremberg, Germany

In 1985 Richter explained: 'When I paint an abstract picture, I neither know in advance what it is meant to look like nor, during the painting process, what I am aiming at and what to do about getting there.' This totally abstract painting is complicated by its title's reference to a named individual.

Born in Dresden, Gerhard Richter defected to West Germany in 1961 to escape the repressive regime in East Germany. He continued his studies at the Dusseldorf Art Academy during a dynamic creative period where he studied alongside Konrad Fischer, Blinky Palermo and Sigmar Polke. In 1963 they staged an exhibition in a furniture shop called 'Living with Pop: A Demonstration for Capitalist Realism' – a term for their local variation on Pop Art that commented on Germany's newly voracious consumer culture.

Following the success of Capitalist Realism, Richter began making paintings based on photographs (sometimes personal, other times anonymous subject matters), blurring their representational content. Abstract works then materialized alongside his photo paintings, beginning with the 'Colour Charts' in 1966, which utilized industrial paint charts and were partly inspired by his interest in Pop Art's strategies of repetition, and Blinky Palermo's geometric abstraction. The pair visited New York in 1970, intensifying their dialogue with Minimal and Conceptual Art in America.

In 1976 Richter began his gestural, multicoloured abstract paintings alongside his photorealist works. His process involves the quasi-mechanized application of paint on a grand scale using a squeegee, which is dragged across the surface to create intense colour mixtures and endlessly rich surface textures and patterns, often relying heavily on chance effects.

In 1987 he further collapsed the distinction between representational content and abstraction by introducing his 'Overpainted Photographs'. Richter has continued his dedication to the 'Abstract Paintings', while in 2011 he debuted a new series, the 'Strip Paintings'. These works remix painterly creation for the digital era: they are digital prints based on photographs of Richter's 'Abstract Paintings' that are then divided, stretched and recombined as thin vertical slices. The series is an abstraction of abstraction.

KEY EVENTS

1972: Represents Germany at the Venice Biennale and features in documenta 5 in Kassel.

1977: The artist begins to make sculptural works using painted grey glass – beginning his interest in opacity and reflection.

2002–7: Richter is invited to design a monumental stained-glass window for the famous cathedral of Cologne, where he has lived and worked since 1983. He produces an abstract design of 11,500 glass squares, inspired by his 'Colour Chart Paintings'.

RASHEED ARAEEN
b.1935

Rasheed Araeen arrived in London in 1964, having graduated in civil engineering from NED University of Engineering and Technology in his hometown of Karachi, Pakistan, two years prior. He had already begun to make abstract paintings in Karachi, but in London he was inspired by modern British sculptors Anthony Caro and Phillip King to abandon painting for three-dimensionality. Despite his lack of formal artistic training, Araeen quickly forged his ground-breaking and idiosyncratic version of Minimalist sculpture in Britain – and yet his impact on this artistic discourse at the time was marginalized because of his ethnicity.

Araeen's late 1960s sculptures were handmade in wood and metal, in contrast to many American Minimal sculptors whose works were manufactured in factories. The criss-crossing diagonals of his cuboid linear lattices are reminiscent of the window grilles he designed as a young engineer in Karachi. Like Charlotte Posenenske, Araeen intended for visitors to his exhibitions to rearrange his precarious stacks of serial modular units, creating endless visual options. He also made ephemeral work for outdoor public spaces, such as *Chakras* (1969–70), for which he floated sixteen bright orange disks in the water of St Katharine Docks, London.

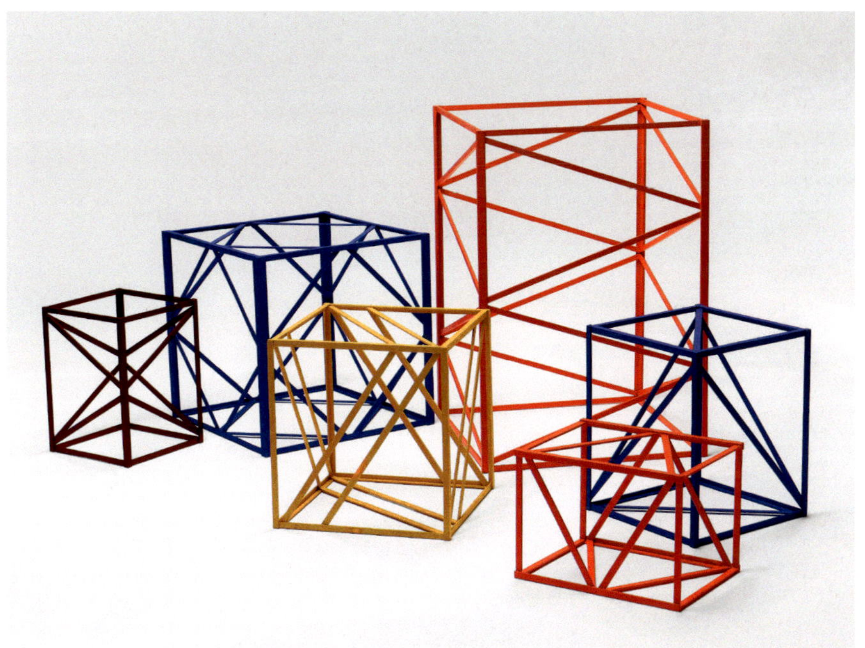

Rasheed Araeen
*One Summer
Afternoon*, 1968
Emulsion and acrylic on
wood: 6 painted wood
constructions of various
sizes, maximum:
74 x 50.5 x 50 cm
(29 x 19 x 19 in.),
minimum: 33.5 x 24 x
24.5 cm (13 x 9 x 9 in.)
Centre Pompidou, Paris

**For Araeen, the
participatory and
interactive aspect of this
six-part work disrupts
the severe symmetry
of the structures with
the element of chance
created by the viewers'
engagement.**

Alongside his artistic practice Araeen's work as a writer, editor and curator sought to address imbalances in the way non-white artists were analysed and given critical consideration by the Eurocentric art press. Araeen's artworks of the 1970s and 1980s became more overtly political in their subject matters and often incorporated film and multimedia. In more recent years Araeen has returned to abstract wall paintings and geometric structures, creating new configurations for social spaces internationally.

KEY EVENTS

1987: Araeen launches the academic journal *Third Text*, addressing art in a global context.

1989–90: Araeen curates 'The Other Story: Afro-Asian Artists in Post-War Britain' at the Hayward Gallery, London, a group exhibition that aims to correct the erasure of black and minority ethnic artists' major contributions to narratives of contemporary British art. Featured abstract artists included Frank Bowling, Li Yuan-chia and Francis Newton Souza.

2017–18: 'Rasheed Araeen: A Retrospective' opens at Van Abbemuseum in Eindhoven, the Netherlands.

EVA HESSE
1936–70

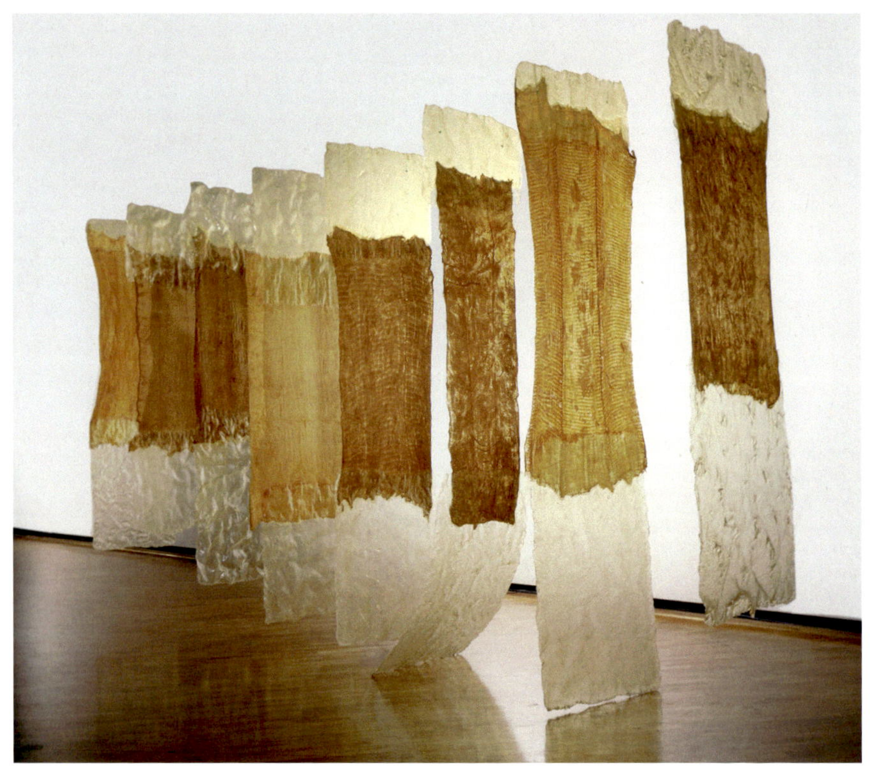

Eva Hesse
Contingent, 1969
Cheesecloth, latex,
fibreglass, installation,
variable: 350 x 630 x
109 cm (137⅞ x
248⅛ x 43 in.)
National Gallery of
Australia, Canberra

The luminescent
properties of works
such as her eight-part
suspended sculpture
Contingent seem to
almost trap light, in
which colour is both
absent and present. The
gradual clouding of the
latex and resin over the
years should not obscure
the fact that when this
sculpture was made, its
materials were almost
entirely transparent
– with certainly none
of the yellowing that
characterizes its
appearance today.

Hamburg-born Eva Hesse was evacuated from Germany on the Kindertransport via Holland and the United Kingdom, to settle with her family in New York at the age of three. She studied at the Pratt Institute, Brooklyn, and the Cooper Union, followed by a BFA at Yale University, where she studied under the renowned abstract colourist Josef Albers.

In 1963–4 Hesse spent a year in Kettwig-am-Ruhr, Germany, with her then-husband, sculptor Tom Doyle. During this time she had a studio in an abandoned textiles factory where she began experimenting with low reliefs using string and cord that hinted at abstracted and sexualized body parts. Hesse's work matured upon her return to New York in 1965, when she renounced the reliefs' acidic colours for a monochromatic palette of grey hues. The half-painting, half-sculpture *Hang Up* (1966) demonstrates this tactile use of the 'grayscale'. Over the next few years, Hesse would begin to deploy the textures, translucency and pliability inherent in her chosen materials of latex, fibreglass and resin, in material installations that disrupted the rigid Minimalist reliance on grids and seriality. Her reconfiguration of repetition transformed the grid into something less grounded and certain, but more open to a humanizing element. As the artist stated: 'If something is absurd, it's much more exaggerated, more absurd, if it's repeated.'

In 1969 Hesse debuted her momentous *Expanded Expansion* (made of rubberized cheesecloth and fibreglass poles) in the radical group exhibition 'Anti Illusion: Procedures/Materials' at the Whitney Museum of American Art, New York, which is often credited with defining what came to be known as Process Art. Process artists undid certain assumptions of sculpture, including rigid and coherent forms, to embrace chance, disorder, irregularity and the forces of gravity upon loose or unsculpted materials. Hesse died of a brain tumour on 29 May 1970 at the age of thirty-four.

KEY EVENTS

November 1968: Hesse's only New York solo show of sculpture during her lifetime, 'Chain Polymers', opens at Fischbach Gallery, New York.

1968–9: Hesse is included in the installation-focused exhibition 'Nine at Leo Castelli', organized by artist Robert Morris at the Castelli warehouse in New York, alongside Process artists such as Richard Serra and Keith Sonnier.

December 1969: *Contingent* is shown in the group exhibition 'Art in Process IV' at the Finch College Museum of Art, New York.

LEE UFAN
b.1936

Lee Ufan was born in a rural village in south-eastern Korea during the country's occupation under Japanese colonial rule. In 1956 he interrupted his painting studies at Seoul National University to move to Tokyo, where he undertook a philosophy degree at Nihon University. By the end of the 1960s Lee had become a leading artist and theorist within the Japanese art movement Mono-ha (School of Things), alongside sculptor Nobuo Sekine. The group reflected the changing status of art in a post-colonial industrialized world by rejecting representation in favour of direct engagement with natural and raw industrial materials in large-scale sculptures of stones, soil, glass and steel. It shares some affinities with Arte Povera in Italy and Process Art in the United States. As the artist explained in a 2014 interview: 'In an effort to break away from the conventional way of thinking that concentrated solely on making and look at things anew, we asked: how does bringing in the unmade open up a new dimension of expression and change both the made and the unmade? That movement became Mono-ha.'

In 1973 Lee was appointed Professor at Tama Art University, which prompted his return to painting and led to his identification with the Korean school of Dansaekhwa (Monochrome Painting). Lee controlled the intense physicality of his painting by carefully regulating his breathing in alignment with his systematic brushstrokes. The presence of the body – which marks the painting's spatial relationship to the passing of time – is crucial to understanding Lee's serial monochromes of this era. Throughout his career Lee has published a vast body of philosophical writings, which underpin his understanding of the art object as a physical affirmation of being in the world.

Lee Ufan
From Point, 1979
Glue and mineral pigment on canvas, 161.9 x 130.2 cm (63¾ x 51⅜ in.)
Private collection

This work forms part of a major series made by Lee between 1972 and 1984, which focuses on the repetitive power of painting a systematic grid of square brushstrokes, which mark the canvas with powdered cobalt-blue pigment suspended in animal-skin glue. The horizontal sequence unfolds until the colour is exhausted and the artist begins again.

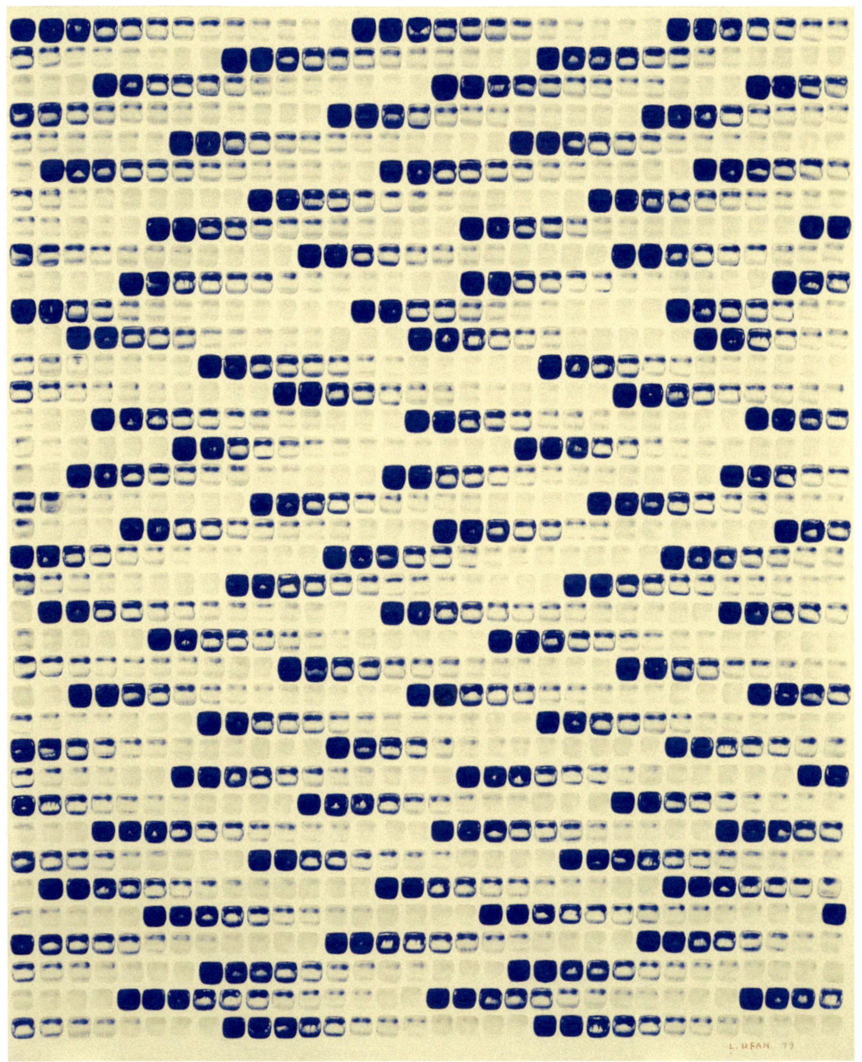

KEY EVENTS

1969: His essay 'From Object to Being' is published, winning
a prize for critical writing.

2001: Awarded the thirteenth Praemium Imperiale (Painting),
Tokyo.

2010: The Lee Ufan Museum, designed by architect Tadao Ando,
opens on the Japanese island of Naoshima.

2019: The major retrospective 'Lee Ufan: Inhabiting Time' opens
at Centre Pompidou-Metz, France.

137

DANIEL BUREN
b.1938

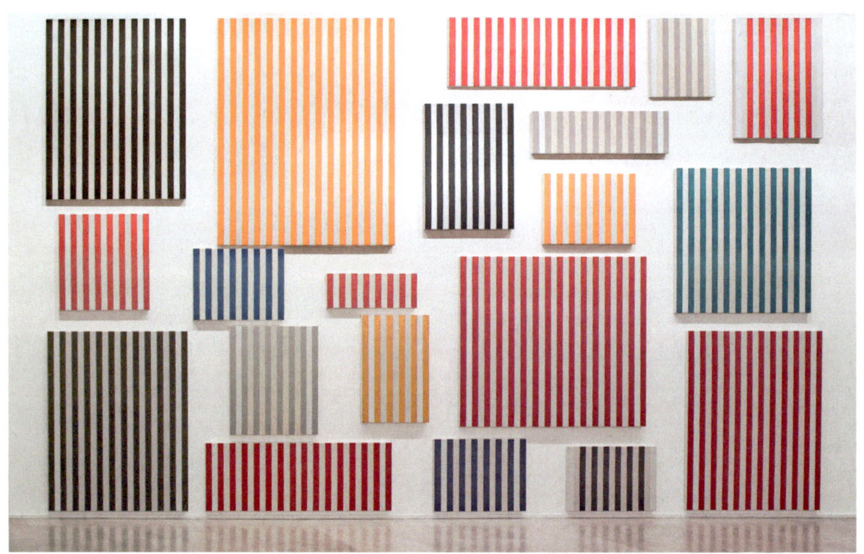

Daniel Buren
Murs de peintures,
1966–77
Acrylic paint on woven
cotton canvas with
alternating 8.7 cm
(3½ in.) wide stripes
Musée d'Art Moderne
de la Ville de Paris, Paris

**This group of twenty
paintings was made over
a period of eleven years;
the differences in their
shapes and colours are
offset by the uniform
striped structure and the
strict formal arrangement
on the wall.**

French Conceptual Artist Daniel Buren's early career was spent trying to find a new visual language for painting that removed all vestiges of illusionism, representation and gestural expression. In 1966, after a sustained period of trial and error, Buren achieved the format with which he would work consistently from this point onwards: a commercially printed design of repeating stripes 8.7 cm (3½ in.) wide, alternating between white and one other colour. Using this system, the artist avoids composition and allows no distinction between the material and its design (the canvas or paper, and the paint on it). His practice can be described as abstract in two senses: the abandonment of painting and the self-effacement of the artist.

An explicitly political dimension in Buren's work emerged around the May 1968 student uprisings in Paris: overnight and without permission he pasted a green-and-white paper version of his work onto 200 billboards around the city, obscuring commercial advertisements with his banal and repetitive stripes. Buren also translated his brutally simple format onto sandwich boards, which he hired two men to wear around Paris for the performance *Sandwich Men* in 1968.

Since 1967, most of Buren's works have been made in situ, which is to say, they are realized as artworks by complete reliance on the architectural, institutional or public context in which they are exhibited. As the artist wrote in 1998: 'My works are totally dependent on the places for which they were designed; they actually upset the traditional, supposed autonomy of the work of art.' Quite often, his works enter or overlap with non-art spaces to confuse the distinction between an exhibiting space and what lies beyond, in the real world (ranging across surfaces from boat sails to commuter train doors).

KEY EVENTS

1968: Buren's first solo exhibition takes place at the Apollinaire Gallery, Milan.

1972: The artist is selected to participate in curator Harald Szeemann's documenta 5, which cements his role within global Conceptual Art.

1986: Buren is awarded the top prize – The Golden Lion – at the Venice Biennale for his solo representation of France.

JUDY CHICAGO
b.1939

Although better known today for her radical feminist works of
the 1970s and 1980s such as *The Dinner Party* (1974–9), Judy
Chicago's sculptural practice from 1965 to 1973 was aligned with
Finish Fetish: a high-gloss, west coast variant of Minimalism. Based
in Fresno and Los Angeles, California, she enrolled in an auto-body
painting school – as the only woman in a class of 250 – to learn the
car industry's lacquering techniques that enabled her to fuse surface
and colour. Some of her earliest sculptures take the form of car
hoods, but she quickly adopted a more strictly abstract vocabulary
of reduced geometric shapes, generated through diagrams, patterns
and systems and realized as large-scale sculptures.

In contrast to the austere and often monochrome palettes
of the New York Minimalists, the Finish Fetish artists favoured
pastel and candy hues that evoked the sun-drenched landscapes
and consumer-led commercialization of California. At the time of
making the majority of her Minimal sculptures the artist was known
as Judy Gerowitz; in 1970 she changed her last name to Chicago
(her hometown), announced publicly via two advertisements in
Artforum magazine. This decision was prompted by her experience

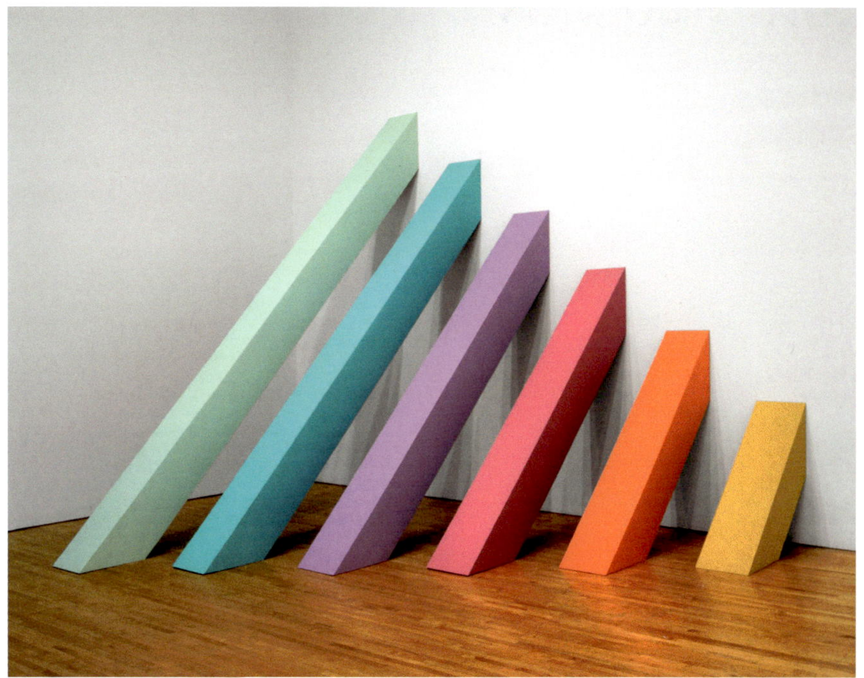

Judy Chicago
Rainbow Pickett,
1965/2004
Latex paint on canvas-
covered plywood,
301.6 x 301.6 x 335.3 cm
(118¾ x 118¾ x 132 in.)
Collection of Waldman
Family Charitable Trust,
Mountain Center (CA)

**This six-part sculpture
is named after Wilson
Pickett, the sixties
soul singer. Its separate
slanting diagonals
connect wall and floor,
moving gradually from
cool to warm tones like a
colour wheel equivalent
to a musical scale.**

of repeated sexist denigrations and erasures of her work from institutional and commercial art spaces.

Around 1968 Chicago began producing her temporary interventions known as 'Atmospheres'. These works reconfigured pyrotechnic firework displays as site-specific performances that drenched the landscape in coloured smoke: an abstract, immersive gesture that was equally an attempt to 'feminize' the male-dominated southern California art scene.

KEY EVENTS

1966: The artist's sculpture *Rainbow Pickett* is included in curator Kynaston McShine's 'Primary Structures: Younger American and British Sculpture' at the Jewish Museum, New York.

1972: Chicago collaborates with Miriam Schapiro and members of the Feminist Art Program, California Institute of the Arts, Los Angeles, to create the immersive installation *Womanhouse*.

2020: San Francisco's de Young Museum stages the first ever full retrospective of Chicago's practice.

HOWARDENA PINDELL
b.1943

Howardena Pindell's large-scale, multicoloured paintings of the early 1970s are shimmering, iridescent abstractions constructed using labour-intensive methods, with the paper hole punch as her primary tool. These processes subsequently generated material for the artist to create further works, entirely different in appearance and yet still utilizing the circle as their fundamental repeating form. As she explains, the paintings were ‹made by spraying synthetic polymer resin through templates. I constructed the templates using strips of punched paper. I had saved the dots of paper punched from oak tag, an off-white paper. Numbering each dot by using a radiograph, a needle, and tweezers, I created two- and three-dimensional works made of collaged, punched, and numbered dots.' Pindell had created a dual system of making whereby the 'waste' of the punched holes from her templates became the core material for the textured surfaces of her collages.

Pindell earned her Masters of Fine Art at Yale University, where she studied Josef Albers' colour theory course, to which she credits her complex understanding of colour – alongside her deep respect for Georges Seurat's Pointillism. As well as creating her abstract collages and paintings, Pindell became the first African-American woman to be hired as a curator at the Museum of Modern Art (MoMA), New York, where she worked in the Prints and Illustrated Books department for twelve years (1967–79). Her practice of this time is broadly aligned with Postminimalism – a term encompassing numerous artists, including Eva Hesse and Lynda Benglis, whose

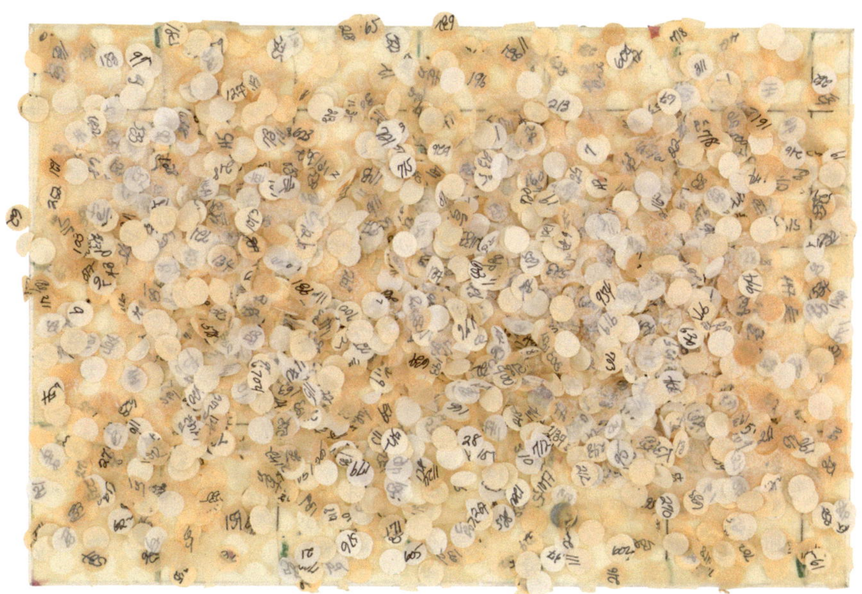

Howardena Pindell
Untitled #58, 1974
Mixed media on board,
12.75 x 20.32 cm
(5 x 8 in.)
Rose Art Museum,
Brandeis University,
Waltham

Considering the wider context for her practice, Pindell notes: 'Black aesthetics, for me, means being conscious of African art . . . I think one can also use abstraction and have a black aesthetic because of the way abstraction has been handled in Africa through the use of geometry and patterns.'

work explores the performance and physicality of materials subjected to natural forces such as gravity, and loosens the rigid systems (geometric permutations and gridded structures) prevalent in Minimalism.

The artist does not see a separation in her work between its aesthetic qualities (the beauty of her abstract colours, shapes and textures) and its critical qualities that reflect subtly on social and political concerns, particularly those connected to her experiences as a black female artist. Pindell reminds us of the ever-present cultural dimension of abstract art, which is never produced in a vacuum.

KEY EVENTS

1977: Pindell has a solo exhibition at the influential non-profit art organization Just Above Midtown (JAM) in New York, run by Linda Goode Bryant.

1986: An important solo exhibition is staged by The Studio Museum, Harlem, New York.

2017: Pindell's work is featured in the major survey show 'We Wanted a Revolution: Black Radical Women, 1965–1985' at the Brooklyn Museum, New York.

143

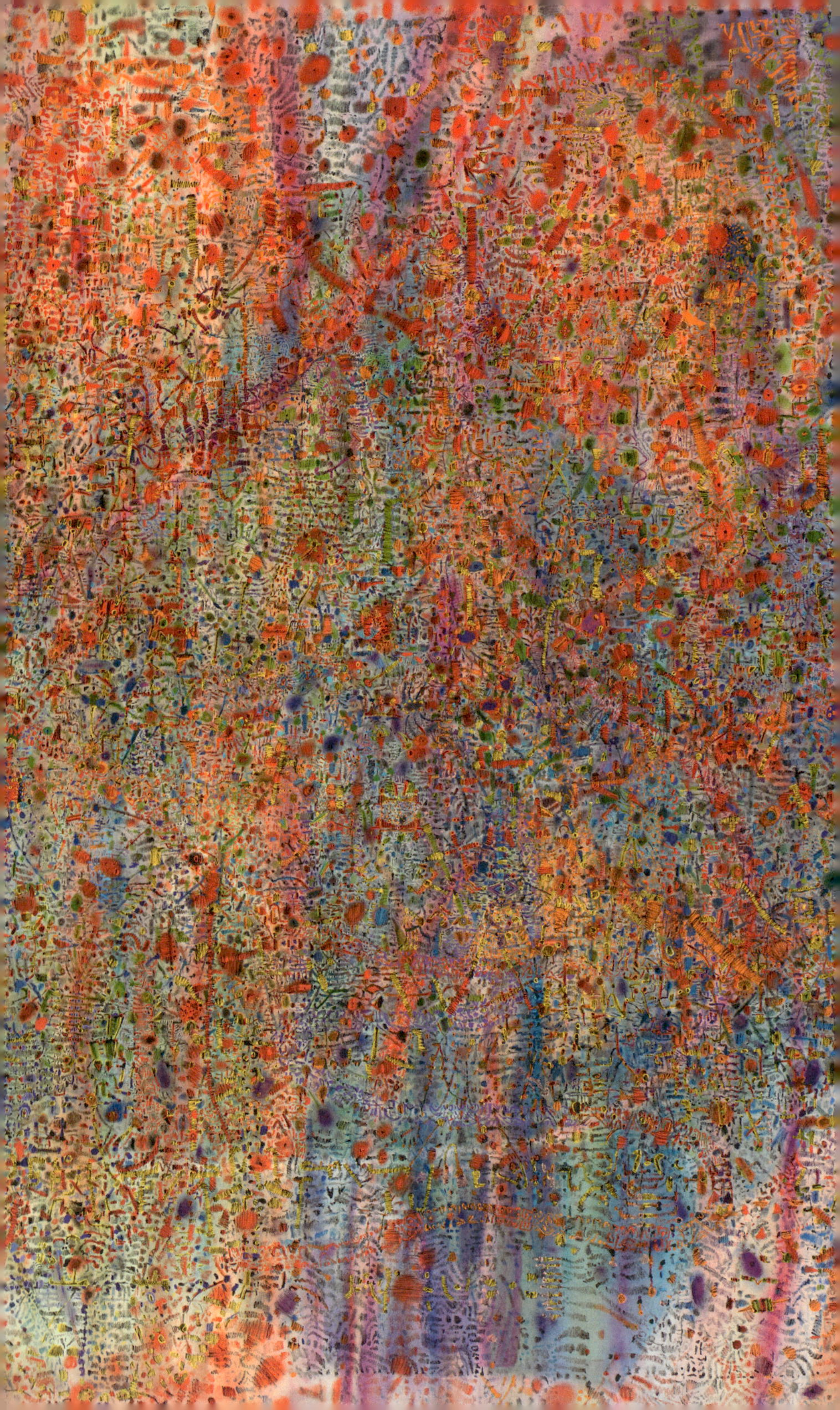

ABSTRACTION IN THE DIGITAL AGE

-

Abstraction's defining quality lies in its
openness . . . By opening our understanding of
art to a multiplicity of possible interpretations,
abstraction is inherently multidirectional:
it de-centres the boundaries that separate 'art'
from commonplace definitions of what it is not

-

Kobena Mercer

2006

HELEN PASHGIAN
b.1934

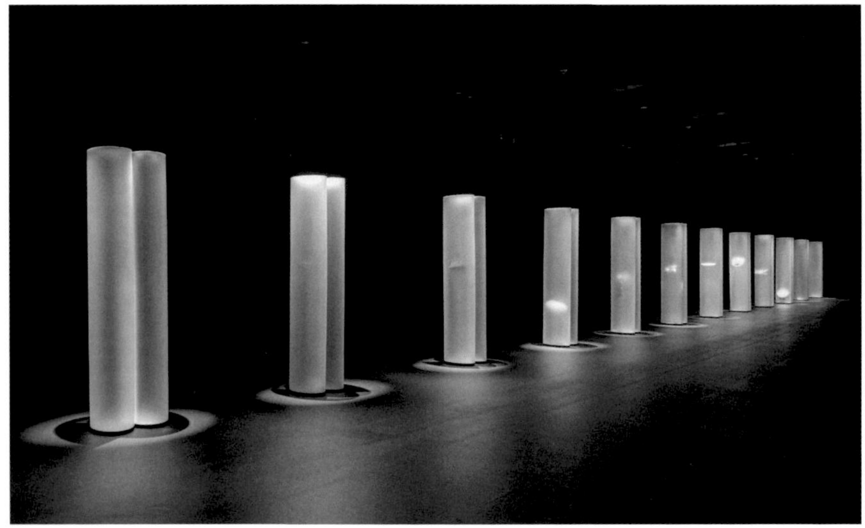

In the 1950s Pashgian trained as an art historian in New York and Boston, specializing in seventeenth-century Dutch painting with a particular interest in Johannes Vermeer and his mastery of light. After her east coast studies, she returned to her native Pasadena, California, where she started making sculpture in the late 1960s. She became part of a loose group of abstract artists working with the translucent and prismatic properties of newly available industrial materials including coated glass, epoxies, fibreglass and resin. This became known as the Light and Space movement of Southern California. These artists shared an interest in altering the viewer's perception of space through immersive installations that blurred the boundaries between the art object, its surrounding environment and light conditions, and the bodies of the exhibition visitors.

In her three-dimensional works, Pashgian treats light as both the medium and object of her practice, utilizing materials that absorb, reflect and refract light. Working with a fabricator to produce her sculpture, her favoured processes include the casting and moulding of resins and acrylics into distinctive discs and spheres. This can involve heating a solid plastic sheet until it is soft and pliable, then transforming it into a sinuous three-dimensional shape by using a wooden mould. These elliptical shapes are often suspended within freestanding columns, appearing as enigmatic inner sources of light. Pashgian also allows for a wide range of colours within her work, which reference the sun-dappled atmosphere of California. Of critical importance to the works' appearance is their final, intensive stage of sanding and polishing. The artist does not allow for any trace of human labour to remain on the surface of her sculptures. She believes that even a single scratch disrupts the viewing experience of looking, moving and encircling these solid objects that appear like liquid light.

Helen Pashgian
Untitled, 2012–13
Formed acrylic,
dimensions variable
Los Angeles County
Museum of Art,
Los Angeles

The artist described this major twelve-part installation by explaining: 'I think of the columns as "presences" in space – presences that do not reveal everything at once. One must move around to observe changes: coming and going, appearing and receding, visible and invisible – a phenomenon of constant movement. It touches on the mysterious, the place beyond which the eye cannot go.'

KEY EVENTS

1970–71: Pashgian is artist in residence at the California Institute of Technology, Pasadena.

2011: Pashgian's work features in the major group exhibition 'Phenomenal: California Light, Space, Surface' at the Museum of Contemporary Art San Diego.

2013: Awarded the Distinguished Women in the Arts Award by the Museum of Contemporary Art, Los Angeles.

SHEILA HICKS
b.1934

Nebraska-born Hicks studied at Yale University under many
abstract artists including Josef Albers, whose colour theories
and exercises profoundly affected her development as an artist.
He also introduced Hicks to his wife, the artist Anni Albers,
whose influential practice centred on pictorial hand-weavings that
integrated the language of geometric abstraction with ancient Latin
American textiles. The art historian George Kubler taught a course
at Yale on Pre-Columbian art that gave a wider context to Hicks's
interest in Latin American visual cultures. She began to experiment
with textiles alongside her painting practice. With the support of
the Alberses, Hicks was awarded a Fulbright scholarship to study
painting in Chile from 1957 to 1958, where she also encountered
Andean weaving techniques. In 2004 Hicks reflected on the impact
that Josef and Anni Albers had on her early years as an artist:

> I realized that Josef had awakened me to the world of colour and
> ways of using colour. At the same time, Anni had helped me to
> think about structure. There's a basic structure to everything.
> Biologists know this, but artists don't necessarily see this
> right away. There I was thinking colour and thinking structure
> simultaneously. In addition I was developing my powers of
> observation – visual.

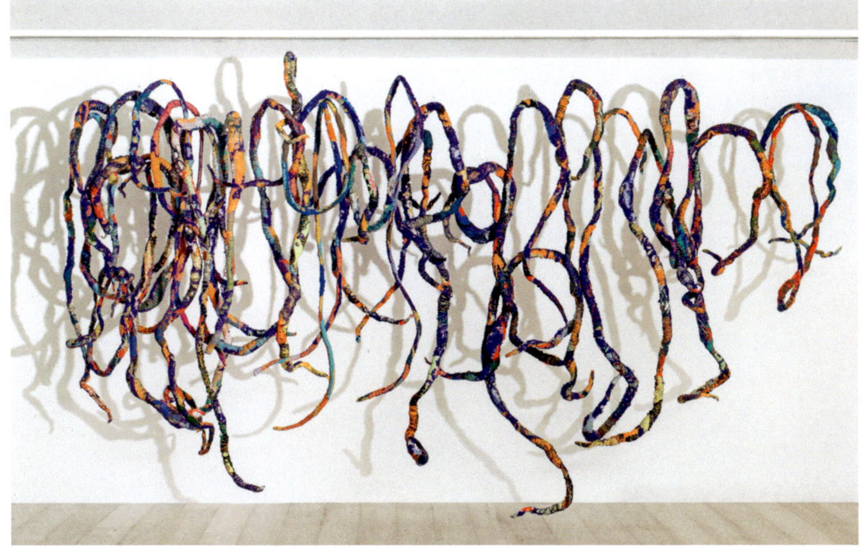

Sheila Hicks
*Baôli Chords/Cordes
Sauvages Pow Wow,*
2014–15
Cotton, wool, linen, silk,
bamboo and synthetic
fibres, twenty-six
elements: each 250 x
20 cm (98½ x 7⅞ in.)
Private collection

**This multicoloured
installation binds
together a wide range
of natural and synthetic
fibres into tightly wound
branch- or root-like
structures, freed from
the ground or the tree to
snake among each other
and dance freely against
the gallery's white walls.**

After finishing her studies, Hicks spent the years 1959 to 1964 living and working in Guerrero, Mexico. She has been based in Paris since 1964, although she travels extensively across the globe. Hicks spent much of the 1960s producing commissioned textiles for corporate locations including CBS television headquarters and IBM's Paris head office. Her large-scale installations always include an architectural dimension, considering the specific features of the spaces in which she is working. Her textile work uses both natural and synthetic fibres in a huge variety of bright colours. The fibres are woven, knotted, braided, embroidered and combined with a host of additional materials including paper, wood, silk and copper. She calls her small-scale experimental weavings *minimes* (French for minimal) and makes most of these pieces on the same hand loom she has kept for over fifty years.

KEY EVENTS

1969: The artist's work is featured prominently in a group exhibition of contemporary weavers, 'Wall Hangings', at the Museum of Modern Art (MoMA), New York.

2010: Hicks is awarded the Smithsonian Archives of American Art Medal.

2019: Her solo retrospective exhibition 'Campo Abierto/Open Field' opens at The Bass Museum of Art, Miami.

DÓRA MAURER
b.1937

Budapest native Maurer originally studied painting and printed graphics at the Hungarian Academy of Fine Arts in the late 1950s. She became an important member of the country's independent avant-garde group of artists, designers and poets who challenged the state-sanctioned cultural output of the socialist period, leading many study circles and workshops ranging across film, photography and printmaking, organizing exhibitions and editing art publications. From 1968 she split her time between Budapest and Vienna for thirty years, as one of the few Hungarian artists able to travel and exhibit both inside and outside the country. During this time, she developed a practice centred on a conceptual investigation of movement, repetition and incremental change – as expressed through photographic series such as *Reversible and Changeable Phases of Movements* (1972), which documented simple actions and gestures in sequential grid formations.

Her commitment to teaching throughout her career has led to many interdisciplinary and collaborative experiments including Super 8 film, drawing and performance workshops. At its core, her practice is a research-based investigation, a problem solving through visual means. Since the mid-1980s Maurer's practice has been focused on paintings of abstract shapes dominated by curving, overlapping planes, foreshortened geometry and spatial inversions. However, she does not consider herself a painter. As Maurer explains: 'I make experiments, I change methods without restraint, and I think in formal oppositions.'

Dóra Maurer
Overlappings (Irregular) 4,
2009–2010
Acrylic on canvas and
wood in five parts,
450 x 233 cm
(177¼ x 91¾ in.)
Vintage Galéria, Budapest

This work's five separate panels are painted to suggest a transparency that is not present in reality: the 'overlaps' are illusory, implying a layering of colours to heighten the suggestion of three-dimensionality.

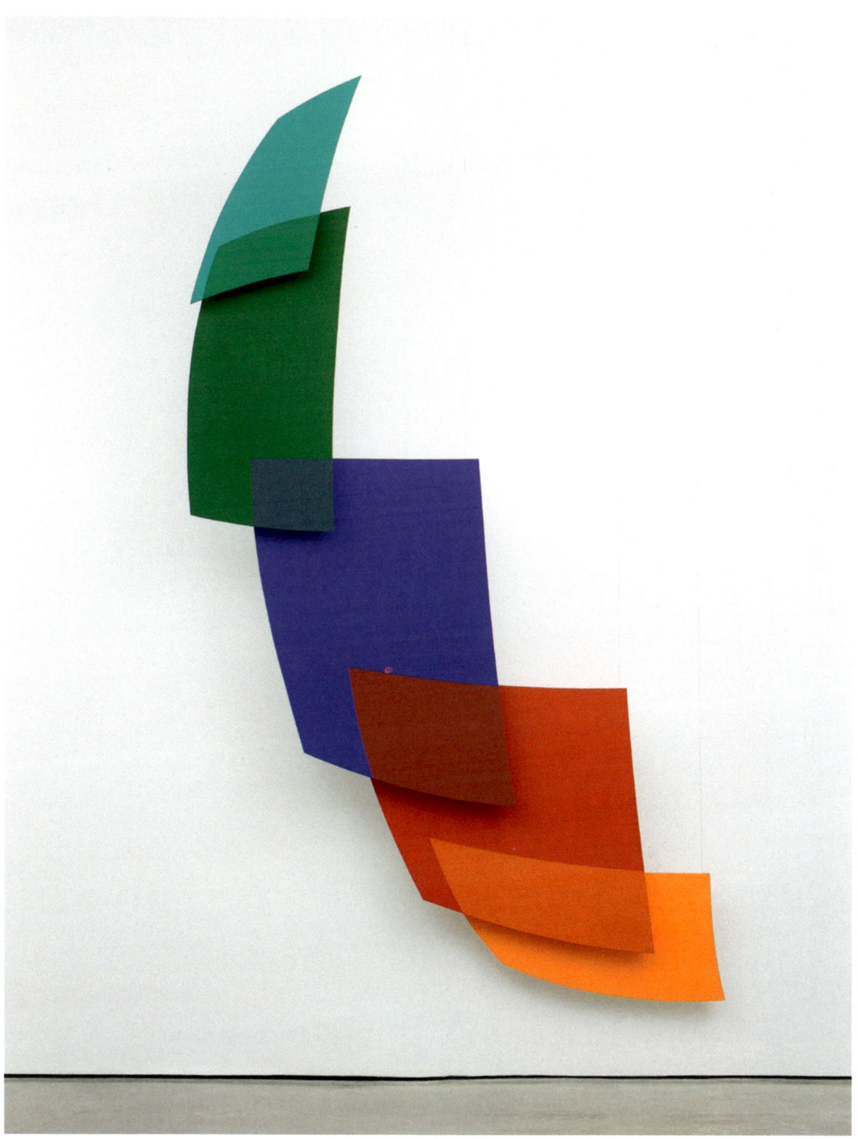

KEY EVENTS

1982: Maurer creates a painting directly on the wall of a tower
room in Castle Buchberg am Kamp, Austria. This installation
marks her shift into painting.

2019–20: Tate Modern stages a major exhibition of Maurer's work
from the 1970s to 2019.

TAKESADA MATSUTANI

b.1937

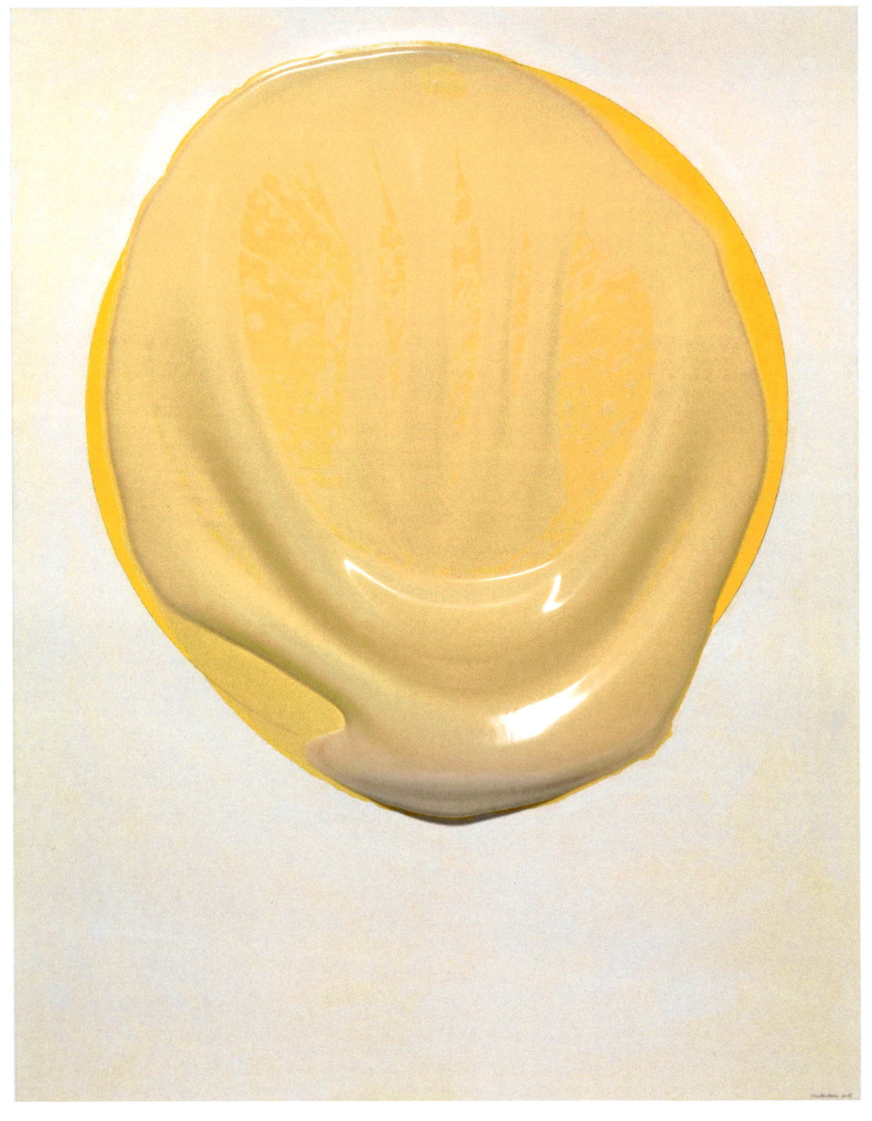

Takesada Matsutani
Propagation 15-2, 2015
Vinyl adhesive and
acrylic paint on
canvas and plywood,
146 x 114 cm
(57½ x 45 in.)
Centre Pompidou, Paris

**Reflecting on his interest
in evoking temporal flux
in 2010, the artist said:
'A flow, the flow of time,
this flow that you have
no idea when it started or
when it will finish – from
there, I tried producing
a visual form. Whether
I was able to stop time
within the work was
doubtful . . . Time flows
incessantly.'**

Born in Osaka, Matsutani grew up in the Kansai region of
Japan, which after the Second World War became the location
of the country's only major post-war art movement to receive
international acclaim and attention: Gutai (its literal translation
is 'embodiment' or 'concreteness'). After studying at Osaka's
Municipal School of Arts and Crafts in the 1950s and teaching
himself about western contemporary art through books, Matsutani
developed an abstract painting practice around 1960. With his
acceptance into the group by founder Jirō Yoshihara, Matsutani
officially joined Gutai in 1963, an occasion marked by his first solo
exhibition at the Gutai Pinacotheca, Osaka. His work is identified
with certain materials: graphite, vinyl glue (an industrial product
newly available in the 1960s) and *sumi* ink (a solid ink powder
used primarily in calligraphy and brush painting); and with chance
processes that often involve the artist's breath – such as inflating
bubbles of vinyl glue directly on the canvas, using a straw.

In 1966 a major event changed the course of his life and work:
Matsutani won a competition organized by the Institut Français in
Kyoto that included a six-month stay in France. After travelling
throughout Europe, the artist settled in Paris – where he would
establish his permanent residency by the end of the decade. His
commitment to Gutai never wavered, and he continued to return
to Japan regularly, participating in all the Gutai group exhibitions
until its formal disbanding upon Yoshihara's death in 1972. In Paris
he joined Atelier 17, the studio of British printmaker Stanley William
Hayter, from 1967 to 1971, where he became Hayter's assistant and
met his future wife, the artist Kate van Houten, who introduced him
to the technique of silkscreen printing.

Inspired by Zen Buddhism, the concept of the void, and his
interest in cellular structures, propagation and other biological life
cycles, alongside abstracted references to body organs and orifices,
Matsutani's practice is an organic meditation on impermanence and
lived experience.

KEY EVENTS

1977: The artist begins making his graphite *Streams* and other
large-scale works that are hybrids of performance
and installation.

2019: Centre Pompidou organizes 'Takesada Matsutani', the
largest retrospective exhibition to take place in his adopted
home country of France.

EL ANATSUI
b.1944

El Anatsui makes shimmering, abstract wall hangings by utilizing discarded everyday materials in vast quantities, including metal graters and, beginning in 2001, his signature material of flattened aluminium seals and caps from liquor bottles. Born in Anyako, Ghana, the artist undertook his fine art degree and postgraduate training in Kumasi before moving to Nsukka, Nigeria, in 1975. A decade later he joined the Aka Circle of Exhibiting Artists, based in Eastern Nigeria. He taught sculpture and design at the University of Nigeria in Nsukka until his retirement in 2011. Over the decades his practice has encompassed geometric wood reliefs and sculpture in terracotta, clay and metalwork.

His intricate, multipart assemblages are the result of extremely delicate and physically demanding processes of manual labour: the bottle caps are crushed, rolled, twisted and cut before being threaded together using copper wire. These humble individual elements are stitched into a single, indivisible whole: a mosaic-like textural field that undulates in its vastness. As a commentary on excessive consumption and waste within systems of industrial manufacturing, El Anatsui's working method does not obscure the branding or design of his recycled objects, reminding us of the global capitalist economy from which they have emerged. El Anatsui synthesizes his formal material enquiry – producing resolutely

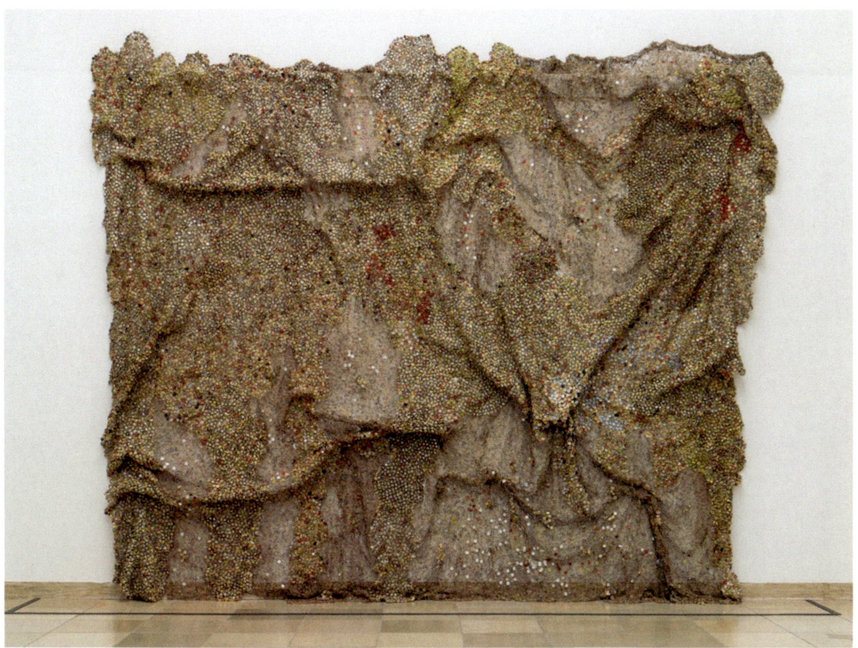

El Anatsui
Dusasa II, 2007
Found aluminium
and copper wire,
546.1 x 655.3 cm
(215 x 258 in.)
Metropolitan Museum
of Art, New York

The artist explains that the title of this work, *Dusasa*, can be translated from the West African language Ewe as a 'communal patchwork made by a team of townspeople'. This alludes to his collaborative method of working alongside many assistants to fabricate his large-scale installations.

non-representational works – with references to many visual and linguistic traditions of West African art, design and textiles such as Ghanaian *kente* and *adrinka* cloths, alongside the histories of slavery, colonization and post-colonial conditions, and the precarity of globalization and environmental catastrophe today, alluded to by works like *Rising Sea*, 2019.

KEY EVENTS

2015: The artist receives the Golden Lion for Lifetime Achievement at the Venice Biennale.

2019: El Anatsui makes his largest ever work, *Second Wave*, for the façade of the Haus der Kunst in Munich, utilizing thousands of bottle caps and offset printing plates.

155

TOMMA ABTS

b.1967

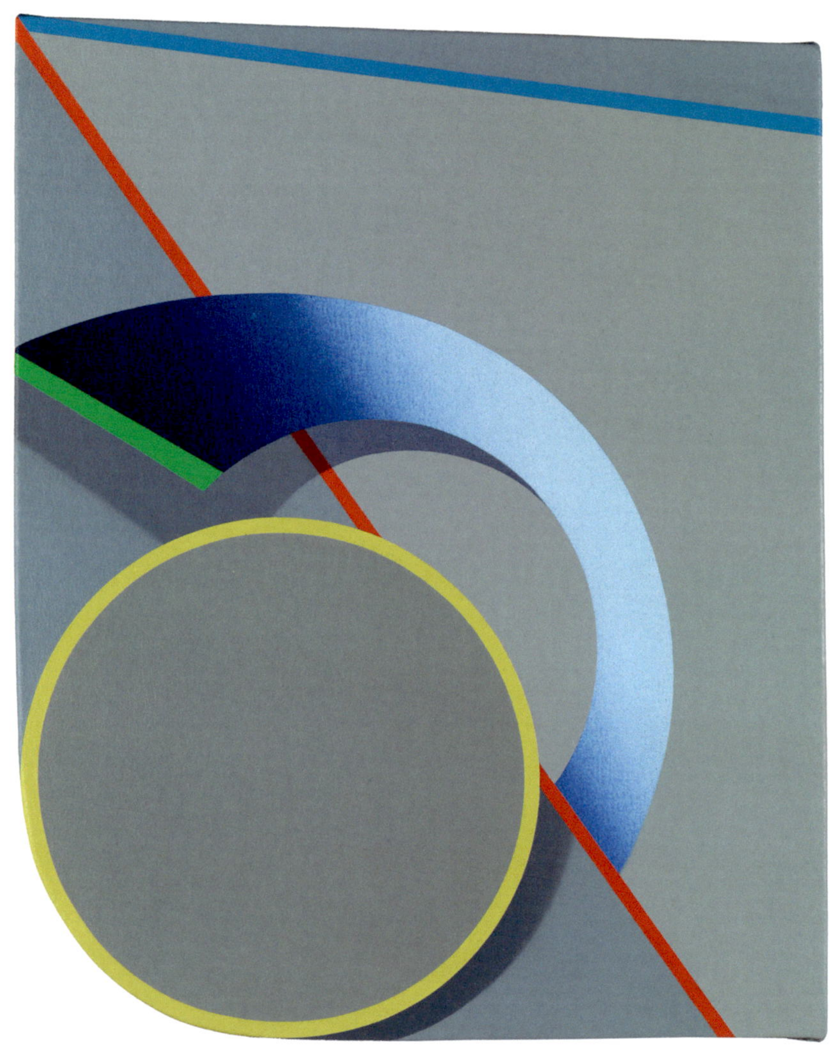

Tomma Abts
Oeje, 2016
Acrylic and oil on canvas,
48 x 38 cm (18⅞ x 15 in.)
Private collection

While the actual bottom-left edge of this canvas is meticulously curved, its surface circular forms are painted with invented shadows cast in different directions, creating a contradictory internal logic that reveals the painting's own artifice. *Oeje*, like all of Abts's titles, is taken from a German dictionary of first names.

London-based Abts was born in Keil, Germany, and studied at the Hochschule der Künste in Berlin from 1988 to 1995. She is devoted to a particular size for her paintings: a rectangular format of 48 cm (19 in.) height by 38 cm (15 in.) width. This self-imposed restriction allows for a totally intuitive process of making, using an abstract language of geometric and biomorphic shapes and planes, with no preparatory sketches or pre-planning before she begins the painting itself. Of her working method, Abts explains: 'Making a painting is a long-winded process of finding a form for something intuited.' Her paintings have many layers, as Abts's sequential stages of decision making, revisions and overpainting gradually arrive at the final image.

The artist has recently made bronze and other metal casts of canvas surfaces, stripping her work of its multicoloured aspect and returning it to a monochromatic richness almost redolent of Byzantine icon paintings. In common with many abstract artists from the first half of the twentieth century, such as Malevich and Rozanova, Abts prefers the term 'non-objective' to describe her work. As she clarifies:

People often use the term abstract to describe my paintings. I don't consider them abstract because I'm working from a somewhat indistinct and hazy place towards a very specific and concrete image. I am constructing an image from nothing and try to define it very clearly, so that it becomes legible. At the same time, I want it to be as open as possible.

This oscillation between precision and openness defines Abts's practice. She often utilizes deft optical illusions to suggest three-dimensional depth within her flat surfaces.

KEY EVENTS

2006: Abts wins the Turner Prize in London, which is awarded by Japanese Conceptual artist Yoko Ono.

2018: The Serpentine Galleries, London, and The Art Institute of Chicago, Chicago, co-organize the touring solo exhibition 'Tomma Abts'.

JOHANNA UNZUETA
b.1974

Santiago-born Unzueta moved to New York in 2000, where she began to make sculptural works in felt, often recreating household and industrial objects to reflect on the human dimension of manufacturing processes.

Since 2015 Unzueta has produced large-scale, freestanding abstract drawings on large sheets of paper that she has tinted with indigo-blue, fustic-yellow and other natural dyes. They are transformed into three-dimensional objects through the support of transparent frames, secured to bases of recycled timber. The artist recalls that: 'In the beginning, I was thinking about the elemental mathematical exercises of set and subset, and also how this is somehow related to the idea of collaboration and community.' The drawings utilize pin holes and other techniques to emphasize their double sidedness. To create their perfect shapes, Unzueta uses embroidery hoops from her collection of hundreds. The results are delicate oval, circular and tessellating geometric forms activated by light and suggestive of textiles. Through these subtle but complex gestures, Unzueta inscribes traces of indigenous craft processes and Latin American histories of geometric abstraction into her practice, disrupting distinctions between art and craft, and the traditional and the contemporary.

The artist writes of her drawings that: 'They are muse exercises in which natural designs become a new point of observation. Here, a new set of references is taking shape in the form of biological observations of life, plants and the sciences.' Their abstract patterns

Johanna Unzueta
December 2014, January, February, March 2015
NY, 2014–15
Watercolour and pastel pencil on watercolour paper, 107 x 107 cm (42⅛ x 42⅛ in.)
Collection of the artist

Creating works that are both diagrammatic and deeply connected to the human body, Unzueta views her abstract drawing process as a meditative act. She explains: 'I don't use rulers, I actually use my hands and fingers, or other parts of my body to measure and I calculate their relationships by eye.'

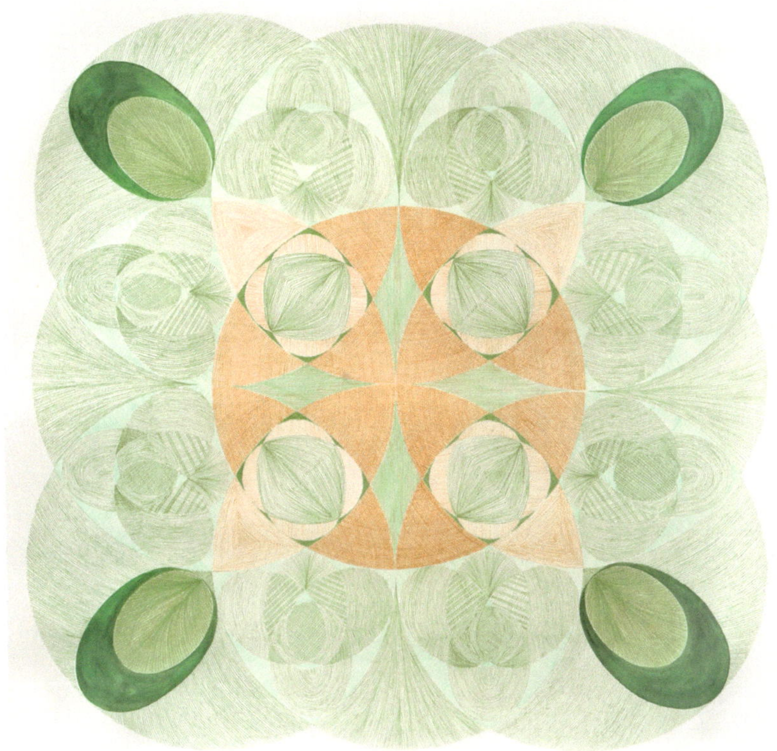

are inspired by nature's 'golden ratio' – a symmetry that can be seen in natural structures such as insect wings or the petal formation of flowers. These drawings take many months for the artist to create. The duration of her labour is indicated by their titles, which list the place(s) and year(s) of their production, indicating her engagement with ideas of progress, abstracted labour, and their implications for human existence and evolution.

KEY EVENTS

2018: The artist participates in the tenth Berlin Biennale with an outdoor wall mural and her freestanding drawings.

2020: 'Tools for Life', her first solo exhibition in Britain, opens at Modern Art Oxford.

159

RANA BEGUM

b.1977

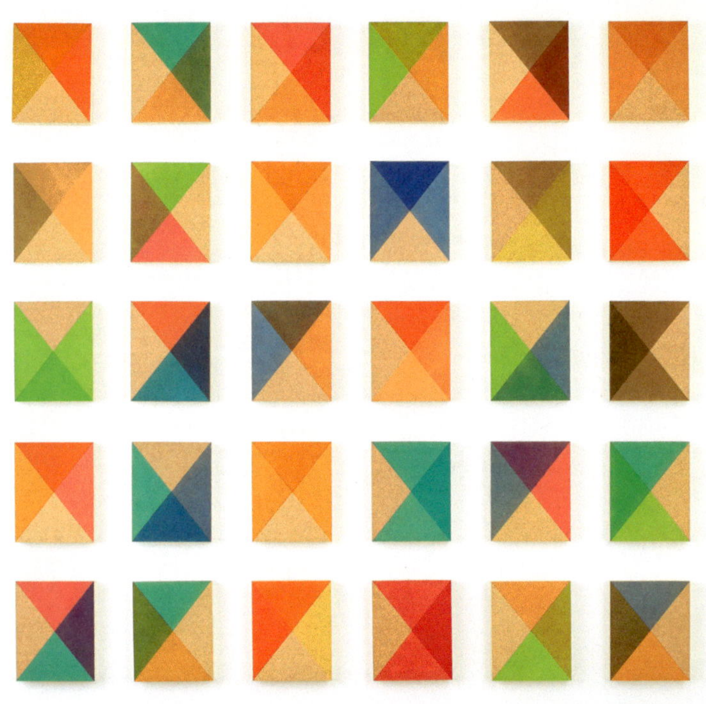

Rana Begum
No. 786 Painting, 2018
Acrylic on MDF, thirty
panels, 165 x 170 x 4 cm
(65 x 67 x 1⅝ in.)
Private collection

**The artist is interested
in how light can change
our perception of colour:
each of these thirty MDF
panels is divided into four
triangles of overlapping
washes of acrylic
paint, creating a grid
that is both rectilinear
and diagonal in its
organization of space.**

A graduate of Chelsea College of Art and Design and the Slade
School of Fine Art, Bangladeshi-born Begum lives and works in
London, where she takes inspiration from the constantly changing
modular structures and empty spaces of its urban landscape.
Influenced by Constructivism, Minimalism and the geometric
designs of Islamic art and architecture, Begum's work oscillates
between two and three dimensions. She often uses the folding
principles of origami to 'activate a two-dimensional composition',
as the artist describes one of her sculptural processes.

Begum explains her interest in the simple abstract forms that
underpin all of her work: 'I am perpetually drawn to basic geometric
shapes because they facilitate my core interests of colour and
light rather than detracting from them.' She realizes these shapes
in a huge variety of industrial and functional materials including
aluminium, cement tiles, copper, glass, painted MDF, Perspex,
reflectors and powder-coated steel, while also working with more
artisanal products such as handmade bamboo baskets to create her
canopy-like architectural installation *No. 764 Baskets*, 2017–18.
Begum sourced the baskets from traditional basket makers in
Bangladesh. The artist titles all of her works numerically, to avoid
foregrounding any one interpretation from her rich palette of
sources and inspirations.

Like many abstract artists Begum believes that the viewer of
her work plays an important role in its activation: 'In life we are in
constant motion, seeing things change and shift around us. I felt
the need to reflect these transitions and changes within my work.
I rely upon both natural light and the interaction of the viewer to
achieve this.'

KEY EVENTS

2016: Her public art commission, *No.700 Reflectors*, for Lewis
Cubitt Square, King's Cross, London, utilizes 30,000 bike
reflectors.

2017: Begum's solo exhibition 'Light Space Colour' opens at the
Sainsbury Centre for Visual Arts, Norwich, and tours to Djanogly
Art Gallery, University of Nottingham.

ZHAO YAO
b.1981

Zhao Yao was born and raised in Luzhou, Sichuan province, China, and studied in the Design Arts Department of Sichuan Fine Arts Institute in Chongqing. Now living and working in Beijing, since 2011 Zhao has developed an ongoing series of works titled *A Painting of Thought*, whose sharply delineated geometric shapes and patterns are taken from Chinese children's games and brainteaser puzzles designed to develop logical thinking. Zhao applies these symbols using thick layers of acrylic paint onto sourced textiles (sometimes handmade, sometimes machine-made), whose existing patterns and surface textures disrupt the rational logic of the puzzles and their shapes. He suggests of this series that 'the whole format is very similar to the artistic training we receive for abstract art'.

Zhao's use of found puzzle imagery and everyday fabrics rather than artist's canvas reveals his interest in pointing to the possible limits of originality for abstract painting in the digital age. By working with the seemingly innocuous visual format of children's games, his paintings draw attention to the ways in which socially agreed codes of knowledge formation, logical reasoning and problem solving are transmitted across generations. Zhao's practice has an almost melancholic quality, recognizing abstraction's mundane reality in the digital sphere. To counteract this feeling of digital-image exhaustion, the artist imbues his practice with a spiritual dimension, signalling the symbolic and utopian aspects of abstract art that have been present throughout its more than century-long existence.

In 2012 Zhao carried seven paintings to be blessed by a living Buddha (Rinpoche) at the Moye Temple in Qinghai province close to the Tibetan border. Four years later he repeated this journey, bringing his huge fabric work *Spirit Above All* to be blessed by more than a hundred Rinpoches and carried up the mountain, where it lay outdoors for more than five months. This intensely physical process was inspired by the region's commonplace Buddhist ritual of transporting embroidered *Thang-ga* devotional paintings to be exposed to the elements for a day on the mountainside.

Zhao Yao
A Painting of Thought I-10, 2011
Acrylic on found fabric, 140 x 100 cm (55⅛ x 39⅜ in.)
Courtesy of Beijing Commune

Zhao's paintings emphasize the systematic nature of mass production, and its relationship to the mechanics of abstraction. As the artist makes clear, 'everything here is readymade. Readymade images, readymade colours, readymade fabric, and a readymade understanding of painting.'

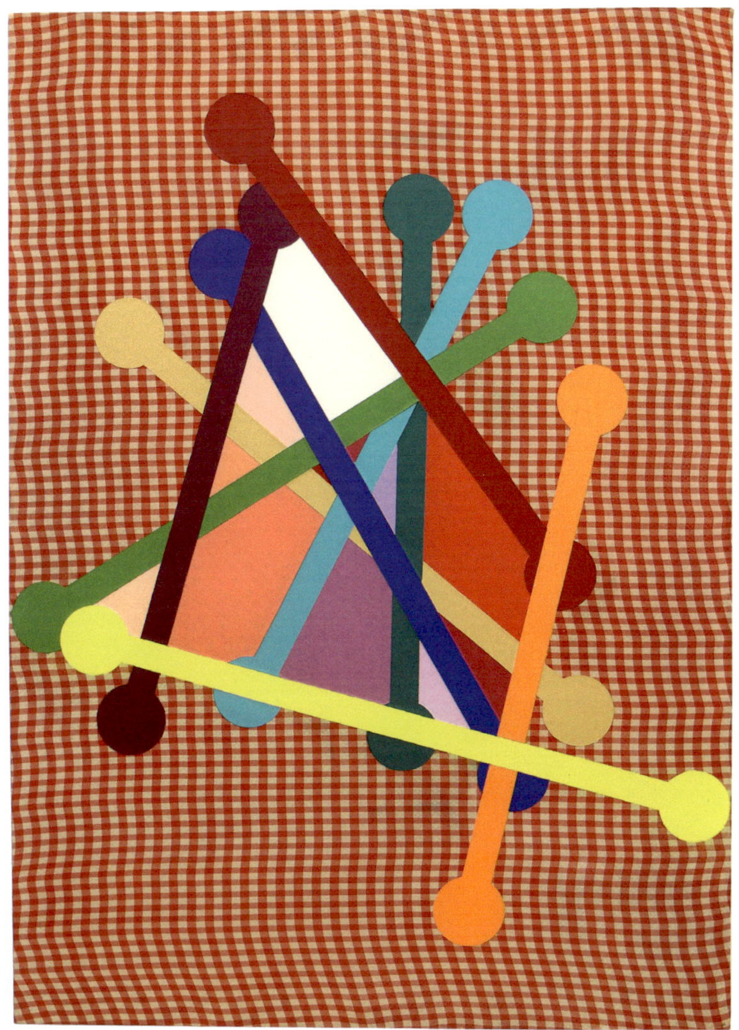

KEY EVENTS

2015: Zhao is included in the group exhibition 'Adventures of the Black Square – Abstract Art and Society 1915–2015' at Whitechapel Gallery, London.

2016: The artist realizes his first sculptural work, *A Sculpture of Thought I-192*, at the Cass Sculpture Foundation, West Sussex.

18 May 2018: Zhao receives permission to hire the iconic Beijing Workers' Stadium to temporarily display *Spirit Above All*, a colossal, multicoloured abstract fabric work measuring 116 x 86 metres (127 x 94 yards) on its football field.

TOMM EL-SAIEH
b.1984

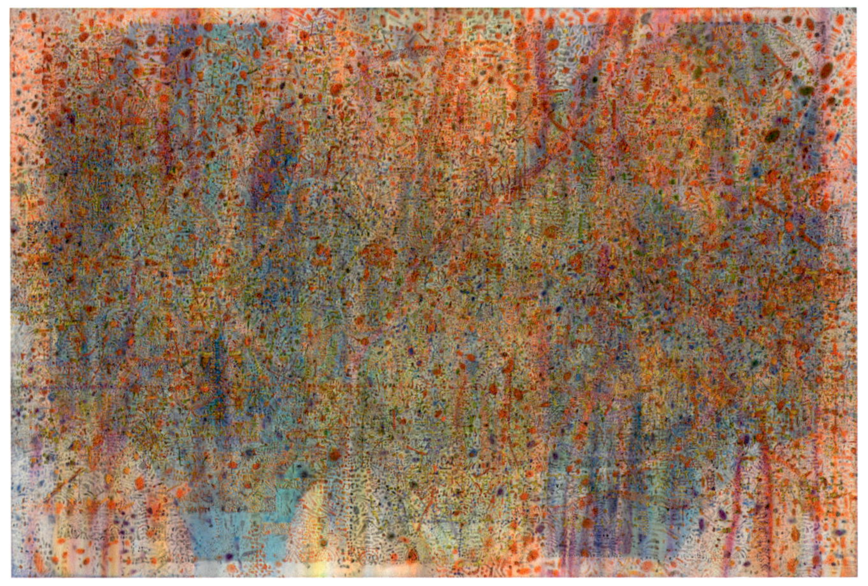

Tomm El-Saieh
Walking Razor, 2017–18
Acrylic on canvas, 243.8
x 365.8 cm (96 x 144 in.)
Collection of Rubell
Museum, Miami

The artist believes that 'abstraction lends itself more to the idea of music. It's more about the feeling.' The title of this painting is inspired by the lyrics of 'Stepping Razor', a 1977 song by Jamaican reggae musician Peter Tosh.

Born in Haiti to an Israeli mother and Palestinian-Haitian father, Tomm El-Saieh was raised in Miami and studied at the New World School of Arts in his home city. During his upbringing the artist was also taught by many masters of Haitian painting, whose work was rooted in narrative traditions and the religious iconography of Voodoo. His family has run an art gallery in the capital Port-au-Prince since the 1950s, which El-Saieh now directs.

In his all-over abstract compositions that accumulate thousands of tiny dashes, marks, rubbings and erasures, the artist sees a connection to the musical rhythms, patterns and vibrations that infuse Haitian symbolic painting, despite his work's obvious absence of image or storytelling. Of how his paintings relate to his Haitian American identity, El-Saieh says: 'I find abstraction is a place that isn't necessarily about resisting the things that make me who I am, but a space where there's ambiguity.'

Embracing this duality in his work, El-Saieh understands his paintings as hybrid forms, in terms of their geographic complexity, their assimilation of modernist forms including the grid and monumental abstract scale and also in their hybridity concerning digital and analogue space. While they are non-representational, we might understand these paintings as complex constellations of information – even screens of encrypted or networked data, the type that constantly surrounds us. El-Saieh's work is a reminder that abstract art is an always politicized mode of visualizing the world around us, rather than an isolated space of purity or simplicity.

KEY EVENT

2017–18: El-Saieh's debut solo museum show opens at the Institute of Contemporary Art, Miami. His work also features in the New Museum Triennial, 'Songs for Sabotage', in New York.

MAJOR GROUP EXHIBITIONS OF ABSTRACT ART

1910–29

1910
First 'Jack of Diamonds' group exhibition in Moscow features Wassily Kandinsky, Natalia Goncharova, Mikhail Larionov, Liubov Popova and Kazimir Malevich.

1911
Public unveiling of Cubism takes place at the Salon des Indépendants, Paris.

1911
Kandinsky debuts his monumental near-abstract painting *Composition V* in Munich at the first exhibition of The Blue Rider group.

1912
Autumn Salon, Paris, features Cubist works alongside two of Kupka's *Amorpha* paintings (1912); their startling abstraction is captured by the newsreels.

1915
'Tramway V: First Futurist Exhibition of Paintings', Petrograd

1915–16
'The Last Exhibition of Futurist Painting 0,10' in Petrograd launches Suprematism and includes Malevich's *Black Square*.

1922
'Congress of the International Union of Progressive Artists' in Düsseldorf advocates for abstract Constructivist art as a shared avant-garde language.

1922
'First Russian Art Exhibition' in Berlin is sanctioned by the Soviet government and is organized in part by Naum Gabo.

1923
'International Exhibition of New Art', Łódź, Poland

1927
'Machine-Age Exposition', New York, juxtaposes modern abstract art (including Gabo, Pevsner and Stażewski) with architecture, industrial design and engineering.

1930–49

1930
Group exhibition of 130 artists, including Kandinsky, Mondrian and Taeuber-Arp, is staged in Paris by the Cercle et Carré group, led by Joaquín Torres-García and Michel Seuphor.

1931–6
Regular exhibitions held by artist group Abstraction-Création, established by Hans (Jean) Arp, Albert Gleizes, Jean Hélion, Auguste Herbin, František Kupka, Theo van Doesburg and Georges Vantongerloo.

1934–5
'Unit One' touring group exhibition including British abstract artists Barbara Hepworth and Ben Nicholson

1935
First 'all abstract' exhibition in London staged by The Seven and Five Society.

1936
'Cubism and Abstract Art' – a major group exhibition is organized by Alfred Barr at the Museum of Modern Art, New York.

1937
Major group exhibition 'The Constructivists' at Kunsthalle Basel, Switzerland

1938
'International Exhibition of Surrealism' in Paris features many biomorphic abstract works.

1946
First edition of Salon des Réalités Nouvelles, Paris: an annual art exhibition devoted exclusively to abstract art, accompanied by a journal of the same name.

1949
First Progressive Artists' Group exhibition at Bombay Art Salon presents a pluralist mix of abstract and figurative paintings and sculptures.

1950–65

1951
First São Paulo Biennial establishes Concrete Art in Brazil.

1951
'Ninth Street Art Exhibition', New York, brings together many first- and second-generation Abstract Expressionists to define the New York School.

1956
'This is Tomorrow', an experimental interactive group exhibition (equally abstract and representational) is staged by the Whitechapel Gallery, London, in collaboration with the Independent Group.

1959
The first Neo-Concrete group exhibition is staged in Rio de Janeiro, Brazil.

1959
Neo-Concrete emphasis at the São Paulo Biennial, which also includes the abstract group exhibition 'Non-Figurative South African Art'.

1959–60
'Sixteen Americans', group exhibition, The Museum of Modern Art, New York

1960
'Konkrete Kunst', Zurich, is organized by leading Concrete artist Max Bill.

1963
GRAV (Groupe de Recherche d'Art Visuel) stages its *Labryrinth* at the third Paris Biennial, comprised of twenty kinetic installations.

1965
In New York, 'First Group Showing (Works in Black and White)', the only exhibition of Spiral art collective

1965
'The Responsive Eye', Op Art group show at The Museum of Modern Art, New York

1966

Group exhibition 'Primary Structures: Younger American and British Sculptors' at the Jewish Museum, New York, is quickly seen as one of the defining moments of Minimalism.

1966

'First World Festival of Negro Arts', interdisciplinary cultural festival in Dakar, Senegal

1967

'Serielle Formationen (Serial Formations)' at Frankfurt University includes artists Judd, LeWitt, Martin, Rosenenske and Stella, in the first German exhibition to explore Minimalism.

1969

Era-defining exhibition of Minimal, Conceptual and Process Art: 'Live in Your Head: When Attitudes Become Form' at the Kunsthalle Bern is curated by Harald Szeemann.

1969

Group exhibition of Process Art: 'Anti Illusion: Procedures/Materials' at the Whitney Museum of American Art, New York

1969

'Art in Process IV' at the Finch College Museum of Art, New York, opens in December.

1970

'Information' group show of Conceptual Art at the Museum of Modern Art (MoMA), New York

1972

'Documenta 5', Kassel, Germany

1973

First posthumous exhibition of Emma Kunz's drawings at Aargauer Kunsthaus, Switzerland

1982

'The Exchange between Artists, 1931–1982: Poland–USA' group exhibition at the Musée d'Art Moderne de la Ville de Paris, Paris

1986

'The Spiritual in Art: Abstract Painting 1890–1985' at the Los Angeles County Museum of Art features Hilma af Klint's work for the first time in a public exhibition.

2004

'Beyond Geometry: Experiments in Form, 1940s–70s' at the Los Angeles County Museum of Art (LACMA)

2006

Global touring group show 'High Times, Hard Times: New York Painting, 1967–1975' reappraises this moment of abstract painting in New York.

2007

'The Geometry of Hope: Latin American Abstract Art from the Patricia Phelps de Cisneros Collection' is organized by the Blanton Museum of Art, Texas, surveys geometric abstraction in Latin American art from the 1930s to 1970s.

2012–13

'Inventing Abstraction 1910–1925: How a Radical Idea Changed Modern Art' at the Museum of Modern Art, New York

2014

'Other Primary Structures' at the Jewish Museum, New York, offers an updated, global retake on its iconic 1966 'Primary Structures' show.

2014

'Variations: Conversations in and Around Abstract Painting', Los Angeles Museum of Contemporary Art, features artists including Mark Bradford and Julie Mehretu.

2014

'Abstract Drawing', a group show at Drawing Room, London, is curated by artist Richard Deacon.

2015

'Adventures of the Black Square: Abstract Art and Society 1915–2015' group exhibition at Whitechapel Gallery, London

2017

'Magnetic Fields: Expanding American Abstraction, 1960s to Today' organized by the Kemper Museum of Contemporary Art, Kansas City, focuses on abstract art by female artists of colour.

2018

'Shape of Light: 100 years of photography and abstract art' at Tate Modern, London

2020

'Taking Shape: Abstraction from the Arab World, 1950s–1980s', a touring group exhibition is organized by the Grey Art Gallery, New York University, New York.

GLOSSARY

Abstract Expressionism: a new approach to abstract art developed by a diverse group of artists, mainly based in New York in the 1940s and 1950s, rooted in gestural mark-making and spontaneous actions thought to emerge directly from the unconscious.

Abstraction-Création: an association founded in Paris in 1931 by a group of forty-one artists to promote abstract art. It evolved from earlier abstract groups including Cercle et Carré and De Stijl. Many of its members were exiles from Nazi Germany and Stalinist Russia, and associated abstract art with freedom and political resistance.

Action Painting: term coined by art critic Harold Rosenberg in 1952 to describe those Abstract Expressionists (most notably Jackson Pollock) who used physically expressive gestures deploying brushes, sticks or paint poured directly from the can onto large-scale canvases, often on the floor.

Anti-Form: term coined by the American artist Robert Morris in 1968 to describe an approach to post-Minimalist sculpture that rejects fixed forms and shapes in favour of slumped, gravity-bound piles and spills of loose materials.

Art Informel: European post-war style of abstract painting, which promoted improvisation, gestures, chance processes, rough textures and collaged materials.

Bauhaus: influential German school of art and design founded in 1919 by architect Walter Gropius. It was forced to close by the Nazis in 1933. Many important abstract artists including Josef Albers, Wassily Kandinsky, Paul Klee and László Moholy-Nagy taught there.

Biomorphic: term used to describe abstract shapes that recall biological and microbial forms and other motifs found in nature.

Black Mountain College: an experimental and progressive art school in North Carolina, operational from 1933 to 1957.

Blaue Reiter, Der (The Blue Rider): influential group of Expressionist painters, mainly based in Munich, Germany, who used non-naturalistic colour palettes and near-abstract deconstructed forms in their landscape and still-life paintings.

Cercle et Carré: Paris-based artists' group formed in 1929 by painter Joaquín Torres-García and artist/critic Michel Seuphor to promote abstract art.

Color Field Painting: phrase used to describe a second-generation style of Abstract Expressionism that soaked and stained vast fields of colour into the canvas with little sharp definition or delineation. Post-painterly Abstraction is a related term.

Complementary colours: opposites on the colour wheel that have a harmonious relationship of balance and contrast, for example, red and green, and orange and blue.

Conceptual Art: a type of art that considers the idea or concept to be more important than the finished artwork. In 1969 artist Sol LeWitt declared that: 'Conceptual artists are mystics rather than rationalists. They leap to conclusions that logic cannot reach.'

Concrete Art: international term coined by De Stijl leader Theo van Doesburg in his 1930 *Manifesto of Concrete Art*. Advocating for the concrete reality of an object, it avoided symbolic interpretation. The term can describe geometric abstract art that flourished in Europe in the 1930s and Latin America in the 1940s and 1950s.

Constructivism: art movement emerging in Russia around 1915 that was concerned with both the material and spatial presence of an object, and with creating a category of useful, industrial art based on technical constructions of primary colours and geometric shapes.

Cubism: artistic movement pioneered by Pablo Picasso and Georges Braque in around 1907, which presented multiple, fragmented perspectives on the depiction of objects and people within one compositional space.

Dansaekhwa: Korean art movement (also known as Tansaekhwa) founded in the 1950s that committed to the universal nature of monochromatic abstract painting and sculptures.

De Stijl: Dutch artists' group and journal established by Theo van Doesburg and Piet Mondrian in 1917 that advocated for a geometric approach to abstract art and design encompassing painting, furniture, interior design and architecture.

Direct carving: form of sculpting where the material, often stone or wood, is directly incised by the artist's tools, rather than via casting or moulding processes.

Expressionism: an artistic approach, often associated with modern German art movements, in which the appearance of reality is distorted to evoke the artist's inner emotions. Often relies on non-naturalistic colour schemes and vigorous, expressive brushstrokes.

Futurism: Italian art movement founded by Filippo Marinetti in 1909, which moved towards abstract painterly experiments to capture the speed and energy of the modern world.

Geometric abstraction: abstract art that uses the shapes of geometry, such as circles, squares and triangles, to create a visual language with no direct real-world reference point.

Gestural: a way of describing painting that retains the traces of the artist's brushstrokes, actions or gestures undertaken during the process of making. Synonymous with 'painterly'.

Gutai: a post-war Japanese art association established in 1954 by Jirō Yoshihara that used abstract strategies to express the bodily, elemental experience of engaging with humble materials, including paper, ink, newspaper and mud, through actions and performances.

Hard-Edge Painting: term coined in 1959 by the art critic and historian Jules Langsner to describe West-Coast abstract painters. Later applied to artists including Ellsworth Kelly and Frank Stella.

Impasto: painting technique that builds up thick layers or wedges of paint on the canvas, creating an almost three-dimensional surface.

Installation Art: artwork, frequently mixed media, that is defined by the limits of a physical space or room.

Kinetic Art: work that incorporates movement – such as Naum Gabo's sculptures using electric motors or Alexander Calder's mobiles reliant on air currents.

Minimalism: movement of artists working in the 1960s to reduce abstract art to simple geometric forms, using industrial materials to create a spatial relationship to the body of the viewer.

Modernism: a period generally agreed to span the 1860s to 1950s, and which included the emergence of abstract art. Post-modernism was a reaction against the idealism and universality of modernism.

Mono-ha (School of Things): Japanese artists' group based in Tokyo in the mid-1960s that rejected representation and embraced raw material properties.

Monochrome: an artwork created using only a single colour.

Neo-Concrete: term used by the Brazilian avant-garde in the late 1950s to describe the new wave of artists reconfiguring the severity of Concrete Art by introducing a more emphatic bodily presence within abstraction.

Neo-Plasticism: phrase first used by Piet Mondrian to describe the wholly abstract (plastic) nature of his paintings.

New York School: a catch-all term for the group of artists associated with Abstract Expressionism in the 1940s and 1950s.

Non-objective: inspired by Plato's belief that geometry is the most ideal expression of beauty, this term is associated with early pioneers of geometric abstract art.

Op Art: short for 'optical art', describes abstract art that uses perceptual and physiological effects to suggest the instability and movement of its pure colour geometric elements.

Orphism: a term devised by French poet and art critic Guillaume Apollinaire in 1912–13 to describe Sonia and Robert Delaunay's prismatic abstract colour compositions, also known as Simultanism, referencing the ancient Greek poet Orpheus.

Picture plane: flat surface of a painting, and its orientation in space.

Serial Art: uses a pre-established set of rules to determine its composition and visual appearance, often exhausting all variations within a given set – for example, Sol LeWitt's sculptures based on open and closed cube permutations. Associated with Minimalism.

Suprematism: Kazimir Malevich's revolutionary Russian movement, inaugurated with the exhibition '0,10' in Petrograd (1915).

FURTHER READING

Althaus, Karin, Mühling, Matthias and Schneider, Sebastian, eds., *World Receivers: Georgiana Houghton – Hilma af Klint – Emma Kunz* (Hirmer Verlag and Lenbachhaus, Munich, 2019)

Alvarez, Mariola V. and Franco, Ana M., eds., *New Geographies of Abstract Art in Postwar Latin America* (Routledge, London, 2018)

Babaie, Sussan and Zand, Roxanne, *Geometry and Art in the Modern Middle East* (Skira, New York, 2019)

Baker, Simon and de l'Ecotais, Emmanuelle, eds., *Shape of Light: 100 Years of Photography and Abstract Art* (Tate Publishing, London, 2018)

Blazwick, Iwona, ed., *Adventures of the Black Square: Abstract Art and Society 1915–2015* (Whitechapel Gallery, London, 2015)

Dickerman, Leah, ed., *Inventing Abstraction 1910–1925: How a Radical Idea Changed Modern Art* (The Museum of Modern Art and Thames & Hudson, London/New York, 2012)

Fer, Briony, *On Abstract Art* (Yale University Press, London/New Haven, CT, 1997)

Gabriel, Mary, *Ninth Street Women: Lee Krasner, Elaine de Kooning, Grace Hartigan, Joan Mitchell, and Helen Frankenthaler: Five Painters and the Movement That Changed Modern Art* (Little, Brown, New York, 2017)

Godfrey, Mark, *Abstraction and the Holocaust* (Yale University Press, London/New Haven, CT, 2007)

Hoffmann, Jens and McShine, Kynaston, eds., *Other Primary Structures* (Yale University Press, London/New Haven, CT, 2014)

Lind, Maria, ed., *Abstraction*, Documents of Contemporary Art series (MIT Press and Whitechapel Gallery, Cambridge, MA/London, 2013)

Linsley, Robert, *Beyond Resemblance: Abstract Art in the Age of Global Conceptualism* (Reaktion, London, 2017)

Mercer, Kobena, ed., *Discrepant Abstraction* (Institute of International Visual Arts (inIVA) and MIT Press, Cambridge, MA/London, 2006)

Meyer, James, *Minimalism: Art and Polemics in the Sixties* (Yale University Press, London/New Haven, CT, 2001)

Moszynska, Anna, *Abstract Art*, World of Art series (Thames & Hudson, London/New York, 2020)

Nickas, Bob, *Painting Abstraction: New Elements in Abstract Painting* (Phaidon, London/New York, second edition, 2014)

Siegel, Katy, ed., *Abstract Expressionism* (Phaidon, London/New York, 2011)

Terraciano, Emilia, *Art and Emergency: Modernism in Twentieth-Century India* (I. B. Tauris, London, 2017)

INDEX

Main entries are in **bold**.

Abstract Expressionism/
Expressionists 62—91,
96, 122, 168
Abstraction-Création
17, 28, 35, 41, 44,
48, 168
Abts, Tomma **156—7**
Aka Circle of Exhibiting
Artists, Nigeria 154
Albers, Anni 120, 148
Albers, Josef 102, 120,
135, 142, 148
Anatsui, El **154—5**
Andre, Carl 110
Araeen, Rasheed **132—3**
Arp, Hans (Jean) 17, 26,
28, 29, 44, 47, 82
Art Informel 81, 168
Art International
(magazine) 127
Art Students League 64,
75, 86, 96, 100, 124
Arte Povera 136
Artforum (magazine) 140
Artists International
Association (AIA) 54
Arts Magazine 91
Asawa, Ruth **120—21**

Bacon, Francis 91
Baj, Enrico 60
Balla, Giacomo **14—15**
Ballets Russes 15
Bauhaus 7, 13, 22, 28, 51,
102, 120, 168
Baumeister, Willi 126
Baziotes, William 67
Bearden, Romare 73
Begum, Rana **160—61**
Benglis, Lynda 142
Benton, Thomas Hart 75
Bill, Max 107
Blaue Reiter, Der 13,
22, 168
Bloc, André 45
Blok Group 37, 48
Blue Rider, The *see* Blaue
Reiter, Der
Bombay Bhulabhai Desai
Institute 114
Bowling, Frank **90—91**,
133
Brâncuși, Constantin
47, 82

Braques, Georges 18, 47
Bryant, Linda Goode 143
Buren, Daniel **138—9**

Calder, Alexander 102
Camargo, de Sérgio 102
Capitalist Realism 131
Caro, Anthony 132
Castellani, Enrico 60
Cendrars, Blaise 27
Cercle et Carré 28,
48, 169
Chicago, Judy **140—41**
Choucair, Saloua Raouda
56—7
Clark, Lygis 98, 99, 112
Color Field Painting 68,
76, 85, 89, 169
Conceptual Art 51, 82,
122, 131, 139
Concrete Abstraction/
Art 96, 98, 104, 106,
112, 169
Constructivism/
Constructivists
20, 30, 31, 35, 36,
41, 48, 49, 54, 96,
161, 169
Cruz-Diez, Carlos **102—3**
Cubism 7, 18, 19, 20, 26,
30, 36, 41, 47, 48,
70, 169
Cunningham, Merce 120

D Group 94
Dada 28, 29
Debschitz, Wilhelm
von 28
de Kooning, Willem 71
Delaunay, Robert 26
Delaunay-Terk, Sonia
26—7, 57, 96
de Menil, John and
Dominique 64
Depero, Fortunato 15
De Stijl movement 18, 19,
48, 169
Diebenkorn, Richard 89
Doesburg, Nelly van 47
Doesburg, Theo van 17, 19
Donkey's Tail group 20
Doyle, Tom 135
Dreier, Katherine S. 23

Edwards, Melvin 91
El-Saieh, Tomm **164—5**
Expressionism 7,
13, 26, 48, 170

see also Abstract
Expressionism

Farmanfarmaian, Monir
Shahroudy **100—1**
Farroukh, Moustafa 57
Fauves 26
Feminist Art Program 141
Figaro, Le 15
Fischer, Konrad 131
'Five, The' 11
Fontana, Lucio **52—3**, 60
Frampton, Hollis 110
Francis, Sam 81
Frankenthaler, Helen 76,
84—5
Fuller, R. Buckminster
120
Futurism 15, 16, 20, 21,
25, 26, 30, 170

Gabo, Naum **34—5**, 47
Gaitonde, V. S. 114
Gilliam, Sam **88—9**
Gleizes, Albert 17
Gorky, Arshile 64
Gottlieb, Adolph 81, 85
GRAV (collective) 105
Greenberg, Clement 76,
85, 91
Gropius, Walter 51
Groupe Espace, Le 45
Grupo Frente 106, 112
Gutai artists 153, 170

Hafif, Marcia 100
Hamilton, Richard 55
Hartigan, Grace 85
Hayter, Stanley William
153
Hélion, Jean 17
Hepworth, Barbara 35,
41, 47, 69
Herbin, Auguste 17
Herrera, Carmen 93,
96—7
Hesse, Eva 117, **134—5**,
142
Hicks, Sheila **148—9**
Hockney, David 91
Hofmann, Hans 70, 85
Houten, Kate van 153

Impressionism 7, 18, 57
Independent Group 55

'Jack of Diamonds'
group 25

Johns, Jasper 83
Joppolo, Beniamino 53
Judd, Donald **124—5**, 127

Kaisserlian, Giorgio 53
Kandinsky, Wassily
12—13, 22, 35
Kelly, Ellsworth 78,
82—3, 85
Kinetic Art 102, 170
King, Phillip 132
Kitaj, R. B. 91
Klee, Paul **22—3**, 114
Klein, Yves **58—9**, 60
Kline, Franz 81, 86
Klint, Hilma af **10—11**, 43
Kobro, Katarzyna 20,
36—7, 48
Krasiński, Edward 49
Krasner, Lee **70—71**, 75
Kubler, George 148
Kunz, Emma **42—3**
Kupka, František **16—17**

Leck, Bart van der 19
Lee Ufan **136—7**
Le Fauconnier, Henri 30
Léger, Fernand 41, 57
Lentz, Stanisław 48
Lewis, Norman **72—3**
Lewitt, Sol **122—3**, 127
Li Yuan-chia 133
Lichtenstein, Roy 85
Lippard, Lucy 122
Lissitzky, El **32—3**, 36
Louis, Morris **76—7**, 85
Lye, Len **68—9**

Macke, August 23
McShine, Kynaston 141
Malevich, Kazimir 9,
20—21, 25, 30, 33,
35, 36, 157, 166
Malini, Milena 53
Manzoni, Piero **60—61**
Marc, Franz 22
Marinetti, Filippo
Tommaso 15
Martin, Agnes 43, **78—9**,
127
Martin, Kenneth 54, 55
Martin, Leslie 47
Martin, Mary **54—5**
Masson, André 44
Matsutani, Takesada
152—3
Maurer, Dóra **150—51**
Mercer, Kobena 145

Metzinger, Jean 30
Minimalism/Minimalists
    51, 82, 100, 110, 114,
    122, 123, 124, 126, 127,
    128, 131, 132, 135, 140,
    143, 161, 170
Mitchell, Joan 85
Mohamedi, Nasreen
    114—15
Moholy-Nagy, László
    50—51, 171
Moilliet, Louis 23
Mondrian, Piet **18—19**,
    41, 47
Mono-ha (School of
    Things) 136
Moore, Henry 35, 69
Morellet, François 102,
    104—5
Morris, Robert 100, 135
Moscow
    Museum of Painterly
    Culture 13
Moss, Marlow **40—41**
Motherwell, Robert
    67, 86
Munich
    Academy of Fine Arts
    13
Münter, Gabriele 13

Namuth, Hans 75
Nash, Paul 47
Neo-Concrete Art 98,
    106, 107, 112, 171
Neo-Plasticism 18–19, 171
Nevelson, Louise 83, 100
New Realism 59
New York School 85
Newman, Barnett 63,
    66—7, 73, 89, 96, 119
Nicholson, Ben 39, 41,
    46—7, 69
Nicholson, Sir William 47
Nobuo Sekine 136
Noland, Kenneth 76,
    77, 85
non-objective art 20,
    21, 157
Nouveau Réalisme 59
Nuclear Movement art
    group 60

Oiticica, Hélio **112—13**
Olitski, Jules 85
Ono, Yoko 157
Onsi, Omar 57

Op Art 102, 109, 171
Otero, Alejandro 102

Palermo, Blinky 131
Pape, Lygia 99, **106—7**,
    112
Paris
    Autumn Salon (1912)
    16, 17
    Louvre Museum 27
Pashgian, Helen **146—7**
Pei, I. M. 81
Pevsner, Antoine 35
Picasso, Pablo 17, 47, 75
Pindell, Howardena
    142—3
Polke, Sigmar 131
Pollock, Jackson 71, **74—5**,
    89, 100
Pop Art 98, 110, 131
Popova, Liubov 25,
    30—31, 166
Porset, Clara 120
Posenenske, Charlotte
    126—7, 132
Postminimalism 142—3
Process Art 135, 136
Pryde, Mabel 47

Rauschenberg, Robert 86
Reinhardt, Ad 67, 82, 119
Restany, Pierre 59
Richter, Gerhard **130—31**
Riley, Bridget 103, **108—9**
Rothko, Mark **64—5**, 67,
    78, 81, 96
Rozanova, Olga **24—5**,
    30, 36, 157
Ryman, Robert **128—9**

Scarpa, Carlo 53
Schapiro, Miriam 141
Schoenberg, Arnold 13
Serpa, Ivan 112
Serra, Richard 135
Seurat, Georges 109, 142
Seven and Five Society,
    The 69
Social Realism 72, 75
Socialist Realism 21
Société Anonyme 23
Sonnier, Keith 135
Soto, Jésus Rafael 102
Soulages, Pierre 81
Souza, Francis Newton
    133
Spatialism 52—3

Spiral (collective) 73
Stażewski, Henryk **49—9**
Stella, Frank 100, 103,
    110—11, 127
Stepanova, Varvara 31
Sterne, Hedda 73
Still, Clyfford 67
Stockholm
    Royal Academy of Fine
    Arts 10
Strzemiński, Władysław
    36, 48
Studio 35, New York:
    Artists Sessions
Stumpf, Lily 22
Suprematism/
    Suprematists 7, 20, 21,
    25, 30, 33, 36, 48, 171
Supremus group 25, 30
Surrealism/Surrealists 29,
    44, 47, 64, 75
Symbolism 18
Szeemann, Harald 129,
    139

Taeuber-Arp, Sophie 26,
    28—9, 44
Tatlin, Vladimir 35, 36
Tawney, Lenore 78
Torres García, Joaquín 98
Truitt, Anne **118—19**
Twombly, Cy **86—7**

Union of Youth (society)
    25
Unit One 47
UNOVIS (Advocates for
    the New Art) group
    33, 36
Unzueta, Johanna **158—9**

Valentim, Rubem **98—9**
Vantongerloo, Georges
    17, 19
Vautier, Ben 61
Vézelay, Paule **44—5**
Vienna
    Academy of Fine Arts
    16
Volpi, Alfredo 98, 99

Warhol, Andy 110
Warsaw
    Foksal Gallery 48—9
Weeks, John 55
Whitten, Jack 91
Wigman, Mary 29

Woodridge, Sally B. 121
Works Progress
    Administration 76

Yoshihara, Jirō 153

Zagrodzki, Janusz 37
Zao Wou-Ki **80—81**
Zeid, Fahrelnissa **94—5**
Zhao Yao **162—3**

PICTURE ACKNOWLEDGEMENTS

Front cover: Photo Christie's Images/Bridgeman Images; **2, 27** Davis Museum at Wellesley College, MA. Gift of Mr Theodore Racoosin. © Pracusa 2014083; **8, 24** Ekaterinburg Museum of Fine Arts; **11** Courtesy The Hilma af Klint Foundation, Stockholm. Photo Moderna Museet, Stockholm; **12** The State Tretyakov Gallery, Moscow; **14** The Solomon R. Guggenheim Foundation. Peggy Guggenheim Collection, Venice. Photo akg-images. © DACS 2020; **17** National Gallery, Prague. © ADAGP, Paris and DACS, London 2020; **18** Tate, Liverpool. Photo Tate; **19** Philadelphia Museum of Art. A. E. Gallatin Collection, 1952; **21** The State Tretyakov Gallery, Moscow; **23** The Metropolitan Museum of Art, New York. The Berggruen Klee Collection, 1987. Photo The Metropolitan Museum of Art/Art Resource/Scala, Florence; **29** Private collection. Photo akg-images; **31** State Museum of Contemporary Art, Thessaloniki. George Costakis Collection; **32** Yale University Art Gallery, New Haven. Gift of Collection Société Anonyme; **34** Solomon R. Guggenheim Museum, New York. The Work of Naum Gabo © Nina & Graham Williams; **37** Museum Sztuki, Łódź. © Ewa Sapka Pawliczak; **38, 55** Arts Council Collection, London. © The Estate of Mary Martin; **40** Tate, London. Photo Tate; **43** Emma Kunz Zentrum, Würenlos. © Emma Kunz Zentrum; **45** Tate, London. Photo Tate. © Paule Vézelay/Bridgeman Images; **46** Tate. Photo Tate. © Angela Verren Taunt. All rights reserved, DACS 2020; **49** Zachęta – National Gallery of Art, Warsaw; **50** The Moholy-Nagy Foundation, Ann Arbor; **53** Rachofsky Collection, Dallas. © Lucio Fontana/SIAE/DACS, London 2020; **56** Tate. Photo Tate. © Saloua Raouda Choucair Foundation; **58** Museo Nacional Centro de Arte Reina Sofia, Madrid. Photographic Archives Museo Nacional Centro de Arte Reina Sofia. © Succession Yves Klein, c/o ADAGP, Paris and DACS, London 2020; **61** Centre Pompidou, Paris. Photo Centre Pompidou, MNAM-CCI, Dist. RMN-Grand Palais/image Centre Pompidou, MNAM-CCI. © DACS 2020; **62, 77** National Gallery of Art, Washington, DC. Gift of Marcella Louis Brenner. © Board of Trustees, National Gallery of Art, Washington, D.C; **65** The Metropolitan Museum of Art, New York. Photo The Metropolitan Museum of Art/Art Resource/Scala, Florence. © 1998 Kate Rothko Prizel & Christopher Rothko ARS, NY and DACS, London; **66** The Museum of Modern Art, New York. Gift of Mr and Mrs Joseph Slifka. © The Barnett Newman Foundation, New York/DACS, London 2020; **69** Stills Collection – Ngā Taonga Sound & Vision, Wellington. Courtesy the Len Lye Foundation; **71** Collection of Audrey Irmas, Los Angeles. © The Pollock-Krasner Foundation ARS, NY and DACS, London 2020; **73** National Gallery of Art, Washington, DC. Gift of the Collectors Committee. Courtesy Michael Rosenfeld Gallery LLC, New York. © Estate of Norman Lewis; **74** Stedelijk Museum, Amsterdam. © The Pollock-Krasner Foundation ARS, NY and DACS, London 2020; **79** Solomon R. Guggenheim Museum, New York. Gift of Lenore Tawney, 1963. © Agnes Martin/DACS 2020; **80** Private collection. © DACS 2020; **83** The Museum of Modern Art, New York. Gift of the artist. © Ellsworth Kelly Foundation; **84** Yale University Art Gallery, New Haven. Gift of Howard Sloan, BA 1945, and Mrs Sloan. © Helen Frankenthaler Foundation, Inc./ARS, NY and DACS, London 2020; **87** Courtesy Archives Fondazione Nicola Del Roscio. Photo Mimmo Capone, Rome. © Cy Twombly Foundation; **88** National Gallery of Art, Washington, DC. Anonymous Gift. © ARS, NY and DACS, London 2020; **90** Lowinger Family Collection. Photo Hales Gallery. © Frank Bowling. All Rights Reserved, DACS/Artimage 2020; **92, 97** Crystal Bridges Museum of American Art, Bentonville, Arkansas. Photo Edward C. Robison III. © Carmen Herrera **95** Istanbul Museum of Modern Art Collection. Eczacıbaşı Group Donation. Photo Reha Arcan. © Raad Zeid Al Hussein/Istanbul Museum of Modern Art ; **99** MASP, São Paulo. Doação Ana Dale, Antonio Almeida e Carlos Dale Junior, 2017. © Mendes Wood DM/Almeida & Dale/Instituto Rubem Valentim; **101** Museum of Contemporary Art, Chicago. Gift of the artist in honour of Abolbashar Farmanfarmaian, PhD in Political Sciences, University of Chicago, 1952, and Albert A. Robin Estate by exchange. Photo Nathan Keay/MCA Chicago. Courtesy the artist's family; **102–3** Cruz-Diez Art Foundation, Houston. Photo Atelier Cruz-Diez, Paris. © Carlos Cruz-Diez, ADAGP, Paris and DACS, London 2020; **105** Centre Pompidou, Paris. Photo Centre Pompidou, MNAM-CCI, Dist. RMN-Grand Palais/image Centre Pompidou, MNAM-CCI. © François Morellet; **107** Courtesy Hauser & Wirth. Photo Paula Pape. © Projeto Lygia Pape; **108** National Galleries of Scotland, Edinburgh. Purchased 1974. © Bridget Riley, 2020. All rights reserved; **111** Tate, Liverpool. Photo Tate. © Frank Stella. ARS, NY and DACS, London 2020; **112–3** César and Claudio Oiticica Collection. © César and Claudio Oiticica; **115** Private collection. Courtesy Talwar Gallery, New York/New Delhi. © The Estate of Nasreen Mohamedi; **116, 134** National Gallery of Australia, Canberra. Courtesy Hauser & Wirth. Photo Bridgeman Images. © The Estate of Eva Hesse; **118** National Gallery of Art, Washington, DC. Gift of the Collectors Committee. © annetruitt.org/Bridgeman Images; **121** Courtesy Estate of Ruth Asawa and David Zwirner, New York. Photo Maris Hutchinson. © Estate of Ruth Asawa; **123** San Francisco Museum of Modern Art. The Doris and Donald Fisher Collection. © ARS, NY and DACS, London 2020; **124–5** Seattle Art Museum. Gift of Anne Gerber. Photo Susan Cole. © Judd Foundation/ARS, NY and DACS, London 2020; **127** Courtesy Dia Art Foundation, New York. Photo Bill Jacobson Studio, New York. © Estate of Charlotte Posenenske, Frankfurt; **129** Courtesy the artist and Xavier Hufkens, Brussels. Photo Bill Jacobson; **130** Neues Museum, Staatliches Museum für Kunst und Design, Nuremberg. Loan from the Böckmann Collection. © Gerhard Richter 2020; **133** Centre Pompidou, Paris. Photo Centre Pompidou, MNAM-CCI, Dist. RMN-Grand Palais/Georges Meguerditchian. © Rasheed Araeen. All Rights Reserved, DACS 2020; **137** Private collection. Photo Christie's Images/Bridgeman Images. © Lee Ufan/ADAGP, Paris and DACS, London 2020; **138** Musée d'Art Moderne de la Ville de Paris. Photo Eric Emo/Musée d'Art Moderne/Roger-Viollet. © DB-ADAGP Paris and DACS, London 2020; **141** Collection of Waldman Family Charitable Trust, Mountain Center, CA. Photo © Donald Woodman/ARS, NY. © Judy Chicago. ARS, NY and DACS, London 2020; **143** Rose Art Museum, Brandeis University, Waltham. Courtesy the artist and Garth Greenan Gallery, New York; **144, 164** Collection of Rubell Museum, Miami. Courtesy CENTRAL FINE, Miami. Photo Armando Vaquer. © Tomm El-Saieh; **146** Los Angeles County Museum of Art. Purchased with funds provided by Carole Bayer Sager on the occasion of the 2014 Collectors Committee. Photo Museum Associates/LACMA/Art Resource NY/Scala, Florence. Courtesy the artist and Lehmann Maupin, New York, Hong Kong, and Seoul; **149** Courtesy Alison Jacques Gallery, London. © Sheila Hicks; **151** Courtesy Vintage Galéria. Photo White Cube/Ben Westoby. © the artist; **152** Centre Pompidou, Paris. Photo Centre Pompidou, MNAM-CCI, Dist. RMN-Grand Palais/Philippe Migeat. Courtesy the artist and Hauser & Wirth; **155** The Metropolitan Museum of Art, New York. Purchase, The Raymond and Beverly Sackler 21st Century Art Fund; Stephen and Nan Swid and Roy R. and Marie S. Neuberger Foundation Inc. Gifts; and Arthur Lejwa Fund, in honour of Jean Arp, 2008. Courtesy the artist and Jack Shainman Gallery, New York. © El Anatsui; **156** Private collection. Courtesy the artist and greengrassi, London. Photo Marcus J. Leith; **159** Collection and courtesy of the artist. Photo Rodrigo Pereda; **160** Private collection. Courtesy the artist. Photo Philip White; **163** Courtesy the artist and Beijing Commune

–

To my mother Helen, who made everything possible – especially art

–

First published in the
United Kingdom in 2020 by
Thames & Hudson Ltd, 181A High
Holborn, London WC1V 7QX

First published in the United States
of America in 2020 by
Thames & Hudson Inc., 500 Fifth
Avenue, New York, New York 10110

Abstract Art © 2020
Thames & Hudson Ltd, London
Text © 2020 Stephanie Straine

Design by April
Edited by Caroline Brooke Johnson
Picture research by
Nikos Kotsopoulos

British Library Cataloguing-in-
Publication Data
A catalogue record for this book is
available from the British Library.

Library of Congress Control
Number 2020931753
ISBN 978-0-500-29575-5
Printed and bound in China by
Toppan Leefung Printing Ltd

Be the first to know about
our new releases,
exclusive content and
author events by visiting
thamesandhudson.com
thamesandhudsonusa.com
thamesandhudson.com.au

Front cover: Kazimir Malevich, *Suprematist Composition*, 1916 (detail). Private collection

Title page: Sonia Delaunay-Terk, *Electric Prisms* (*Prismes électriques*), 1913 (detail of page 27). Davis Museum at Wellesley College, Wellesley, MA

Chapter openers: page 8 Olga Rozanova, *Non-objective Composition*, 1916 (detail of page 24). Ekaterinburg Museum of Fine Arts, Yekaterinburg; **page 38** Mary Martin, *Compound Rhythms in Blue*, 1966 (detail of page 55), Arts Counsil Collection, UK; **page 62** Morris Louis, *Beta Kappa*, 1961 (detail of page 103). National Gallery of Art, Washington, DC; **page 92** Carmen Herrera, *Cerulean*, 1965 (detail of page 97). Crystal Bridges Museum of American Art, Bentonville, AR; **page 116** Eva Hesse, *Contingent*, 1969 (detail of page 134). National Gallery of Australia, Canberra; **page 144** Tomm El-Saieh, *Walking Razor*, 2017–18 (detail of page 164). Collection of Rubell Museum, Miami

Quotations: page 9 Kazimir Malevich, 'From Cubism and Futurism to Suprematism: The New Realism in Painting', untitled leaflet distributed at '0,10' exhibition (December 1915), reproduced in *Herman Berninger, Jean Pougny, 1892–1956* (Ernst Wasmuth, Tübingen, 1972), p.53; **page 39** Ben Nicholson, 'Notes on Abstract Art' (1941), *Art in Theory 1900–2000*, edited by Paul Harris and Charles Wood (Tate Publishing, London, 2003), p.399 (article first published in *Horizon*, London, October 1941). Reproduced by permission of the Tate Trustees; **page 63** Barnett Newman, 'The Plasmic Image' (1943–5), reprinted in *Abstract Expressionism: Creators and Critics, an Anthology*, edited by Clifford Ross (Harry N. Abrams, New York, NY, 1990), p.127. © 2019 The Barnett Newman Foundation/Artists Rights Society (ARS), New York, NY; **page 93** Carmen Herrera, quoted in Helena da Bertodano, 'Art's Hot New Thing (Aged 95¾)', *Sunday Telegraph*, London, 19 December 2010. © Carmen Herrera; **page 117** Eva Hesse, exhibition catalogue statement, *Art in Process IV* (Finch College Museum of Art, New York, NY, 1969). © The Estate of Eva Hesse. Courtesy Hauser & Wirth; **page 145** Kobena Mercer, 'Introduction', in *Discrepant Abstraction*, edited by Kobena Mercer (Institute of International Visual Arts [inIVA] and MIT Press, Cambridge, MA, and London, 2006), pp.7–8. © Kobena Mercer